# Contents

# Development and Handicap

*For Betty and Victor*

# Development and Handicap

Vicky Lewis

Basil Blackwell

First published 1987

Basil Blackwell Ltd
108 Cowley Road, Oxford, OX4 1JF, UK

Basil Blackwell Inc.
432 Park Avenue South, Suite 1503
New York, NY 10016, USA

*British Library Cataloguing in Publication Data*
Lewis, Vicky A.
Development and handicap.
1. Handicapped children
I. Title
155.4'5        BF721

ISBN 0-631-13632-0
ISBN 0-631-13633-9 Pbk

*Library of Congress Cataloging in Publication Data*
Lewis, Vicky A., 1948–
Development and handicap.

Bibliography: p.
Includes index.
1. Handicapped children—Development. 2. Child development. 3. Handicapped children—Care. I. Title.
RJ137.L49 1987    649'.15    86-24309
ISBN 0-631-13632-0
ISBN 0-631-13633-9 (pbk.)

Typeset in 10 on 12 pt Plantin
by DMB Typesetting (Oxford)
Printed in Great Britain

# Preface

The idea for this book arose out of an option course I have taught to third year psychology undergraduates for a number of years. Before taking this course all the students have taken courses that examine the development of the non-handicapped child. The third year option course aims to take their understanding of development a stage further and asks what can be learned about the process of development by studying the development of children who are handicapped in a variety of ways. The suggestion that it should form the basis of a book came from Cathy Urwin, who contributed to the course in its early days.

Throughout the book, and indeed in its title, I have used the term handicap, rather than a term such as children with special educational needs. There are several reasons for this. The idea for the book was initially discussed with publishers in the late 1970s, and the title *Development and Handicap* emerged without any intention of it being used as the published title. At this time the term handicap was fairly widely used, whereas now there is a strong preference for less stigmatized terms, a preference which I personally support. However the title stuck: this was partly because the children whose development is described in this book are different from normal children and from many children with special educational needs. In most cases the ways in which they are different can be specified in non-educational terms as well as in educational terms; for example, they may be different in the extent of their visual or auditory abilities, in their chromosomes, or in terms of a motor restriction. In contrast, the difficulties facing many other children with special educational needs can only be specified in terms of their actual needs. Although most of the children described in this book will have special educational needs, it is the specificity of their difficulties which has led me to include them, and to retain the label handicap. However, it is important to realize and remember that for many of them, although their difficulty may be a handicap in the sense that it prevents them from following a normal course of development, their difficulty may not prevent them from reaching levels of

...pment similar to those reached by normal children. Thus a handicap ...affect development, but not necessarily preclude it.

...writing the book I have deliberately chosen to use the pronoun 'she' ...er than 'he', except where I refer to particular individuals who are male. ...he vast majority of non-fiction books refer to individuals as 'he', unless they are developmental texts and want to refer to parents when 'she' is commonly used. While many authors, especially those writing books since the late 1970s, acknowledge that their use of 'he' does not preclude the female members of the species, I have chosen to reverse the situation. Thus in this text, unless otherwise specified, 'she' should be taken to refer to both male and female.

There are a great many people who have contributed to this book in one way or another and I am grateful to them all. It is impossible to mention everyone. However, there are some to whom I am particularly indebted. My first thanks go to all the children and families that I have worked with over the years. Their interest in my work and willingness to talk with me and share their problems and achievements have fostered my interest in the development of children with special educational needs. Peter Bryant supported my particular interest in children with Down's syndrome, both while I was a doctoral student and afterwards. I am grateful to Cathy Urwin who persuaded me to embark on writing the book. More recently, Graham Gibbs has made many suggestions about ways of clarifying what I am trying to say and, more than anyone else, has encouraged me throughout. The many students who have taken my course at Warwick have contributed an enormous amount; I have learned a great deal from organizing the course and by talking with them. Dennis Bancroft, Jill Boucher, Glyn Collis and Ann Lewis read and commented on drafts of each chapter. Their comments were invaluable and spurred me on to finish the book. My thanks also go to Grant MacIntyre and Adam Sisman for their encouragement. Finally, Philip Carpenter has been a helpful, patient and supportive editor. I am grateful to you all.

# 1

# The handicapped child

## Introduction

### Why study handicapped children?

This book is about handicap. It is also about development. However, it does not just describe the development of handicapped children, rather it examines this development as a way of furthering our understanding of the processes underlying development in general. Any account of development needs to be able to explain how individual normal children develop and how, when there is a handicap, the developmental process is altered. An understanding of how a particular handicap may change the course of development in an individual child can also illuminate our understanding of what may be going on in the normal child; for example, it may alter the emphasis any explanation places on particular experiences.

This is not a new approach. A number of other writers have pointed to the value of studying the development of handicapped children for elucidating the developmental process (e.g. Cicchetti and Stroufe, 1978; Cicchetti and Pogge-Hesse, 1982; Cicchetti and Schneider-Rosen, 1983; Wode, 1983). Cicchetti and various co-workers have argued that such studies can throw light on prerequisites for particular developments, and may clarify the relationship between separate areas of development such as cognitive, social and linguistic developments. Wode in particular points to the value of studying the language development of blind children as a way of extending our understanding of how language develops.

However, there is a problem with this approach which is pointed out by Urwin (1983). Urwin, writing about the development of communication in blind children, argues that it is important to consider the handicapped child's development with care. If their development is underestimated the role of handicap in development may be overestimated. In studies of handicapped children it is important to be sure that what we are looking at is genuine development and neither an artifact of the situation nor of our expectations of how a handicap may influence the course of development. We also need to be certain that any conclusions we reach as to the role of a handicap in development cannot be attributed to some other problem or difficulty.

This book is not only about theory. It is also about ways in which handicapped children may be helped in their development. Although the book examines theoretical and practical implications in separate chapters, it is not intended that they should be seen as separate. A theoretical account which can explain the development of both normal and handicapped children is of great value in deciding how the handicapped children may be helped and in indicating what the priorities for help should be. Theory is also valuable as a way of guiding further research. Conversely practical suggestions which are tried, and prove to be positive, can be a useful way of testing any theory. The theory must be able to accommodate the results of any intervention. However, it does not follow that the theory underlying a successful intervention necessarily explains how that development normally comes about. For example behaviour modification, which is based on learning theory, may be used successfully to teach some of the features of language behaviour to a mentally handicapped child, but this does not mean that learning theory explains the language acquisition of a non-handicapped child.

## How the book is organized

The book considers five areas of handicap, blindness, deafness, motor handicap, Down's syndrome and autism. The development of children with each of these handicaps is described separately in chapters 2–6. Chapter 7 considers some practical implications of the studies which are discussed in these five chapters, and chapter 8 examines some theoretical implications of the studies. The remainder of this first chapter describes each of the handicaps, and discusses their incidences and causes. The final section of this chapter indicates some of the difficulties in studying handicapped children. Readers whose main interest is in the psychological consequences of handicap should move to the final section of this chapter. The remaining sections of this first chapter can be used as a reference source for details of the handicaps as and when required.

## Some facts about handicap

The incidence of any handicap will depend on a variety of factors. One of the most important factors is the way in which the handicap is defined: how the child who is handicapped is identified as handicapped and different from the child who is not handicapped. Definitions of handicap are subject to many influences, two important ones being the knowledge that we have and the views and attitudes of the society in which we live. Whatever definition is adopted it is important to realize that there is, from a psychological point of view, no true definition of handicap and no definitive cut-off point.

The two influences of knowledge and attitude cannot be separated. The sort of knowledge that is collected and the way in which it is understood and used will depend to a great extent on social and political pressures. This can be illustrated by examining the reasons why more children are identified as handicapped today than in past centuries, or even a few decades ago.

There are at least three reasons why we are more aware of handicap today than in the past. One is the nature of work and the shift in developed countries from rural communities to industrialized urban areas. The second is due to developments in education, and the third relates to advances in medicine. These factors can be illustrated by considering some of the changes which have happened in Britain. Following the Industrial Revolution (1750s to 1830s) people who were unable to adapt to the changing living and working conditions became more noticeable. At the same time it became increasingly necessary to provide education so that young people could be prepared for the rapidly changing demands of work. The provision of education itself also led to the identification of those children who could not cope, and with this came the beginnings of provision for the handicapped, often separate from the rest of society. The increased urbanization led to increases in disease as a result of poor sanitation, and this was followed by an increasing awareness of factors important for health and of ways of preventing and treating disease. Industrialization has also led to many technical developments, a number of which have enabled the dissemination of information and knowledge, for example, television and radio.

Over the years knowledge has accrued and values and attitudes have changed. From the point of view of handicap, one of the most significant developments was that of the intelligence test at the turn of this century. Originally Binet was commissioned to devise a test which would distinguish those children who would benefit from education from those who would not. Since these early beginnings, the psychometrics business has exploded on either side of the Atlantic, not always with positive consequences. We have also seen changes in how intelligence is conceptualized, and in the sort of legislation which is made concerning the handicapped.

For these sorts of reason we are much more aware of handicap today than previously. However, many people are still surprised by how many children are identified as handicapped. Warnock (1978) concluded that 'up to one in five children at some time during their school career will require some form of special educational provision.' Using fairly pragmatic criteria, Wynn and

Wynn (1979) concluded that about 1 per cent of children are so severely handicapped that they require and will continue to require considerable help with many or all basic living skills such as dressing, washing and feeding, and a further 10 per cent are handicapped such that they are unlikely as adults to find more than the humblest sort of employment. Wynn and Wynn report general agreement with these figures across surveys in Canada, France, USA and Britain. This means that on average one child in ten will have no employment prospects or very reduced prospects at the end of childhood as a result of their own characteristics.

As Wynn and Wynn point out in their excellent book, these figures will vary depending upon a variety of factors. In particular, more of the most severely handicapped children are currently surviving, and surviving for longer, because of improved medical treatments, whilst the incidence of children with less severe handicaps has tended to decrease in the most developed countries as a result of improvements in health care and living conditions generally. For example they report that in the 1920s only about 10 per cent of babies with Down's syndrome reached school age, whereas the corresponding figure in the 1970s was seven or eight times higher. For children with less severe handicaps there are quite marked differences of incidence between developed countries. Wynn and Wynn cite the figure of 5 per cent for Sweden, a country which has promoted a great deal of health awareness among the general population, compared to 10 per cent for Britain and France. They suggest that the equivalent figure for the USA may be even higher.

Thus the incidence of handicap is not fixed but will shift from year to year and from country to country. But wherever it is looked at and although definitions vary, the actual numbers involved are large. Wynn and Wynn estimate that in Britain 130,000 children under 15 are very severely handicapped, with about 30,000 handicapped children being born each year. Babson and Benson (1971) estimate that in the USA 50,000 babies a year are born with severe malformations, and a further 300,000 have some degree of learning difficulty, ranging from mild to severe. These numbers alone argue for the necessity of including the study of handicapped children in any account of development.

In many cases of handicap the cause is unknown and, even though knowledge of handicap is increasing all the time, it seems unlikely that the causes of all handicaps will ever be known. One reason for this is that different factors can influence an individual child's development at different times. For example, the environment of the child after her birth can mitigate the effects of adverse perinatal factors and vice versa, so that a baby of low birth weight born into a caring, stimulating environment is less likely to have learning difficulties later than a baby of similar birth weight who is reared under less supportive conditions.

Handicaps originate at different stages of development: before birth (prenatally); at around the time of birth (perinatally); and after birth (postnatally). In general, the earlier in development a handicap originates, the more severe it is, with the most severe handicaps being caused during pregnancy. The French Government (Wynn and Wynn, 1979) estimated that 35 per cent of all handicapping conditions which are identified in the first 12 months of life actually originate in the first 12 weeks of pregnancy. The British National Child Development Study (Bradshaw, 1975) found that 71 per cent of those children who had a severe handicap at the age of 7 years had a defect which originated either before birth or around the time of birth. A similar figure was reported in a survey of handicapped adults who were dependent on social security carried out by the USA Department of Labor. In addition, this survey found that in 94 per cent of the cases the disability was the result of some nervous system defect (Niswander and Gordon, 1972).

Prevention of handicap is much easier for handicaps originating later on in pregnancy than for handicaps originating in the first three months. The proportion of children with Down's syndrome, a chromosomal disorder originating at conception, as a function of the number of children with severe mental handicap, may actually be increasing. Wynn and Wynn (1979) cite figures of 21 per cent and 32 per cent of all severe mental handicap as attributable to Down's syndrome for France in 1968 and Sweden in 1975 respectively. Chromosome aberrations cause at least one-third of all cases of severe mental handicap, and these will remain despite improvements in antenatal care.

Unlike chromosome anomalies, cerebral palsy, which results from damage to the brain, originates later in pregnancy. Data from the Danish Cerebral Palsy register for 1950–9 shows that 89 per cent of the cases originated at or before birth, the remainder being due to some postnatal infection of the brain or an accident (Glenting, 1976). If this is the case, then countries which have improved their antenatal care programmes should have a reduced incidence of cerebral palsy. Data from both Sweden and Denmark support this. For the period 1954–8 the incidence in Sweden was 22 per 10,000 births and for the period 1967–70 it was 13 per 10,000 births (Hagberg, 1975; Hagberg et al., 1975a, b). Over this period Sweden reduced the incidence of cerebral palsy by over 40 per cent. In Denmark a reduction of 22 per cent was achieved between the mid-1950s and mid-1960s, bringing the incidence down to 20 per 10,000 births (Glenting, 1976).

This discussion shows that handicaps originate at different points in development and that this has implications not just for incidence but also for ways of reducing the number of children who are handicapped. It is very important for research to continue to try to unravel the causes of handicap. Research is important for prevention, and also for the individual with the handicap and for those around her. In many cases knowledge of the cause may not help to alleviate the condition although there are exceptions, a notable example being phenylketonuria where severe mental handicap can be prevented by strict dietary control. However, knowing what has caused their child to be handicapped may be very important for the parents of the child. If they know the cause then they have something on which to focus their anger or distress or even guilt. If the cause is not known some parents may spend time worrying about things they may have done or may not have done which could be responsible for the handicap. This may affect their attitude and behaviour towards their child. Knowledge of the cause of their child's handicap is obviously of direct relevance if they decide to have a further child, and if the child wants to have children later on.

In addition, although two children may be said to have the same handicap, the exact nature of their handicap may vary and this may be due at least in part to the handicaps being the result of different causes. Thus knowledge of the cause may have implications for development.

In the sections which follow I have tried to provide a clear description of five areas of handicap. I have also tried to point out features of each handicap which may be of particular relevance to how the children develop.


*Blindness*

Most blind children can see something, even though their vision may be very limited or restricted to only a small portion of their visual field. The nature of the vision that a child has is important because of its implications for development. For example, a child who has peripheral vision but no central vision will not be able to see what is straight ahead of her, but will be able to see things off to the side, as if holding opaque discs a short distance from each eye and looking straight at them. Such a child will be unable to read print, but may be quite mobile and run around freely. In contrast, a child with only central vision, as if looking through a long tube, may be very cautious in her movements but be able to read print. Yet another child may have vision which is blurred at all distances and positions, whilst another may be extremely near sighted. Both of these children are likely to move about cautiously, although the near sighted child may be able to read print and to inspect objects visually if she holds them right up to her eyes. The child with blurred vision at all distances is unlikely to be able to do either of these things. Some of these differences in the nature of the blindness are characteristic of certain eye conditions which will be examined later in this section.

The method most commonly used for assessing how much and how clearly a person can see (their visual acuity) is the Snellen chart, the chart of letters or digits of decreasing size seen in most opticians' premises. This measures distance vision under controlled conditions. For a person with normal sight the Snellen reading will be 6/6 in metric measurement (or 20/20 in imperial measurement). This means that the person can see at 6 metres (20 feet) the letters she should be able to see at 6 metres (20 feet). If you have 6/12 vision this means that something that a person with 6/6 vision can see at 12 metres needs to be brought to 6 metres for you to be able to see it clearly. If you have 3/60 vision something which the normal eye could see at 60 metres would have to be brought 57 metres nearer, to a distance of 3 metres for you to be able to see it clearly. Beyond 3/60 vision, sight is usually measured by the distance at which the person can accurately count the number of fingers held up. Some blind people may not be able to perceive even fingers, but they may have some light perception. Light perception is similar to what a sighted person would see with her eyes closed when something solid is passed between a light and her eyes. Other blind people may not even have light perception.

Although a person's visual acuity is important, what they can do with the vision they have is more important. For example, two children may have 6/60 vision, but one be very near sighted and the other not. As the person gets older her visual efficiency may improve, although her acuity remains much the same, because she gets better at using the vision she has. In fact, the use which a visually handicapped child makes of her residual vision may be an indicator of her intelligence, and of the sort of support and learning opportunities she has had. There are various scales which can be used to assess the school child's residual use of her vision, for example the Barraga Visual Efficiency Scale (Barraga, 1970), and the Look and Think Checklist (Tobin et al., 1978). Neither of these just measures what the child can see, but assesses the sense that the child makes of what she can see.

Blindness has been defined both legally and educationally. The legal definition states that a person is blind either if she has a central visual acuity of 3/60 or less in her better eye with correcting glasses, or if her central visual acuity is better than 3/60 and she has a peripheral field defect such that the widest angle that the visual field subtends is no greater than 20 degrees, that is, less than a sixteenth of the peripheral field. Partially sighted people are those with visual acuities between 3/60 and 6/60 in the better eye after all necessary medical or surgical treatment has been given and compensating lenses provided. Mittler (1970) gives the following educational definition of blind and partially sighted pupils:

Blind pupils – those who have no sight or whose sight is or is likely to become so defective that they require education by methods not involving the use of sight. Partially sighted pupils – pupils who by reason of defective vision cannot follow the normal regime of ordinary schools without detriment to their sight or to their educational development, but can be educated by special methods involving the use of sight.

All these definitions of blindness and partial sightedness will include children with a wide range of visual impairments, and for this reason many recent writers have begun to use the term visually handicapped in preference to blind. The term blind implies that the person cannot see, whereas the term visually handicapped implies that vision is impaired, but not that the person is necessarily unable to see anything. In this book the terms blind and visually handicapped will be used interchangeably to refer to those people who would be defined legally as blind; those who would be defined as partially sighted will be referred to as partially sighted.

Blindness is fairly infrequent and its incidence depends on the age of the population examined. Many sighted people have never met a blind person, and those who have most probably know an elderly blind person rather than a blind child. The incidence of blindness in childhood also varies with age, since some children become blind, whilst others are born blind. It also varies with the country in which the child is born. Blindness is much more common in Third World countries than in developed countries and this is due to the fact that a number of diseases which are fairly common in Third World countries are associated with blindness. Most of these could be prevented. The prevalence of blindness amongst the school population in the UK was given as 1.37 per 10,000 of the population by Vernon in 1972. For the partially sighted the corresponding figure was 2.66. Of these children half of the blind and almost a quarter of the partially sighted had at least one other handicap. In terms of actual numbers, Dobree and Boulter (1982) suggest that about 200 children under the age of 15 are registered as blind every year in England and Wales. About half of these children are blind from birth, that is congenitally blind. Figures for the USA are given as about 10 per 10,000 school aged children, three of these being considered blind for educational purposes. It has been estimated that in the USA 36,800 people under 18 are severely visually handicapped (Garwood, 1983).

In 1978 there were probably no more than 3,500 children in England and Wales who were identified as visually handicapped and requiring special education. However, events can alter this. For example, it has been estimated that the epidemic of maternal rubella, or german measles, in the USA in 1964–6 led to 30,000 children with eye defects which was a dramatic increase over the previous years.

Visual defects have many different causes, although in possibly as many as half the cases of congenital blindness the cause is unknown. Most children who have some form of visual defect have something wrong with their eye or eyes. However, the defect can be due to atrophy of the optic nerve or some brain damage. With optic nerve atrophy the extent of the child's vision depends on the number and location of the damaged fibres. It is usually congenital, that is present at birth, but seldom inherited. When brain damage causes blindness the eyes are usually normal and the blindness is secondary to some brain malfunction. These children often have additional severe handicaps.

However, in most cases of blindness something is wrong with the eyes which, in a condition known as anophthalmia, are actually missing. In retinoblastoma, a malignant tumour develops on the retina, the light sensitive cells at the back of the eye, and if untreated by removal of the eye (enucleation) and radiation therapies the tumour can spread along the optic nerve to the brain. The age of onset of the tumour varies, and can be inherited. These children may be particularly bright (e.g. Williams, 1968; Witkin et al., 1971), although the exact nature and explanation of this superiority is not clear (Warren, 1977).

The most common cause of blindness is congenital cataract, in which the lens of the eye is cloudy. If the opacity of the lens is very dense the lens may be removed and glasses provided, although the person's vision is still likely to be poor. This condition is sometimes inherited.

Another inherited condition is albinism and is the result of a partial or total lack of pigment from the eyes, and also from the hair and the skin. The irises, that part of the eyes which is normally coloured blue, green or brown, are usually very pale and, because the eyes cannot screen out bright light, these children are very sensitive to light, or 'photophobic'. The functioning of the retina may also be affected. Individuals with albinism can usually read print. They may also show nystagmus, a condition in which the eyes shift rapidly from side to side.

Congenital glaucoma is a further condition which is usually inherited. The normal eye is filled with fluids which are being produced and reabsorbed all the time. In glaucoma the outflow of one of the fluids, vitreous humour, is impaired and as more is produced pressure builds up and constricts the blood vessels which nourish the retinal cells. Unless the pressure is relieved surgically the retinal cells die, those at the periphery first, resulting in reduced peripheral vision.

In a further condition the eyes are oval rather than round and, because the lens cannot accommodate sufficiently, the image falls short of the retina, resulting in myopia, or shortsightedness. The more elongated the eye ball the greater the myopia.

A condition which results in peripheral vision is macular degeneration, where the light receptor cells in the central portion of the retina have failed to develop or have been destroyed by disease. If the mother contracts rubella (german measles) in the first three months of pregnancy, the baby may be born with cataracts and other problems, notably deafness.

In retrolental fibroplasia small portions of the retina may be left intact. This is relatively infrequent now, but was more frequent in the 1940s and 1950s before its cause was known. It is due to an excess of oxygen, which may be administered at birth to premature underweight babies to keep them alive and to try to prevent brain damage. The oxygen excess causes the retinal blood vessels to grow abnormally, leading to retinal damage, although small portions of the retina may remain healthy.

In retinal dysplasia the retina fails to develop properly resulting in little or no vision. This condition can be inherited.

Some children may become blind later on in their lives through direct injury or as a result of an infection such as meningitis, where the membrane covering the brain and spinal cord becomes inflamed. These children are said to be adventitiously blinded, and the visual experiences they have had, particularly if extensive, are likely to have implications for their developmental progress.

## Deafness

When I think of deaf people I immediately imagine two categories: those whom I assume cannot hear at all and who probably use a sign language I cannot understand, and the hard-of-hearing, commonly people who have gradually become increasingly deaf as they have got older. It is clear that deafness varies, and in fact the variation is much greater than my first two groups suggest. Deafness is, however, rarely total.

Deafness can vary in several ways. It is not just a case of how deaf a person is, but also the nature of the deafness: for example, can she hear high notes as well as she can hear low notes? This is important information because it has implications for learning to speak, for whether or not a hearing aid would be useful and for education. It is also important as a background for understanding the deaf child's developmental difficulties.

Deafness is graded along two scales. One is intensity which is measured in decibels (dB) or units of sound. The normal threshold for hearing pure tones is O dB. The second scale is frequency, measured in Hertz (Hz). Here the range for the normal ear is from about 20 to 20,000 Hz, and the frequencies which are important for speech fall between 250 and 4,000 Hz.

On the intensity scale a loss of about 20–5 dB is hardly significant. Even up to 40 dB a person could hear speech if she listened carefully but, compared to a hearing person, she would be slower to notice that someone was speaking. A person with a loss of up to 55 dB could hear sounds but would have difficulties interpreting them, although a hearing aid might help. These people are described as partially hearing. By using a hearing aid it is usually possible to gain about 30 dB, and in certain cases more. Hearing aids are not really useful unless the person's hearing loss is greater than 40 dB. With smaller losses the gains in intensity that are possible using an aid are counteracted by the distortion which occurs. Aids are of most use for losses between 40 and 55 dB.

Losses of over 55 dB present increasingly severe problems, with the person who has a loss of over 90 dB perhaps being able to hear a very loud noise close by, such as a pneumatic drill, but more on the basis of the vibration produced than the noise itself. These people are deaf. Usually a hearing aid will not be of any use, although it may help some people, particularly when the loss occurs after some language has been acquired. In certain cases amplification is actually painful and so cannot be used: this is called loudness recruitment.

When measuring a person's ability to hear it is necessary to find out if the person can hear tones of different frequencies as well as intensities, since the pattern of intensity loss can vary over the frequency range. The pattern of loss is important as it can tell us something about what aspects of speech the person can hear. This is because although vowels and consonants are complex sounds made up of many different frequency components, they can be distinguished on the basis of frequency. The frequency components of vowels are concentrated below 1000 Hz whilst the frequency components of consonants tend to fall above 1000 Hz. A person with a high frequency loss will tend only to hear the vowel sounds of speech, and this makes speech very difficult to interpret. Being able to hear consonants is much more useful. Another point to note is that consonants are of weaker intensity than vowels. This means that a person who has a 55 dB loss across the whole frequency range will hear more vowel sounds than consonant sounds. The superiority of vowels is about 15 dB. Hearing aids can be designed to raise the intensity of certain frequencies or to reduce the intensity of others. This will be particularly useful for a person who has a greater loss of the high frequencies than of the low frequencies. By selectively reducing the amplitude of the lower frequencies the frequencies characteristic of consonants will be made more salient and this will aid the person's perception of speech.

Deafness is also described in terms of how the person functions. In Britain, the Ministry of Education (1962) provides a definition in terms of the educational needs of deaf and partially hearing children:

[D]eaf pupils . . . pupils with impaired hearing who require education by methods suitable for pupils with little or no naturally acquired speech or language . . . [P]artially hearing pupils . . . pupils with impaired hearing whose development of speech and language, even if retarded, is following a normal pattern, and who require for their education special arrangements or facilities though not necessarily all the educational methods used for deaf pupils.

Similar definitions, although not restricted to children and therefore not specific to education, have been adopted in the USA:

A deaf person is one whose hearing disability precludes successful processing of linguistic information through audition, with or without a hearing aid. A hard of hearing person is one who, generally with the use of a hearing aid, has residual hearing sufficient to enable successful processing of linguistic information through audition. (Report of the Ad Hoc Committee to Define Deaf and Hard of Hearing, 1975)

Like visual handicap, there is tremendous variety in the nature and extent of deafness, and from a developmental point of view it is especially important to be able to assess the impairment. Unfortunately it is difficult to make accurate hearing assessments of very young children, although there are developments in this area, some of which will be described later. In general children who are deaf, that is have losses greater than 55 dB, are identified in the first year, but children who have a smaller loss may go undetected for much longer.

The problem is how to measure the sorts of sounds a deaf child can hear. In the UK babies are routinely screened between 6 and 12 months of age. At this age a hearing baby will respond to a sound-making object which is out of sight and to one side by turning her head towards the sound. A baby who cannot hear the sound will not turn her head. Of course, the baby may not turn towards the sound for other reasons. She may have an attentional problem or some physical disability which prevents her making the head turn. Also a child with a small hearing loss may turn quite accurately to the correct side, and therefore her hearing loss will go unidentified.

Although the head turn test is routine, there are some interesting developments for even earlier screening of hearing, as early as the first few days. In one development the baby lies in a cradle and her movements and her heart and respiration rates are monitored by computer (e.g. Simmons, 1977). Tones of various intensities and frequencies are presented and any physiological reaction from the baby is noted. This sort of equipment can be used to identify babies who show abnormal reactions to sounds and their development could then be monitored very carefully. Another development is of an instrument which is placed in the outer ear canal and makes a short audible click. The resulting vibrations of the ear drum can be detected by a device called a tympanometer. The movement of the ear drum is related to the frequency of the sound and any abnormalities noted. Unfortunately neither of these techniques is widely available.

Measurement becomes easier as children get older. Between about 18 months and 3 years the child can be asked to do certain things, whilst the consonant and vowel structure of the requests and their amplitudes are varied. Also the child's own language may give a good indication of what she can and cannot hear.

At ages over about 3 years a pure tone audiogram can be obtained. This is done for each ear and shows the intensity loss over the frequency range. The procedure requires that the child indicates when she hears a tone, and to achieve this with young children you have to build up to it gradually so that the task is clear to them. In the first instance the child might be taught to respond to the sight of a drum being beaten, then the drum is moved out of sight and beaten. Eventually pure tones are presented for response.

The number of children who are identified as having a hearing impairment increases with increasing age. There are two reasons for this. The first is that as the child gets older it is easier to identify deafness, particularly if it is partial. Second, some children are not deaf when they are born, but they become deaf later on. Kyle and Allsop's (1982a) interviews with deaf 16–65 year olds revealed that 72.6 per cent were deaf at birth, 13.1 per cent became deaf in the first two years, 8.6 per cent between the ages of 3 and 5, and 6.8 per cent became deaf after the age of 5. About 9 per 10,000 school children are either deaf or partially hearing. A report by the Department of Education and Science (1968) shows that in 1954 the rates per 10,000 of the school population for deaf and partially hearing were 6.00 and 1.86 respectively. The corresponding figures for 1967 were 3.93 and 4.68 which shows a fall in the number of deaf children matched by a rise in the number of partially hearing children. This shift over the 13 years towards greater numbers of partially hearing children is most likely the result of earlier screening and assessment and provision of hearing aids. In the USA it has been estimated that between 500,000 to 700,000 children have impaired hearing (Green, 1981).

Deafness seems to affect slightly more boys than girls although the difference is small. However, more deaf boys have additional handicaps – about 35 per cent compared to 30 per cent of deaf girls.

Deafness can be caused by damage to different anatomical areas of the ear, and the characteristics of the deafness which results and the time of onset varies. However, in about a third to a half of deaf children the cause is unknown, although Kyle and Allsop (1982a) report that 54.9 per cent of the deaf 16–65 year olds they interviewed did not know the cause of their deafness, which in 79 per cent was profound. However, since this figure is not based on medical records, it may be an overestimate.

The ear can be divided into three parts, the external ear, the middle ear and the inner ear. The two main types of loss are conductive and sensorineural which result from pathology of, or damage to, the middle ear and the inner ear respectively. Sensorineural deafness is the more common and the more drastic. It involves damage to the sensory hair cells of the cochlea or the auditory nerve and is usually irreversible. A conductive disorder on the other hand is seldom total and is usually reversible. It involves an air bone gap somewhere in the cavity of the middle ear which is spanned by three bones. Mixed conductive and sensorineural losses also occur, and in a few cases there is some central malfunction of the auditory pathways within the central nervous system.

A sensorineural loss can occur prenatally, perinatally or postnatally. By far the most common cause of sensorineural deafness is genetic, probably accounting for 40–60 per cent. In most cases it is carried by a recessive gene such that if both parents are deaf the child is four times more likely to be deaf than if only one parent is deaf. In fact, one or both parents of about 10 per cent of deaf children are themselves deaf.

Children who inherit their deafness seldom have additional handicaps. Unfortunately, the remaining causes of sensorineural deafness often result in other problems as well. About a third of all deaf children have at least one additional handicap.

In the prenatal period the second main cause of deafness is maternal rubella, or german measles, and here the children may also have visual problems, central nervous system damage and congenital heart disease. Rubella results in deafness in about 22 per cent of children whose mothers contract it in the first two months of pregnancy. This is probably the most susceptible period because it is the time during which the inner ear completes its development. Damage from rubella contracted by the mother later in pregnancy is relatively unlikely. As a cause of deafness rubella accounts for about 10 per cent of deaf children, but following the rubella epidemic in the USA in 1964–6 the figure rose to around 40 per cent.

At the time of birth there are two main hazards, incompatibility between the rhesus factors in the blood of the mother and the blood of the foetus, and cerebral anoxia, a restriction of oxygen to the brain. Together, these account for 10–20 per cent of cases, and leave the children not just deaf but often multiply handicapped. The anoxia may be associated with prematurity and compared to full term babies such children are four times more likely to be deaf.

The final group of causes of sensorineural deafness occurs postnatally and is due to bacterial infections of the central nervous system. Such children are commonly multiply handicapped. The main infection is meningitis which results in inflammation of the meninges, the covering of the brain and spinal cord. Less than 5 per cent of children who contract meningitis become deaf, accounting for about 10 per cent of the deaf population. The other, but less common, infection leading to deafness is encephalitis.

The main cause of conductive deafness is otitis media or middle ear infection which occurs and can reoccur in childhood. It seldom results in total deafness but because it may reoccur it can lead to fluctuating levels of hearing.

Finally deafness can result from damage to the auditory pathways within the central nervous system. This may result from the mother being exposed to a teratogen during pregnancy, and probably the most well-known example is that of thalidomide. The critical period for this drug to have its adverse affect on the foetus seems to have been 35–50 days after the woman's last menstrual period: that is, very early on in the pregnancy. There are commonly additional handicaps, which will be described in the next section.

## Motor handicap

I am going to concentrate on three handicaps: spina bifida, cerebral palsy and damage caused by the drug thalidomide. The first two often involve a degree of brain damage, whereas thalidomide damage seldom does although there may be other problems, notably deafness. Thus none of the three handicaps presents straightforward motor problems, and this is a difficulty when interpreting the findings and examining their implications for theory.

## Spina bifida

This term literally means a divided or split spine. What happens is that during the second and third months of pregnancy when the spinal column is being formed, part of the tissue which normally covers the spinal cord fails to fuse over, leaving the cord exposed at that point. In other words the spine is split. In the embryo the spinal cord originates from a flat sheet of cells. A groove forms along the length of this sheet of cells and normally the cells on either side of the groove grow over and eventually meet. This forms a tube called the neural tube which eventually differentiates into the brain and spinal cord, covered by the skull bones and the spinal vertebrae respectively. In spina bifida the cells fail to close over at some point along the length of the groove.

There are several different sorts of spinal damage of this type. In one the vertebrae do not fuse right over but the cord itself is usually undamaged and often all that can be detected is a slight bump in the skin somewhere along the spinal column. This condition is known as spina bifida occulta and since it rarely has any adverse affects on development I shall not be concerned any more with it. The other main type is spina bifida cystica which is subdivided into myelomeningocele and meningocele. Both of these are characterized by a sac-like cyst on the skin's surface which contains membranes and fluid which have escaped through the gap left by the unfused vertebrae. In myelomeningocele part of the spinal cord and attached nervous tissue protrudes through the gap, whereas in meningocele the spinal cord remains in its correct position and only the cord's covering, the meninges, and the fluid surrounding the cord, the cerebrospinal fluid, protrude into the cyst. Not surprisingly myelomeningocele is by far the more serious of the two conditions, and unfortunately it is also the most common, accounting for about 85 per cent of all cases of spina bifida cystica.

Spina bifida can occur anywhere along the spinal column, although it is most common in the lower back, the lumbar region, where the vertebrae close over last. The site of the lesion is important since in myelomeningocele nerves which originate below the lesion will usually fail to operate their respective muscles, thus preventing movement. Nerves to the hips, legs and bladder

originate in the lumbar region. Below this in the sacral region nerves inner-
vating the sphincter muscles of the urethra and rectum originate. So the
primary problems in spina bifida, particularly myelomeningocele, are those of
incontinence and paralysis of the legs.

Unfortunately, in many cases of spina bifida there is an additional problem:
hydrocephalus. This is associated with myelomeningocele in 85 per cent of
cases and involves an accumulation of cerebrospinal fluid around the brain
owing to an obstruction in the normal circulation of this fluid. Unless this
obstruction is bypassed by the insertion of a shunt to drain off the excess
fluid, the build-up of fluid exerts pressure on the brain and skull, causing
damage to the brain cells and enlargement of the head. A consequence of
hydrocephalus may be some degree of intellectual retardation, which makes it
more difficult to ascertain the effects of the motor problems on development.

Spina bifida has been known about for a long time, with descriptions as far
back as 2000 BC. However, until fairly recently, the majority of babies born
with this deformity died in the first few weeks and months after birth, particularly those with severe myelomeningocele and associated hydrocephalus.
These babies died for a variety of reasons, notably some infection of the central
nervous system which attacked the exposed portion of the spinal cord, or
as a direct consequence of the hydrocephalus. The reduction in the mortality
rate was brought about mainly by advances in medicine. In the 1940s the
development of antibiotic treatment enabled previously fatal infections of the
central nervous system to be controlled, and this together with improved
surgical expertise prevented the deaths of many children with spina bifida.
Another advance was the development in 1956 of a shunt to control the
circulation of cerebrospinal fluid. This could be inserted in cases of
hydrocephalus to drain off the excess fluid and direct it back into the blood
system.

In Britain the incidence of spina bifida is about 20 for every 10,000 births,
although the mortality rate for babies born with myelomeningocele is still
around 50 per cent by the end of the first year. Slightly more girls than boys
are affected, the ratio being around 1.3 : 1. The prevalence of spina bifida
varies in different parts of the world. For example it has been reported as
being very low, only 1 or 2 per 10,000 births, in certain Negro communities,
whereas the incidence in Ireland has been found to be as high as 40 or 50 per
10,000 births. Prevalence also varies with the age of the mother, mothers
under 20 and those over 35 being most at risk for producing a spina bifida
baby, and mothers over 40 being most at risk for bearing a child with
hydrocephalus. Families in social classes IV and V run a slightly greater risk,
particularly if the mother is over 30 or if she has three or more children.
Another seemingly bizarre finding is that more spina bifida babies are conceived between the months of April and June than at other times of the year in

England, although there is no peak time for hydrocephalus (Rogers and Weatherall, 1976).

All these factors point to the possibility of some environmental cause and recently the mother's diet has come under scrutiny. The argument is that the mother's diet is likely to be poor if she lives in an industrial area, has little money to spend on food and many mouths to feed. The relationship with the month of conception is interesting since it suggests that it is early on in pregnancy that diet is crucial, namely at the time when the neural tube is formed. In England, in the spring and early summer, food is often expensive and of poor quality because the new season's vegetables are not yet available. At this time the mother's diet may be deficient in certain respects. Various dietary culprits have been considered in the past ranging from blighted potatoes to excessive tea drinking, but vitamins are currently attracting most attention. In 1981 Smithells et al. reported that the likelihood of a woman who had already given birth to a baby with a neural tube defect having another similarly handicapped child was much reduced if the woman took additional vitamins for a month before conceiving and for two months after. This finding has support from other groups of workers (e.g. Holmes-Siedle et al., 1982), and has obvious practical implications.

Despite the attractiveness of this explanation it seems unlikely that it is the whole answer. First, by no means all women living in poor conditions, with large families to support on low incomes and who conceive when fresh food is in short supply, produce children with neural tube defects. Second, some spina bifida babies are born to women in advantageous circumstances. Third, women who have already had a child damaged in this way run a much greater risk of having another one than is true for the rest of the population. Between 3 and 6 per cent of families with one such damaged child conceive a second (e.g. Carter, 1974). It seems likely that there is some complex genetic explanation, such that certain mothers (or fathers) are predisposed to produce a child with neural tube damage given certain environmental conditions, in particular depleted vitamin supplies.

Unlike spina bifida, which is always congenital, hydrocephalus can be either congenital or the result of some postnatal infection, notably meningitis, where the membrane covering the brain and spinal cord becomes inflamed.

### Cerebral palsy

Cerebral palsy has been described as 'a disorder of movement and posture resulting from a permanent, non-progressive defect or lesion of the immature brain' (Bax, 1964). As well as these motor behaviour problems, which can range from barely detectable to almost complete physical helplessness, there may be any or a combination of difficulties in vision, hearing, speech and intellectual ability. Between a third and two-thirds of children with cerebral palsy may also suffer from fits. So even though two children may both be said to have cerebral palsy the differences between them may be much greater than their similarities. This makes it even harder to examine the effects of these children's motor difficulties on development than it is in the case of spina bifida.

Nevertheless, it is the motor difficulties which define this group and several different types of motor problems have been identified. Three-quarters of cerebral palsied people are characterized by spastic movements due to a failure of the muscles to relax so that the movements seem stiff and rigid. This group is described as spastic. This results from damage to the motor cortex. An arm may be held pressed against the body with the forearm bent at right angles to the upper arm and the hand bent against the forearm. The fist may be clenched tightly. The leg is often bent at the knee and rotates inwards from the hip. The person may walk on the outside of their foot so that if both legs are involved a scissored gait results. Their balance may be poor because of the odd way that their weight is distributed. Not all limbs are necessarily affected, although they are in about a third of all spastics. The equal involvement of all four limbs is known variously as quadriplegia, tetraplegia or double plegia. About a quarter are hemiplegic, having a spastic leg and arm on one side of the body. In diplegia, accounting for 20 per cent, all the limbs are involved, but the legs are worse than the arms. In 18 per cent only the legs are affected, known as paraplegia. In a very small proportion, less than 2 per cent in each case, the arms are worse than the legs (bilateral hemiplegia), three limbs are affected, usually two legs and an arm (triplegia), or only one limb is affected, usually a leg (monoplegia).

The second largest group is the athetoid group. This group presents a very different picture. As a result of damage to the basal ganglia these people have an excess of uncontrollable movements which interfere with their normal body movements. Their movements seem to be of a writhing, lurching nature and their heads are often drawn back. Uncontrolled facial grimacing and dribbling is common. Although the lack of motor control is usually generalized to the whole body, in a few people only certain limbs are affected. These are then described by the classification used for the spastic group.

A much smaller group are ataxic. This condition is due to damage to the cerebellum and results in poor coordination of movement and disturbed balance. The person may appear clumsy and unsteady and may have difficulty locating themselves in space. They may rush downhill and fall over, but come to a standstill when they try to walk uphill.

The remaining cerebral palsied people have a variety of motor problems ranging from rigidity of the muscles to complete floppiness or some mixture of the conditions described above.

Cerebral palsy is probably slightly more common than spina bifida with estimates ranging from about 15–25 babies per 10,000 babies born alive. And, unlike spina bifida, which is always congenital, cerebral palsy can develop after birth, as can hydrocephalus. The sex ratio is reversed with marginally more boys than girls being born with cerebral palsy.

Postnatal causes including meningitis account for about 10 per cent of children who are diagnosed as suffering from cerebral palsy. Other postnatal causes of cerebral palsy include encephalitis, and various sorts of trauma, such as fractures of the skull, brain tumours and restrictions of the blood supply to parts of the brain. But the main causes of cerebral palsy occur prenatally or perinatally. Rhesus incompatibility between the blood of the foetus and the blood of the mother and subsequent haemolytic disease of the newborn used to account for 10 per cent of these children, especially those with athetoid cerebral palsy, but this has now largely been prevented by giving the baby a blood transfusion shortly after birth. Maternal rubella is sometimes implicated, but by far the largest identified factor is lack of oxygen, or anoxia, at birth. This can occur for a variety of reasons which may be associated with prematurity, low birth weight or a lengthy labour, and again this has obvious practical implications for prevention.

There have been suggestions that certain mothers may be more likely than others to produce abnormal foetuses. This comes from reports of mothers of cerebral palsied children having had more miscarriages or still births than mothers of normal children. For example, Illingworth (1958) states that mothers of cerebral palsied children have a 35 per cent greater loss than mothers of normal children. This has led to some suggestions, as yet unsubstantiated, of a genetic contribution. However, Hewett (1970) questions this raised incidence, reporting that 15 per cent of her mothers had a history of miscarriages and still births compared to a reported 22 per cent amongst women who mostly gave birth to normal children (Newson and Newson, cited in Hewett, 1970). Also cerebral palsy seldom reoccurs in the same family. In Hewett's own study 14 of the children (8 per cent) had a normal twin, an unlikely finding if there is a large genetic contribution.

### Handicap due to thalidomide

This handicap takes its name from the drug which caused a variety of problems. In nearly all cases there is some type of limb deficiency, and around 45 per cent have at least one absent or vestigial limb. It is the long bones of the limbs which are commonly affected, being either completely missing or shortened, although the range of physical handicap is vast, from the absence of a thumb to no limbs at all. The arms tend to be more affected than the legs, and limbs on both sides of the body are usually affected.

It is the physical handicaps that have been emphasized in much of the publicity surrounding thalidomide, and have come to be associated with it, probably because they are visible. But thalidomide led to many other non-visible problems of which deafness 'probably presents the most serious and largely unacknowledged problem in the whole thalidomide disaster' (Pringle and Fiddes, 1970). They report that 20 out of the 60 children affected by thalidomide that they studied had impaired hearing, seven being profoundly deaf.

The physical and hearing problems are probably the most serious difficulties, although as many as a quarter of people damaged by thalidomide have something wrong with their eyesight, and around 10 per cent have some internal deformity, often of the heart or bowel. Thus, before we can draw any conclusions about the role of motor disability in the development of these children, account needs to be taken of the part played by their other difficulties, especially their hearing problems.

The drug thalidomide was available in Britain in the late 1950s until it was withdrawn at the end of 1961, and it is estimated that about 500 children who were born in Britain between 1959 and 1962 were damaged by it. The damage was caused by their mothers taking thalidomide, a non-barbiturate drug, as a sedative during pregnancy. It seems to have arrested the development of different parts of the embryo according to when it was taken, causing the observed malformations. This particular tragedy has implications for the testing of drugs before they are marketed.

### Down's syndrome

The recognition of Down's syndrome is usually attributed to J. Langdon H. Down (1866), although there are earlier reports of individuals who fit the category (e.g. Séguin, 1846). However, after Down's original paper there were many reports which confirmed his observations. All these reports based their diagnosis on a number of clinical features which are characteristic of Down's syndrome.

A well-known clinical feature of Down's syndrome is the slant of the eyes, which resembles that characteristic of people of oriental origin. The top of the Down's syndrome person's head is flatter than that of non-Down's syndrome people, and their heads are shorter from front to back. The nose is often small with a flattened bridge and nostrils which point forward. The tongue is usually furrowed and becomes increasingly so as the person with Down's syndrome gets older, and the teeth, which often appear later than in the normal child, are normally irregular. The ears too may be different, often small, and in particular the lobes may be reduced in size or even absent.

The hands have attracted much attention. They are typically broad and stumpy, and the little finger is likely to be short and crooked and with only one crease. In many Down's syndrome people there is a characteristic fold across the palm called the four finger crease or simian line. It has been reported that the joints are hyperflexible. A further well-known characteristic is a wide space between the first and second toe, although this also tends to occur in people with other mental handicaps.

If a person possesses four or more of the above characteristics and is retarded in her mental development, she in all likelihood has Down's syndrome. However, it is no longer necessary to rely entirely on these features for a diagnosis. The Down's syndrome person also has a characteristic chromosome pattern which may be examined to confirm a clinical diagnosis.

The chromosome abnormality was not identified until 1959, although Mittwoch in 1952 concluded that the Down's person has 24 pairs of chromosomes. At this time the normal complement of chromosomes was unknown, but in 1956 it was reported as 23 pairs (Tjio and Levan, 1956). These pairs are distinct and, with the exception of the two chromosomes determining the individual's sex, they are assigned numbers in order of decreasing chromosome size from 1 to 22. Pairs of chromosomes are assigned to groups as follows: A, pairs 1–3; B, pairs 4 and 5; C, pairs 6–12; D, pairs 13–15; E, pairs 16–18; F, pairs 19 and 20; G, pairs 21, 22 and the sex chromosomes. Mittwoch was later shown to be correct in terms of Down's syndrome being genetic in origin, but incorrect in the actual number of chromosomes present. The most usual chromosomal aberration resulting in Down's syndrome is an additional chromosome (e.g. Jacobs et al., 1959). Originally this chromosome was thought to be a number 21, but subsequent work showed that it is probably the slightly smaller chromosome 22 which is trisomic (e.g. Ridler, 1971). To avoid confusion, the numbers of pairs 21 and 22 have been reversed. This karyotype is variously labelled standard trisomy, trisomy 21 or autosomal trisomy G, after the group label, and accounts for about 95 per cent of all Down's syndrome people.

Approximately 3 per cent of Down's syndrome people have yet another type of genetic abnormality, a translocation. Here, the major part of an additional chromosome of the G group is fused on to the major part of another chromosome of the same group or the D group. These two karyotypes are usually referred to as G/G and D/G translocations, respectively, and they each account for about 1.5 per cent of Down's syndrome people. Since two chromosomes have been fused in these translocations, there are 46 chromosomes in each cell as opposed to the 47 in the standard trisomy. In some cases of a translocation, one of the parents is found to be a carrier of the translocated chromosomes. Such a person is normal, but since two of his or her chromosomes are fused together the person will only possess 45 chromosomes.

The remaining 2 per cent of people with Down's syndrome have two or more different cell types, one of the cell types having a Down's syndrome karyotype and the remainder one or more other karyotypes. These people are called mosaics.

There have been a number of attempts to differentiate the different Down's syndrome karyotypes clinically but generally without much success (e.g. Johnson and Abelson, 1969). One of the problems is that there are so few of the translocation and mosaic types that any large scale study is very difficult. However, recently there has been a growing interest in the dermatoglyphic patterns of the Down's person's hands and feet (e.g. Rodewald et al., 1981), although these are not generally used in making a diagnosis. The Rodewald et al. paper reports a significant correlation between the percentage of trisomic cells in 17 mosaic Down's individuals and the presence of dermatoglyphic palmar patterns characteristic of Down's syndrome. They also found that 20 per cent of the children had one parent with dermatoglyphic patterns characteristic of Down's syndrome. This finding has implications for identifying people who may be at risk of conceiving a child with Down's syndrome.

Down's syndrome is often associated with some additional problems. The two most common ones are various sorts of cardiac malformation and hearing disorders. It is very unclear just how many Down's people have cardiac anomalies. Berg et al. (1960) report an average figure of around 19 per cent, with the percentage figure varying in individual studies from 7 to 70 per cent. The actual figure may be much higher since many heart defects may go undetected. The incidence also tends to be age related, since heart disorders are often a cause of death in the Down's baby's first year. A hearing loss seems to be quite common in a large number of Down's syndrome individuals with as many as two-thirds having a handicapping loss which may fluctuate over time (e.g. Kehoe, 1978; Cunningham and McArthur, 1981). This problem is obviously important when we examine the way in which the Down's child develops.

Estimates of the incidence of Down's syndrome vary, but there is agreement that it is the most common form of mental handicap. The incidence of Down's syndrome has been explored in two ways: by surveying large populations, often relying on clinical rather than chromosomal diagnosis, or by carrying out chromosome studies of consecutive liveborn babies. The incidence is generally agreed to be of the order of 14–20 per 10,000 births (e.g. Connolly, 1977), although some studies report incidences well outside this range, both lower and higher. However, whatever its actual incidence, the number of Down's children who are conceived is very likely much higher, since it is estimated that somewhere between 60 and 70 per cent of all trisomic 21 foetuses abort spontaneously early in pregnancy (e.g. Lindsten et al., 1981).

Down's syndrome occurs in all populations and social classes and it is often reported that more boys than girls have Down's syndrome. This sex difference in Down's syndrome is further exaggerated by the fact that there is a higher mortality rate in the first few years of life for girls with Down's syndrome than for boys with Down's syndrome (Scully, 1973).

One of the difficulties in determining the incidence of Down's syndrome is that a number of Down's babies die in their first few years of life, so the incidence in the population declines as the population gets older. For example, of Cowie's (1970) sample of 81 Down's babies, 13 (16 per cent) had died before the age of 2 years, 8 (10 per cent) within the first 17 weeks. Cunningham and Sloper (1976) report a similar proportion of deaths (6 out of 37, 16.2 per cent) from their sample of children aged from 14 to 30 months.

Why is there a high mortality rate amongst Down's people, especially young ones? One reason is the prevalence of congenital heart disease. A second reason is that Down's people are much more likely to get infectious diseases than non-handicapped people, and more likely to die as a result of some infectious respiratory disease (Øster et al., 1975). One of the consequences of this is that, with the increasing availability of drugs to combat these sorts of infection, Down's people are living longer now than in the past (e.g Carter and Jancar, 1983). However, despite improved medical care, the Down's person under 5 years or over 40 years is still more likely to die than a person without Down's syndrome (e.g. Richards and Siddiqui, 1980).

The incidence of Down's syndrome increases with increasing maternal age. This relationship between maternal age and Down's syndrome has been confirmed many times. Lindsten et al. (1981) report an incidence of 10 per 10,000 live births for women under 28; 10–20 per 10,000 for women aged 29–33; 20–30 per 10,000 for mothers aged 34–6. By 40 the incidence had jumped to 114.6 per 10,000 births, and at over 40 the incidence was 470.6 per 10,000.

For the majority of people with Down's syndrome the factor causing the chromosomal abnormality is obscure, although there have been plenty of suggestions. As early as 1883 Shuttleworth argued that they were unfinished children whose development for some reason was incomplete. Sutherland in 1899 pointed to syphilis, and J. Langdon H. Down's son (R. L. Langdon-Down) in 1906 pointed to familial tuberculosis. None of these suggestions has had any support and all have been discarded. Other suggestions which have been similarly unsupported include maternal stress, parental alcoholism, thyroid deficiency and a small amniotic sac.

The discovery that Down's syndrome was genetic in origin led to an increasing search for a cause. Interestingly, several decades before this Waardenburg (1932) suggested that Down's syndrome might be due to non-disjunction, a failure of the chromosomes to separate during the formation of the ovum or sperm. However, it is still unclear why this might occur. The association with maternal age has been used to suggest that it has something to do with the forming of the ovum, but Stene et al. (1981) have also pointed to a paternal factor, though this latter suggestion has been questioned (e.g. Hook and Cross, 1982). Observations by Connolly (1977) indicate that environmental factors may be important in determining whether or not a Down's child is conceived. Connolly found that although the birth rate amongst women over 35 in Ireland up until 1974 was falling, there was no sign that the number of children born with Down's syndrome was decreasing. Connolly argues for the existence of a presently unknown teratogenic agent. This view, which is also suggested by Jongbloet (1975), is still in need of direct evidence.

In a very few people with Down's syndrome, the cause will be the inheritance of a translocation, although the mechanism by which the parent acquires the translocation is unknown.

## *Autism*

Autism is not new, although it has only been acknowledged as a condition for 40 years. One of the earliest accounts of a child who is now thought to have been autistic was by Itard (1801/1807). He described a boy deemed to have been raised by wolves who has become known as the wild boy of Aveyron. This boy, Victor, was found at the age of about 10 or 11 living in a wood. Itard's description of Victor makes it quite clear that today he would have been labelled as autistic.

What are the features of autism? For many people the term autism means a withdrawing of oneself from the reality of day to day living, and this is certainly characteristic of these children. They seem to keep within themselves and avoid contact with other people. However, the term autism also carries with it the idea that the person withdraws into herself in order to live in some sort of fantasy world. This is not thought to be part of the autistic syndrome. For this reason the term autism is not an entirely appropriate label for these particular children, but no suitable alternative has been suggested. Interestingly, Wing and Gould (1979) have pointed out that many of the behaviours which characterize autistic children can also be found in non-autistic children. They suggest that it may be more useful to examine this larger group of socially impaired children, rather than to consider subgroups such as autistic children. However, this book will focus on the characteristics of the autistic child.

Kanner was the first person to attempt to classify systematically the behaviour of autistic children in 1943. He extracted a number of features, although he intended that the case studies which he described should serve as the way of diagnosing further children. In his original paper Kanner discusses about ten diagnostic points, but in a later paper with Eisenberg (Eisenberg and

Kanner, 1956) five separate areas are identified. These are the main areas which are usually attributed to Kanner:

1 A profound lack of affective contact with other people. The children show little or no interest in other people, tending not to look at them and failing to demonstrate any sort of emotional response towards them. They are socially withdrawn.
2 An obsessive desire for things to be kept the same. This can range from the order of the books on the bookshelf, to their day to day routine. If there is any change, even a slight one, the child may show great distress, even having a tantrum. This behaviour will last until the change is altered back to how it was. This characteristic is also seen in various rituals they perform which will be repeated over and over again without variation.
3 A fascination with objects. Objects like stones or leaves will be collected. They will be picked up and handled very carefully and with a surprising degree of skill.
4 Communication difficulties. Many of them are mute. If they do have some language, then they seem unable to use it for communicating with other people, and much of it is inappropriate.
5 Good cognitive potential. They look intelligent and thoughtful.

Kanner also stressed that the symptoms must be present from early childhood.

Over the years certain aspects of Kanner's characteristics have been challenged. There are two main challenges, one concerning the intelligence of these children, and the other concerning the primary symptom. Kanner's conclusion that these children were of good cognitive potential was based on observing that they usually look normal and intelligent and often have intelligent professional parents. In addition, he observed that autistic children are often exceptionally good at something, like remembering all the items on a shopping list, or a nursery rhyme after only one hearing. He assumed that this must reflect an underlying intelligence. More recently, psychologists have begun to realize that you do not have to be equally good or bad at everything, and that it is possible for a child who is not very bright to be good at one or two things. The current view of autism is that the majority are intellectually impaired, and that in some children this coexists with isolated skills.

The second challenge to Kanner's original proposal is to question which of the behaviours are most important, or primary, to the condition. Kanner held that the absence of any emotional response to people was of fundamental importance, together with the insistence on things staying the same. One of the problems with this position is that these behaviours cannot account for the other behaviours which go to make up the condition. More recent researchers, notably Wing and Rutter, have argued that the basic impairment is cognitive. They argue that a cognitive impairment leads to problems in communication and language, and that the behavioural and emotional difficulties are secondary to this. Rutter (1983) argued that autistic children have a basic cognitive deficit, basic in the sense that it is fundamental to their handicap, and a deficit in the sense that certain of their cognitive processes are damaged. Such a view is much more compatible with what we know about autism than is Kanner's.

Not all the children who are diagnosed as autistic show all of the behaviours. The severity of the behaviours varies and they generally tend to become less severe as the child gets older. This makes it hard to know where to draw the boundary, to say which children are autistic and which children are not. An attempt has been made to get around this by calling the children who have Kanner's two essential behaviours to a marked degree the nuclear group. Children who have many autistic characteristics, but in whom Kanner's two essential behaviours are not so marked, have been called the non-nuclear group. Children whose behaviour puts them outside these groups are not autistic.

The characteristics of these two groups of autistic children were examined in a survey of all the children aged between 8 and 10 who were living in the former county of Middlesex, England, on 1 January 1964 (Lotter, 1966, 1967a). Of all the children diagnosed as autistic, either nuclear or non-nuclear, a third were thought to have some neurological problem, and less than 20 per cent had an IQ above 70. Two-thirds had shown abnormal behaviour from birth or shortly after. Just under a third had no language, and another third were extremely limited in their use of language.

As Rutter (1983) points out, not enough is known about the processes underlying the behaviours which characterize autism. Until more is known about the cognitive deficits in autism and how they relate to the behaviours which characterize autism, a definitive description of autism will not be possible.

The Middlesex survey in England (Lotter, 1966, 1967a) took as its sample 78,000 8–10 year olds. A preliminary screening for children with autistic-type behaviour identified 135 possible cases. These children were examined more intensively and 54 were found to show some of Kanner's characteristics. Fifteen of these were socially unresponsive and showed an insistence on things not changing, including various rituals which they would engage in repeatedly. These 15 were identified as belonging to Kanner's nuclear group. This is an incidence of 2 in 10,000. A further 20 children showed many of Kanner's characteristics, but without the predominance of the social aloofness and repetitive rituals. These make up the non-nuclear autistic group, with an incidence of 2.5 per 10,000. The remaining 26 children showed some similar behaviours, but were not classified as autistic. The incidence of autism is taken as the number of nuclear and non-nuclear autistic children, which from Lotter's survey was 4.5 autistic children for every 10,000 children aged between 8 and 10. A figure of 4.9 per 10,000 was reported by Wing and Gould (1979) for a population in Camberwell, London. Figures of this order have been found in Denmark (Brask, 1970), although two surveys, one in the USA (Treffert, 1970) and one in Sweden (Gillberg, 1984), reported lower incidences of 2.5 and 2 per 10,000 respectively.

These figures show that there is disagreement as to the actual incidence of autism. This is not surprising since it is fairly infrequent and therefore a large population of children needs to be examined in order to get an accurate figure. Also not all authors agree as to its diagnostic features. In a paper which examines all of these surveys, with the exception of Gillberg's, and discusses their respective drawbacks, Wing et al. (1978) conclude that the incidence of autism is somewhere between four and five children in every 10,000 children. More of these children are boys than girls, although the size of this ratio varies from 16 : 1 (Wing and Gould, 1979) to 1.4 : 1 (Brask, 1970). There is a suggestion that boys predominate amongst the most able autistic children.

Given its incidence, autism has attracted a disproportionate amount of attention. This reflects the fact that it is an especially intriguing handicap about which, despite a great deal of research, there is still confusion. This confusion extends to the research into causes of autism. Many more theories have been put forward as to the cause of autism than would be expected from its relative infrequency (see Wing, 1976, for a detailed account).

The change of emphasis in explanations of the nature of the primary handicap (from that of a problem in forming social relationships to the more recent view of a cognitive disorder of some sort) has been accompanied by a shift in the sort of theories which have been proposed to account for its cause.

In the 1940s and 1950s the source of the problem was often placed with the parents. It was argued that the child was basically normal at birth, but that the way in which she was brought up resulted in her abnormal behaviour. In support of this view many of the early papers described the parents of autistic children as being highly intelligent, but unsociable, unable to show their emotions, cold and detached. They were often professional people, and the impression created was that they were very distant from their children, showing them little affection or warmth. More recently, Kanner (1973) has argued that autistic children inherit certain problems from their parents, and that these difficulties could be made worse by the environment that the parents provide. The role of the parents as a causal factor has been challenged and discredited (e.g. Rutter et al., 1971), and any differences that are found between parents of autistic children and parents of normal children are usually explained as an outcome of caring for a handicapped child.

Further evidence against the idea of autism as due primarily to the environment comes from studies which report that the incidence of autism amongst siblings, although raised, is not as high as would be expected if the environment was so distorted. The prevalence amongst siblings is about 200 per 10,000, about 50 times higher than in the normal population.

Genetic explanations have also been proposed, and indeed the possibility of this was suggested by Kanner (1949). The incidence amongst siblings indicates that if a genetic mechanism is involved it is not straightforward. However, some other evidence does support the notion of a contribution from the genes. For example, in about a quarter of all families with an autistic child there is a history in the family of speech delay. This, of course, could just be an artifact of looking for something slightly different in the family because there is an autistic child.

More substantial support for a genetic element comes from Folstein and Rutter's (1977) study of same sex twins. They identified 11 pairs of identical twins and 10 pairs of fraternal twins in whom at least one of the twins was autistic. Identical twins are genetically identical, whereas fraternal twins have the same degree of genetic resemblance as siblings, on average 50 per cent. In four of the identical pairs, but in none of the fraternal twins, both twins were autistic. Additionally, in five of the remaining seven identical twin pairs, but in only one of the ten fraternal twin pairs, the twin without autism tended to show some cognitive abnormality. These abnormalities varied but most of them involved language difficulties. A problem with this evidence is that twins are much more prone to brain injury at birth than are singletons, so this alone could account for the cognitive abnormality, although the greater likelihood of this disorder in the identical twins needs explaining. Folstein and Rutter went further. They ruled out any possibility of brain injury at birth for the four pairs in which both twins had autism, and for those twins who did not have autism but who had some sort of cognitive disorder. On the other hand, out of all 17 pairs in which only one twin had autism, 12 of the autistic twins possibly had received some brain damage at birth. Folstein and Rutter argue that a cognitive deficit may be inherited and show itself as autism or, in some cases, as some other form of cognitive disorder, usually involving language. Additionally, in some cases the inherited disorder may only manifest itself as autism if some sort of birth injury sparks it off. Certainly problems in the pre-, peri- and neonatal periods are reported as more common in the histories of autistic children than for normal children (Gillberg and Gillberg, 1983). However, these authors do point out that it may be that some of the problems arise because the foetus is abnormal in some way, rather than because the child becomes handicapped as a result of some external factor. Gulliford (1971) points out that encephalitis postnatally can also lead to autism.

This view of brain injury is in direct conflict with Kanner's (1943) paper where he argued that autism should not be diagnosed if there is any sign of a neurological problem. It is now generally accepted that autism is often associated with neurological problems. Garreau et al. (1984) report that out of 74 autistic children 39 had neurological and sensory abnormalities, and that there was no difference between those with and those without these problems with respect to their language, IQ, sex or the severity of their autistic symptoms.

Further support for the view that autism may be sparked off by some sort of brain injury comes from five of Folstein and Rutter's identical pairs in whom one twin had autism and the other twin had some other cognitive disorder. Of these, three of the autistic twins had experienced some injury at birth, whilst their co-twins had not. Interestingly, Garreau et al. (1984) noted that those autistic children with neurological problems were more likely than those without to have had their autistic behaviours noticed from birth, although, of course, as the authors themselves point out, this may be just because the children are being more closely observed because of their neurological problems.

Some further support for the idea of autism being the outcome of an inherited cognitive disorder which may in certain circumstances result in cognitive disorders that are not specifically autistic comes from a study by August et al. (1981). They found that 15 per cent of the brothers and sisters of autistic children had some form of developmental problem, either a language disorder, learning difficulty or mental handicap. This compared with 3 per cent for the siblings of children with Down's syndrome. An alternative explanation of the raised prevalence of difficulties amongst the siblings of autistic children is that the presence of an autistic child can create an abnormal learning environment for any siblings.

From the evidence of these studies it seems quite likely that some genetic mechanism is involved in autism, although how it operates and what damage it causes to the brain is unclear. Certainly, before these studies many researchers had proposed various sites in the brain (cf. Wing, 1976).

One of the problems is that because autism is so infrequent, very small numbers of children are involved. A further problem has concerned the diagnosis of autism. The diagnosis is often not clear, and it seems quite likely that different studies investigating the cause of autism may have used different criteria. If there is a single cause then this problem will have obscured the search for it. This raises a further possibility. Since it is often unclear whether or not a child is definitely autistic it seems quite likely that there may be a number of different causes which manifest themselves in a similar way. Perhaps the search should not be for a single cause but for several.

## Difficulties in studying handicapped children

The study of the development of handicapped children is not straightforward and in this section I want to discuss a few of the problems that arise, before examining the development of some of these children.

The very fact that particular children are grouped together and labelled as blind, or deaf or Down's syndrome suggests that the children in each group share certain characteristics. It is obviously true that they will have certain features in common, but earlier sections of this chapter have demonstrated that the nature of the handicaps of children who might be ascribed the same label may be very different. It is also important to remember that children who share a similar handicap will be different from one another in other ways. Knowing the pathology of the handicap is not enough since each child will have been exposed to different experiences and this alone will influence the effect of the handicap on that child's development. All children are individuals, and this applies as much to those who are handicapped as to those who are not handicapped.

Another difficulty which arises when we begin to explore the consequences of a particular handicap for development is the question of whether the aberrant behaviour or development we observe is primary or secondary to the handicap. Has the handicap caused the behaviour directly or is the behaviour the result of some secondary effect of the handicap? For example, if a handicapped child lives away from her family in some form of residential care and her language development is delayed, the delay may not be a direct consequence of her handicap: rather it may be due to some aspect of the residential environment.

In many studies of handicapped children the development of two or more groups of children is compared. Often this is with the intention of finding out how the handicap has affected development. A difficulty here is to select a group against whom to compare the development of the handicapped children. For example, Down's syndrome children could be judged to be similar in some sense to all of the following: other mentally handicapped children of the same chronological and mental ages; younger non-handicapped children at a similar stage of development; non-handicapped children of the same chronological age; older children with Down's syndrome; their non-handicapped siblings. Any or all of these comparisons could be justified and yet none of them is ideal.

This problem of making comparisons is particularly apparent where some measure of intelligence is required, especially with those children who are sensorily deprived. Should a blind child be assessed just on the verbal items of an intelligence test which has been standardized with sighted children, or should test items be specially designed to take account of the fact that the visually handicapped child cannot see? Both of these approaches have been used with visually handicapped children, although there are drawbacks to each. Specially designed tests such as the Williams Intelligence Test for Children with Defective Vision (Williams, 1956), which was constructed for, and standardized on, visually handicapped children, can only be used to make comparisons within the blind population.

The alternative of using, for example, the verbal scale of the Wechsler Intelligence Scale for Children (WISC, Wechsler, 1974) is also not very satisfactory. Tests which have been standardized on a sighted population are not very reliable when they are used with a different population, and the tester is ignoring those aspects of intelligence which would be assessed by those parts of the test which are omitted. It has been suggested that these particular difficulties could be overcome by comparing the performances of visually handicapped children to the performances of blindfolded sighted children. However, this is not ideal, since even though blindfolded, the sighted children will be influenced by their experience of sight. Also they will be being asked to carry out the items in a very different way from how they would normally, and their performance could not be taken as representative of their real ability.

There are no satisfactory answers to these problems. The study of handicapped children and the interpretation of what is observed is fraught with difficulties. These issues must be borne in mind when examining the development of children who are handicapped.

# 2

# How do blind children develop?

## Introduction

One of the most detailed and fascinating accounts of the development of the blind child is given by Selma Fraiberg in her book *Insights from the Blind* (1977). She makes quite clear in this book that blind children who are thought not to be otherwise handicapped develop differently, not just from sighted children but from one another. She illustrates this by two case histories which she describes in some detail. One of the children, Toni, was first seen at 5 months.

She was five months old ...When her mother went over to her and called her name, Toni's face broke into a gorgeous smile, and she made agreeable responsive noises. I called her name and waited. There was no smile. ... [A]t eight months ... [s]oon after she heard our voices, strange voices, she became sober, almost frozen in her posture. Later, when I held Toni ... she began to cry, squirmed in my arms, and strained away from my body. ... At ten months Toni demonstrated for the first time her ability to reach and attain an object on sound cue alone ... Between eight and ten months ... we would see Toni stretch out on the floor, prone on the rug, and for long periods of time lie quite still, smiling softly to herself ... [A]t ten months ... [s]he was still unable to creep, but the walker provided mobility, and Toni was cruising around the house with tremendous energy and making discoveries and rediscoveries at every port ... she absolutely refused to get into the prone position ... [A]t thirteen months ... she began walking with support - and now also creeping ... she had a small and useful vocabulary, she was using her hands for fine discriminations, and she was now expert in reaching and attaining objects on sound cue ... [B]eginning in the second year ... [w]hen Toni became anxious ... she would fall into a stuporous sleep.

Fraiberg's second case history is of a child called Peter who was almost 9 years old when she first saw him:

He walked uncertainly with support ... paid no attention to me or to my voice and sat or lay on the picnic table absently mouthing a rubber toy. Occasionally he made an irrelevant statement ... After a while he came close to me and fingered me. Then, without any change of facial expression and without any show of feeling, he began to dig his fingernails into the skin of my arm, very hard, causing me to wince with pain ... When Peter lost an object he was mouthing, he showed no reaction to loss and did not search for it ... While his mother was with us, I observed that his reaction to her was in no discernible way different from his reaction to me, to the nurse, or to the dog. At no time ... did he ask a direct question, express a need through gesture or language, or answer a question put to him ... Peter always referred to himself in the third person ... There were no toys to which Peter had any attachment. When he showed transitory interest in objects, he brought them to his mouth, sucked on them, and chewed them. He did not explore them with his hands; ... He still preferred soft foods, ... there were typically much echolalia and toneless repetition of stereotyped phrases.

These excerpts show clearly that blindness can have very different consequences for the development of the individual child. Much of Toni's development parallels that of a sighted child although even for her there are some obvious differences: her delay in reaching and crawling; her period of lying passively on the floor and her later retreat into sleep when anxious. Peter presents a marked contrast, and even though he is much older it seems extremely unlikely that Toni's early progress could lead to this.

I shall now look more closely at particular aspects of the blind child's development. I intend to concentrate on the development of visually handicapped children like Toni who seem to be succeeding, rather than on children like Peter. The reason for this is that my concern is with the effects that blindness necessarily has on development. However, in practice I shall also be commenting on children like Peter because I am interested in the process of development and therefore I shall be discussing why particular developments occur. Children like Peter, where the process seems to have gone wrong, are clearly important to our understanding. Any explanation of why some blind children develop like Toni must also be capable of explaining Peter's less successful development. The discussion will be restricted to visually handicapped children thought not to be otherwise handicapped. However, it is often hard to be sure that the child has no additional handicap especially if the child is born blind. Peter may have had some brain damage which further restricted his development, although neurological tests were negative.

## Motor development

### *When and how do blind babies reach for objects?*

For the child who has little or no sight it seems obvious that she will learn a great deal about her environment by touching and feeling it, but the blind baby is slower to reach out into her environment than the sighted baby. This difference is interesting because it illustrates the role of vision in the development of reaching.

The visually handicapped baby with no effective vision may not reach out for a toy until she is 10-11 months old, or in some cases even later. Peter was not reaching at the age of 9 years. This contrasts with the sighted baby who starts to reach at around 5 months. Why is there this delay for the blind baby? Obviously the sighted baby can see the toy, and this acts as an incentive. Although the blind baby may hear the noise of the rattle, the noise will usually be intermittent and therefore unlike the continuous experience of the toy that the sighted baby has while she looks at it. In the first 8 or 9 months even sighted babies will not search for a toy which has been covered up, so perhaps it is not surprising that the blind baby does not reach for a noise that stops. But it is more complicated than this. For the blind baby to reach she has to know that there is something to reach for, that the sound she hears has a source which is within reaching distance. This discovery must be much easier for the sighted baby who sees objects whilst they emit noises, and when she turns towards a sound she will often see the toy or person who made the noise. The sighted baby will have many more opportunities than the visually handicapped baby to discover that sounds have sources which can be located, and there is even some evidence to suggest that babies may be born with this ability. We do not know anything about this early ability in blind babies, and it seems fairly likely that even if blind babies are born with the ability to turn their eyes towards the source of a sound, this will disappear after their repeated failure to find the source. Alternatively, the behaviour may merely appear to persist. For example, the baby may turn her head, not to locate the sound, but in order to equalize the time at which the sound reaches both her ears. But how does the visually handicapped baby come to realize that sounds have locations and sources? She will probably only discover this as a result of reaching. In view of this what is surprising is the finding that if sighted babies are put in a dark room and a toy makes a noise, they do not reach out towards the sound until about the same age as blind babies (e.g. Bower, 1974). Thus the blind baby's delay is not in reaching for sound - since sighted babies reach for sound at the same age - but a delay in reaching for objects.

In order to reach, the blind baby has to venture out into a space she knows nothing about. When the sighted baby sees a brightly coloured toy she may move her arms and legs and even make contact with the toy by chance. When the blind baby hears the sound of a rattle she may go quiet and still, not because she is uninterested but because she is listening; she is attending to the noise. Before she will reach out the blind baby has to know that there is something out there whose presence is signalled by the noise although, even when she knows that there is an object there, she may not reach for some other reason. However, until she does realize that she can reach out to grasp a toy, objects may just seem to emerge from time to time when they come in contact with her hands. When the blind baby's hand does make chance encounters with objects, these tend not to be repeated. By contrast, the sighted baby repeats the contact, for example, clasping and reclasping one hand with the other. This clasping behaviour, which occurs in sighted babies at about 16 weeks, has not been observed in blind babies (Fraiberg, 1968). However, Fraiberg et al. (1966) did observe that blind babies tend to make tentative finger movements in the direction of a toy just before they start to reach. They interpreted this as a sign that the baby was ready to start reaching.

The problem for the blind baby is that sound does not tell her that there is a tangible object out there in the same way that sight does. It is only from experience that we know that sounds usually come from something tangible. A possible solution to this problem was suggested by Bower (1977). He reported that a blind baby reached for toys while wearing a sonar device on a headband. This device emitted sound waves and the baby seemed able to learn to interpret the reflected echoes to deduce the presence of a toy, how far away it was and its size. This was an exciting development, and although there has been some criticism of the method (e.g. Kay and Strelow, 1977), its implications should not be denied.

What are the consequences of this delay in reaching? Does it actually matter? Fraiberg has commented that there may be wide-ranging implications of such a delay for a baby who will depend on her hands for information later on. She goes further to argue that the blind baby must be able to reach towards a sound before she will begin to crawl (Fraiberg, 1977). This last point has been questioned by Hunt (1981) who observed the reverse order in two blind babies. Nevertheless, it seems likely that mobility will be delayed, and certainly we should expect the baby's understanding of her environment to be affected. Both of these will be considered later. Another consequence emerges when we consider what activities are available to a baby who cannot reach. She can listen to noises, taste things, smell things and feel things which her hands come across. We saw earlier that Toni lay passively on a rug for periods of time in the months before she began to reach and move around, and that as soon as she began to reach and move she refused to lie prone on the rug. Blind babies are often observed to turn to their own bodies in this and other ways for stimulation. This may be the beginning of behaviours called blindisms which can persist well into childhood and beyond.

## Blindisms

Blindisms include pressing and poking the eyes with the fingers, rocking backwards and forwards, spinning round and round in circles, and gazing at bright lights. Many of these sorts of behaviour can also be observed in sighted children but they tend to disappear quite early on. Institutionalized children also tend to exhibit these sorts of behaviour persistently. The behaviours are often interpreted as the blind or institutionalized child's way of increasing her general level of sensory stimulation in the absence of outside stimulation. Unfortunately, whilst the blind child is engaged in blindisms she cannot be experiencing her environment.

Blindisms may also provide an outlet for the blind child's energy (Burlingham, 1965). The blind child, even when she has started to move around, will be more cautious than a sighted child and less able to let off steam by running around; blindisms may provide her with an outlet.

## *How are posture and mobility affected by blindness?*

The blind baby is delayed in many aspects of motor development: for example, rolling over; rising up on to her arms when in a prone position; getting up into a sitting position; pulling up to stand and walking (e.g. Adelson and Fraiberg, 1974). On the other hand, she does not seem to have many problems in developments such as sitting, walking when someone holds her hands, and standing alone. The difference between these two groups of developments is that the first is self-initiated, whereas the second just requires the maintenance of a position which has already been achieved. It is the self-initiated movements which seem to be delayed in the blind child, and this is probably where vision is so important: for example, the sighted baby rolls over to get nearer to a toy, stands up to reach things on the table and walks to a parent on the other side of the room. Just as the blind child does not have the visual enticement to reach, so she does not have the incentive to move around in the space beyond.

However, eventually the blind child will become mobile: there are reports of blind children walking at average ages of 21 months (Norris et al., 1957), and at 15.5 months (Fraiberg, 1977), although we saw that Peter was not yet walking independently at the age of 9 years. Once they do become mobile this will further develop their ability to reach on sound cue: as they move towards a sound it will get louder and vice versa. This reinforces the idea that sounds have sources (Wills, 1970).

The blind child will have to be taught about posture because she does not have the example of other people. Her baby gait with feet slightly apart and arms outstretched will persist unless she is told how older people walk. In addition, although she may be quite able to walk around the house, she may find it extremely difficult to walk as confidently when she goes outside. In the absence of sight the blind child makes use of other cues, mainly auditory, and the sort of auditory cues she gets indoors about spaces and obstacles are likely to be very different from those she perceives outside.

## Perceptual development

*Are the acuities of the other senses heightened?*

It is a widespread belief that the blind person's intact senses are more acute than those of a person who can see. The blind are often even credited with possessing a sixth sense. This is a myth.

There is much evidence to suggest that blind children are actually worse than sighted children on a wide range of tactual and auditory tasks, although this inferiority does diminish as the blind child gets older. This raises two questions: why are blind children actually worse than sighted children and why does the difference tend to disappear?

The two questions are related. One of the functions of being able to see is that it helps us to integrate different sense modalities, and to understand the sensory inputs we receive. The sighted child can watch her hands and feel a toy as she manipulates it and can hear the noise it makes as she shakes it. It will be much harder for the blind child, even in this simple situation, to integrate the different impressions she gets of the toy: how it feels, its texture, size, shape, how pliable it is, that it makes a sound and so on. Vision can help to locate all of these features within the toy. It is a unifying sense; it is a sense through which other senses can be related. Blind children do not have this unifying sense and so perform poorly on tasks which benefit from it. Their inferiority is most marked on complex tasks and tasks requiring some integration, such as tests of spatial relations or of relating information across two or more modalities. On straightforward perceptual discrimination of, for example, weight, sound and texture blind children perform on a par with sighted children.

Vision helps us to interpret our other senses. In many of the experiments comparing blind children and sighted children, the performance of blind children is compared with the performance of sighted children who have been blindfolded. This may well put the sighted children at a disadvantage since they will be doing the task in a different way from how they would normally do it. The blind are not disadvantaged in the same way and yet they still do worse. This has far-reaching implications for children who become blind after a period of useful vision: their early visual experiences, particularly if they are extensive, are likely to be of great benefit in how they use their remaining senses.

Why does the blind child's inferiority diminish as she gets older? The most likely explanation seems to be that the blind child can master the perceptual world and she can make sense of sensory experiences, but that without vision this mastery is much more difficult, and it takes her longer to begin to use the other senses effectively (Gomulicki, 1961). Once she is able to use her other senses effectively, this may give the impression of heightened acuity since she will be particularly attentive to the relevant sensory information, and she may make better use of her intact senses than the sighted person does. However, there is no evidence to support the claim that the sensory apparatus of the blind person is actually more acute: she just uses the senses she has more effectively. Indeed the blind learn to make use of their intact senses to gather information normally available through the visual modality. For example, the blind use echoes to discover about the objects and spaces around them. This ability to substitute one modality for another, as well as being utilized in the sonar devices for young blind children, has been used by Bach-y-Rita (e.g. 1972) in designing touch vision substitution systems. These systems provide blind people with a tactile impression of objects around them. A camera views the environment for the blind person, and a corresponding tactile picture is produced on their body from a matrix of small vibrating or electrical points.

## Cognitive development

A number of difficulties have already been identified which might affect the blind child's cognitive development: a delay in reaching for objects; being slower to initiate movement herself; engaging in self-stimulatory behaviours and less effective use of the remaining senses. These behaviours and slower developments will limit the opportunities she has for experiencing her environment and for making sense of it.

Lowenfeld in 1948 referred to three general restrictions, all of which could have effects for cognitive development. The first was the range and variety of experiences available to the blind child. These will be limited because the blind child's intact senses are unable to bring her direct experience of the same sort that vision can. Second, her ability to get about is reduced. This will affect the opportunities that she has for experience and social contact. Finally, she does not have the same control of her environment and of herself as the sighted child, because she has little or no perception of the space beyond that which she occupies.

All this points strongly to some cognitive impairment in the blind child.

### How intelligent is the blind child?

Kolk (1977) reviewed a number of studies concerned with the intelligence of blind children and concluded that 'in general, average IQ scores do not differ significantly' for blind and sighted children. Tillman (1967a, 1973), however, argues that there are significant differences. Using the Verbal Scale of the

WISC, Tillman reported an average IQ of 92 for 110 blind children aged 7–13, compared with 96.5 for a matched group of sighted children. Tillman (1967b) broke down the scale and found that the sighted children were superior to the blind children on comprehension and tasks requiring the child to spot similarities. There were no differences between the blind children and sighted children on information, arithmetic and vocabulary scales. Others have reported that blind children may actually be superior to sighted children on digit span tasks. The explanation proposed by Tillman is that blind children fail to integrate all the different facts they learn, so that each item of information is kept separate and has a separate frame of reference from every other item. They are not impaired on items which just ask for information, like the arithmetic and vocabulary items, but they are impaired on items such as comprehension or judging similarities, which require the child to relate different items of information. It is as though all the educational experiences of the blind child are kept in separate compartments. If this is correct, then, it may be concluded that, as in perception, vision provides the child with the opportunity to make links between different experiences, links which assist the child in making the most effective use of her experiences.

### What does the young blind child understand about objects?

Blind children reach for objects later than sighted children, and they are slower to get moving. Both of these delays will restrict the blind child's contact with near and further afield objects. Even when they do reach, and are moving around, most of their experience of objects will be through touch. Touch, unlike vision, cannot be used to glance at an object. Visual glances can be very useful to give a general impression but, to use touch without vision, you have to touch one part of an object, then another part and so on. The blind baby's experience of each object will be sequential and much slower than the sighted child's visual experience. It will be much more difficult for the blind baby to understand the total extent of many objects, and to relate one part of an object to another part. Imagine trying to make sense of a car, a tree or a house by touch without any prior visual experience.

Auditory information is also very different from visual information. Unlike vision, which is continuous unless you decide to look elsewhere or the lights are turned off, sounds are seldom continuous. A sound may be heard one minute and absent the next. This will make it more difficult for a blind child to understand that objects continue to exist even when she is not experiencing them.

Is the blind child's understanding of objects similar to that of the sighted child's? One way to look at this is to examine the maturity of the child's object concept. To be said to have a mature object concept a child must be able to represent or imagine an object in its absence. Fraiberg (1968) reported that blind children cannot do this until the age of about 3-5 years. Why is object concept development in the blind child delayed? Fraiberg believes that the delay stems from the blind child giving up searching when she does not find what she is searching for. As a result of this the child may deduce that objects cease to exist when they cannot be found. This belief in itself makes the further development of a mature object concept less likely since there will be no point in the child continuing to search.

However, Fraiberg (1977) has pointed out that the young blind child may have some concept of objects before she begins to reach towards them, but that she shows this in more subtle ways than the sighted child, and these signs may be overlooked. She observed a 6 month old blind child called Robbie move his hands across the table top after he had dropped a toy. At 8 months Robbie's hands made grasping motions when he heard the sound of a favourite toy. These sorts of observation have practical implications for how parents can help their blind baby.

Another way of examining children's understanding of objects is to look at how they play. Blind children tend to engage in less constructive and manipulative play, presumably because they cannot see the end result of what they do. In addition, blind children may not have the same impressions as normal children of objects. The blind child's impressions may be much harder to construct. They also engage in less imaginative play (e.g. Fraiberg and Adelson, 1975; Fraiberg, 1977). During the sighted child's second year her pretend play really takes off: for example, sweeping the floor, making cups of tea and hammering a nail in. Initially this play employs the use of miniature versions of the real objects. These miniatures do not seem to hold the same attraction for the blind child, particularly when they are unlikely to have experienced the extent of the original object, such as a car or a house. The blind child may reject dolls and toy animals because they do not feel right. They are not warm, they feel wrong, they smell wrong, and do not make the right sorts of noises. For the sighted child the looks of a doll are sufficient to represent a baby, but for the blind child the information from the other senses is incongruous with reality. Much of the blind baby's play is repetitive, and this and the lack of fantasy play led Wills (1981a) to suggest that the blind child is still trying to organize her actual experiences, and this is her preoccupation in her play. When she begins to talk there is some evidence that her language may serve as a major vehicle for fantasy (Fraiberg, 1977; Urwin, 1981).

The blind child may have unexpected difficulties in understanding many things we take for granted, and she may be unaware of things which are obvious to the sighted. The first difficulty may stem from the blind child's attempts to understand the world, and may be reflected in mistakes she makes in her attempts to categorize. Gibbs (1981) writes of a blind 6 year old who asked for increasingly long sticks in order to be able to touch the ceiling. The only problem was that he was trying to feel the ceiling in the garden. He did not realize that there was no ceiling outside.

The blind child's understanding of objects will necessarily be very different from that of the sighted child's, and in many cases she may always have a different understanding even as an adult. Again vision tends to be a unifying sense. The outcomes of events which can be observed can be anticipated, and it is easier to extract the rules by which things happen when you can watch the event rather than rely on tactual and auditory information. For example, imagine the different experiences of a blind child and a sighted child when their parent is hammering a nail into the wall. The sighted child can see all the preparations and can watch her parent line up the nail and raise the hammer to hit it. The sound of the hammer hitting the nail may be the first thing that the blind child experiences. In this sort of way vision can often provide a context for events which helps the child make sense of them.

## What does the young blind child understand about herself and other people?

The main objects that the blind baby experiences in her early months will be people. She cannot look around and experience objects visually and, until she begins to explore objects with her hands, her main contact with the world outside will be the sound of people talking and the feel of them touching her and playing with her.

Wills (1968) has suggested that blind children may play less with toys than sighted children because they are more interested in people. Fraiberg's two cases of Toni and Peter illustrate clearly that there can be marked differences in blind children's understanding of people. Toni, in her first year, showed that she knew her mother and responded to her with obvious pleasure, whilst withdrawing from strangers. In contrast, even by the age of 9 years, Peter seemed no more interested in people than in objects, and not particularly interested in either. He showed no recognition of his mother as being in any way special and different from strangers. It is quite obvious that something had gone seriously wrong for Peter. When and how do blind children find out that people are different from objects and, more importantly, what do they know about people?

By as early as the end of the first month blind babies are reported as smiling selectively to their parents' voices (Fraiberg, 1977), and in the next months they will smile readily when their parents play in familiar ways with them but they will squirm when strangers handle them. Their hands become more active and between 5 and 8 months Fraiberg observed that the blind babies obviously enjoyed feeling their parents' faces, yet they only briefly explored the faces of strangers. By this age there is clear differentiation of familiar from unfamiliar people. Nine out of ten of Fraiberg's blind babies were first observed to show negative reactions when held by a stranger, such as crying or struggling to get away, somewhere between 7 and 15 months.

These ages of the emergence of differential reactions to familiar and unfamiliar people are approximately the same as those for sighted babies, although there are some blind children for whom these developments take longer or may never occur. However, differences do emerge when the responses of blind babies and sighted babies to their parents are examined more closely. Consider the situation where the parent walks into the baby's bedroom and, talking to her, bends over her cot. Both blind babies and sighted babies of 5 months of age will smile, and the sighted baby will probably reach out her arms towards her parent. The blind baby will not reach out her arms to the sound of her parent's voice. Fraiberg did not observe this sort of proximity seeking behaviour in her 10 blind babies until 10-16 months. Another difference between blind and sighted babies emerges when we look at how they react to a parent's departure. Sighted babies between the ages of 6 and 9 months protest when a parent leaves, the often reported third quarter of the first year separation anxiety. Fraiberg's children were aged 11-22 months when they first showed this behaviour, with a median age of just under 12 months. This is about the same time as they began to show proximity seeking behaviour. Why are there these marked differences in the ages at which blind and sighted children reach out to their parents and protest at their disappearance?

To answer these questions we need to examine what the children need to know in order to exhibit these sorts of behaviour. Both blind and sighted children have demonstrated their preference for their parents over strangers. When their parents are not touching them, blind children will recognize their parents by their voices, and sighted children will see them as well. To reach her arms out to her parent the child needs to know that her parent is there, and for the sighted child the sight of her parent is sufficient. As we saw in the last section, it takes time for the blind child to realize that sounds have sources which she can reach for. Sound does not of itself convey the presence of an object or person. The sighted baby will track things visually as they move around, and will find objects that she had lost sight of. But this cannot be done as easily with sound since sound is seldom continuous.

The sighted child's visual experiences give her many opportunities to discover that toys which go out of sight continue to exist. For example, she will throw toys out of her cot and see them later on the floor, and she will hear her parents when they are out of sight and see them appear as they come through the door. The blind child has far fewer equivalent experiences. Sounds must seem to appear and disappear unpredictably and, because she is

delayed in reaching for toys and in moving around, she will ha[...]
experiences of finding things. It will seem to her that things appear as [...]
nowhere. For example, toys just arrive in her hands and people pick her [...]
She needs to reach out in order to discover that there are objects around her,
and she needs to know that there are objects around her in order to reach out.
This gives a clue to the blind child's delay in protesting at her parent's
disappearance. Until she realizes that her parents are permanent, even when
she cannot feel or hear them, she will not protest. The sighted child of 8 or 9
months protests when her parents go out of sight because she knows they continue to exist (e.g. Bell, 1970). It takes much longer for the blind child to
understand that things continue to exist when she cannot hear or feel them.

Sighted children may derive much value from familiar routines and
experiences in caretaking (Ferrier, 1978) and in play (Bruner, 1975). Blind
children tend to cling to routine and familiar experiences. This begins to
become apparent during the blind baby's second year. It seems likely that
known routines give them greater security because they can predict what is
going to happen. This seems to reflect the problems they have in making
sense of, and in organizing, their experiences, and will probably contribute to
their anxiety with strangers who are unaware of familiar routines, and may be
hesitant about playing with a child who is blind.

All of this will result in the blind child's greater dependence on familiar
adults. Until she begins to reach for objects, the blind baby will only
experience the objects around her if she is taken to them, or her parents bring
them to her. Not surprisingly, the time when the blind child begins to get
mobile and reach for toys coincides with the beginnings of her becoming
anxious when her parents leave her. She knows that objects and people exist
when she is no longer in contact with them, and because of this she realizes
when they have disappeared. A bit later on she will realize that she can often
find her parents by the sound of their voices or the noise of their movements,
and she will begin to follow her parents from room to room. This is usually
accompanied by a gradual decline in her distress when she realizes her parents
have left her temporarily, because she knows that they must be somewhere.
On the other hand, Fraiberg noted that those blind children in her study,
whose parents went away for extended periods of time, showed extreme
distress even when briefly separated, and regression and panic occurred
during the extended separations.

The main difficulty facing the blind child's understanding that her parents
are permanent is that auditory information is not as consistent as visual
information and unless she is actually in physical contact with her parents or
her parents are talking, the child will not know whether they are still there.
Because of this, when the blind child begins to talk she may try hard to keep
her parents engaged in conversation by, for example, asking persistently what

they are doing. Unlike the sighted child who can keep in contact with her parent visually, the blind child keeps in contact by sound or touch. Her parents' responses will tell her that they are still there and their whereabouts. This may also happen with a stranger, the blind child inundating the stranger with questions. This is perhaps equivalent to the stares of a sighted child.

Another difficulty for the blind child is for her to understand that when her parents are angry with her they are the same parents who love her. The sighted child can see that her parents remain the same and that it is just their tones of voice and facial expressions which change. The blind child hears only the change of tone, and because of her reliance on auditory information it is much harder for her to realize that her parent is still the same. The blind child has a much more piecemeal image of her parent than the sighted child has. This difficulty in reconciling the angry with the loving parent may go part of the way towards explaining the fact that blind children tend to comply with the requests of people who are important to them (e.g. Nagera and Colonna, 1965). If they find it hard to cope with their parents' different emotions, then they minimize the chance of arousing their anger by complying. In a similar way the school aged blind child often has difficulty in dealing with her own age-appropriate aggression (Wills, 1970).

Blind children may be unaware of things we take for granted, for example, that people have two hands. They cannot perceive other people's bodies at a glance as the sighted child can, nor can they look at themselves in a mirror. They can only feel parts at a time, and they may have real difficulties understanding how all the different parts relate to each other, even though many of their actions will be centred on their own body. This may create real problems later on, particularly in societies where touching is taboo. The blind child and adolescent may be especially confused about the differences between the sexes.

It is very likely that blind children will be much slower than sighted children to understand that people can do things for them. A blind baby will not be able to watch the actions of others on objects, or anticipate the end result. She will not be able to observe any visual consequences of her own actions. When the blind child does act on an object, like banging a drum, she may be less likely than a sighted child to repeat the action even though it has auditory consequences because she will not see the delight at her action in her parents' faces. This delight seems to act as a real incentive for the sighted child (Burlingham, 1979). In the first year of the sighted child's life she will be discovering about cause and effect as a result of manipulating toys and objects, and observing the actions of other people. Long before she is able to talk, the sighted child will see a toy she wants, gesture towards it, make noises, look at her parent, and generally make her request quite clear. This reflects an understanding that people can do things. But the blind child will

not gesture or make requesting noises towards objects which are out of re.
until she realizes that there are objects beyond her reach, that they ha
particular locations, and that people can be used to get them for her. She doe
not have sight to prompt her requests. She does not have the opportunity to
observe people bringing objects to her: objects just arrive in her hand. In fact,
it may be some time after the blind child has begun to talk that she shows an
understanding of other people's ability to do things, and this may be marked
by a rapid expansion of her language skills as she realizes that she can use her
language to get people to do things for her.

The blind child's understanding of herself and other people as separate
entities, but sharing certain properties which distinguish them from objects,
comes about more slowly than is characteristic of the sighted child. A study
by Scott (1969) reports that 12-16 year old blind adolescents tended to
conform and were unaware of the extent of the influence of the group. It
seems to be far more difficult for blind people to distinguish themselves from
other people.

### *What does the older blind child understand about quantity?*

There are many concepts that will be difficult for the blind child to comprehend, and some may never have the same meaning as for a sighted child,
for example, colour. In this section I want to look at the blind child's
understanding of quantity.

How does the sighted child develop a concept of quantity? According to
Piaget (e.g. 1983), it is not until the concrete operational stage of development, between the ages of about 6 and 11 years, that the sighted child is able
to use appropriately concepts such as number, volume, weight, mass, classification and seriation. For this development, Piaget held that it was necessary
for the child to have manipulated and acted on her environment through
experiences with, for example, water and sand, plasticine or arranging toy
animals in lines. The blind child has far fewer experiences of her environment
and is much less likely to engage in this sort of play, since much of it is heavily
dependent on a visual component, although there are obvious tactual
impressions. If this sort of opportunity is a necessary prerequisite for such
concepts to develop the blind child will be delayed in acquiring these
concepts.

Many of the relevant studies have indeed reported delays (e.g. Hatwell,
1966; Miller, 1969; Tobin, 1972; Gottesman, 1973). The best known of these
studies is that of Hatwell, who examined conservation. This is the ability to
recognize a quantity, which has been changed perceptually, as still retaining,
for example, the same mass, weight, and volume. Hatwell found that blind
children showed conservation of mass at 10 years and weight at 12 years

approximately, compared to 7 and 8 years respectively for sighted children. On tasks in which the children had to seriate items verbally, Hatwell reported that the blind children performed as well as the sighted children, but Piaget has argued that this verbal ability is insufficient to compensate for the hampered sensorimotor development of the blind (Cromer, 1974). These studies seem to support Piaget's emphasis on the importance of active experimentation for operatory intelligence. When it is limited, as in the blind, delays result.

In contrast to these results, there is an important paper which suggests that blind children may achieve conservation within the sighted age range. Cromer (1973) criticized Hatwell's study on several grounds. For example, Hatwell compared blind children from a rural setting with urbanized sighted children, and the blind children did not start school until two years after the sighted children. Either or both of these differences could account for the observed delays. Cromer himself found that there were no differences between the performances of blind children and sighted children, half of whom were blindfolded, on conservation of mass and amount. Unfortunately, Cromer did not have any blind children aged between 7 and 7¾ and, as Warren (1977) points out, this may be the age at which any differences between the two groups are most marked. Notwithstanding this, Cromer's study certainly failed to confirm the large delays reported by Hatwell.

It seems likely that blind children are slightly delayed in developing the ability to conserve, although the actual delay may not be as great as early reports suggest. However, what is more interesting than the question of delay versus no delay, or how much delay, is the question of the processes underlying the development. Are blind children's conservation skills the end result of the same process as occurs in sighted children or not? Cromer's study throws some light on this issue. As well as reporting the children's responses, he also reports the reasons they gave for making their judgements of conservation or non-conservation. What was particularly striking here was that there were no significant differences between the reasons given by the three groups of children, blind, sighted and blindfolded, for either conservation or non-conservation responses. However, there were marked differences between the reasons given by the non-conservers and the conservers. Most of the non-conservers gave reasons referring to the dimensions of the containers and the conservers mostly gave reasons which acknowledged the transformation, for example, 'Because they were the same before', and 'All you did was change it'. Despite these similarities between the blind and sighted children's reasons, there is a suggestion that the process may be different. In one task ping-pong balls were transferred from one of two identical wire mesh cylinders into a taller, thinner cylinder. Four of the six non-conserving blind children said that there were fewer balls in the tall container; all the sighted

children who failed to conserve, whether blindfolded or not, said that th\
cylinder contained more balls. This suggests that the tactual and vis\
impressions of the children are not equivalent, and may reflect differen\
underlying processes. That the difference is in the process rather than merel\
in the modality of the task is supported by the fact that the blindfolded
sighted non-conserving children gave the same sort of reasons as the sighted
non-conservers, rather than reasons similar to those of the blind non-conservers.

The reasons for the delay are unclear. There may be a carryover of delays
from the sensorimotor period, or the delay may be as a result of restrictions in
the operational period (Warren, 1977). It is hard to differentiate between
these two, and they are probably both involved.

Although the blind child is delayed in certain aspects of her intellectual
development, the delays that are experienced by many of the children are
small. The blind child appears to be able to develop similar concepts to the
sighted child, although the process by which this occurs will often be
different. She is deprived of many of the sensorimotor experiences typical of
the sighted child's first two years, and this raises further questions about the
effect this will have on her language development. Will her language reflect
the limitations of her cognitive development, or provide her with a means of
lifting herself out of her restricting environment?

## The development of communication

*How do blind children and their parents communicate before the
children can speak?*

Unless the child's blindness is obvious at birth as, for example, in
anophthalmia, the parents may first become suspicious when they notice that
their baby does not look at their faces and follow them as they move around
the room. This lack of eye contact may cause the parents to feel rebuffed and
they may withdraw from the baby. If this happens and persists, parent–child
communication may suffer. Some parents may find it hard to talk to their
blind baby, to know what to talk about, and may react either by not talking at
all, or by talking non-stop. Why is it so difficult to communicate with a blind
baby, and how can communication be successful?

Most parents find it relatively easy to talk to a sighted baby. They talk
about what the baby is doing, what they are doing and about the objects and
events that they and the baby can see. It is very different with a baby who
cannot see. The blind baby is not drawn towards the environment by its
visual attraction; she is less likely to engage in play and to handle toys; she
cannot see what her parent is doing; she cannot see all the other happenings
that are going on around her. It must be difficult for a parent to justify talking

or its own sake, to talk to the baby about things of which the baby has no experience.

Parents of sighted babies tend to concentrate their topics of conversation on shared visual experience, even though they have shared auditory, tactual and olfactory experiences. The visual modality tends to dominate the other modalities. But it is the other sort of experiences which the blind baby will have, and on which successful communication can be built. The blind baby may still to the noise of an aeroplane and, if the parents are alert to this response as a sign of attention, they will be able to bring it into their conversation, so that they are talking about things which are experienced by the baby. The stilling in response to a noise by the blind baby needs to be understood by the parents as similar to the sighted child turning to look at something which has attracted her attention.

However, there is a major difference. The sighted child may see something move, point to it, look towards her parent and make a noise herself, initiating a pre-verbal vocal exchange. For the blind child, talking or making a noise will interfere with her listening. The blind child may be listening for listening's sake, and will not herself either initiate any vocal exchange, or draw her parent's attention to the sound. In fact, she may give quite the opposite appearance of withdrawing into herself. Thus much of the onus of initiating early communications will rest with her parents.

The blind child cannot engage in those non-verbal interchanges which rely on vision since she cannot watch the expressions on her parent's face. Instead, she will have to rely on how her parent touches and handles her and on the parent's tone of voice. The tone of voice can convey a great deal of information, for example, anger, liking, irritation, interest. But being able to hear her parent's voice will sometimes cause her confusion because she cannot also see her parent's face. She may hear the angry voice and feel rejected and unloved but, unlike the sighted baby, the blind baby will not see the parent's smile as the anger subsides, and consequently may not understand that her parent still likes her despite the cross tone of voice.

Many of these difficulties should be overcome as soon as the blind baby begins to speak. Language will enable her to discover what is going on around her, to ask questions about her environment, and at last her parents will be able to communicate with her. It is interesting that blind adults communicate quite successfully with sighted children. It is the problems that blindness brings in the early years of childhood which create the difficulties in communication between sighted people and young blind children.

### What problems face the blind child as she learns to speak?

The blind child's learning of language is likely to be a very important development, not just for her but also for her parents. But the process is not straightforward. The blind child does not draw her parents' attention towards events in the environment. She will listen to noises, feel textures and smell odours, but she will not invite her parents to comment on these as the sighted child does by her glance at her parent, or by vocal comment or demand. The blind child will not request objects which are out of reach until she has some idea of their permanence and location. The sighted child has the visual reminder of an out-of-reach toy and so, even before she understands about the permanence of objects, she may demand it. But for the blind child to realize that a sound or smell indicates an object which could be requested is much more complex. She also needs to know that people can do things for her and act as agents. The sighted child will make non-verbal requests of her parents before she can make verbal requests. She will point and make noises and look backwards and forwards between them and whatever it is that she wants. The blind child is unlikely to use her parents in this way, and may not make requests of them until she has the necessary language. For the blind child, language itself may be necessary for a full understanding of the agency of others and the existence of further afield objects.

It has been suggested that the sighted child's requesting behaviour may develop out of her reaching behaviour. Initially she sees a toy she would like which happens to be beyond her reach; nevertheless she reaches towards it, but fails to make contact with it. If her parents are watching this sequence they may fetch the toy and give it to her. As her parent moves towards the toy, the child catches sight of this movement and looks at her parent, and then back at the toy. This sequence of behaviour directed towards gaining an out-of-reach toy may gradually develop until, when the child sees an out-of-reach toy she would like, she points to it, looks at her parent and so on. As well as getting the toy for their child the parents are also likely to make some appropriate comment, for example, 'Oh, you'd like the duck, would you?', thus labelling the toy and providing the child with guidance into one use of language. This sort of sequence cannot happen for the visually handicapped child. She is not aware that she is surrounded by potential playthings which she could request, and although she does eventually reach out to objects which make a noise, it is unlikely that she will develop pointing behaviour as a way of directing another person's attention.

It is important that the blind baby's parents talk to her about things which are meaningful to her and of which she has experience. Just as parents of sighted children provide the verbal labels for what their child sees, for example, 'Ooh, look, that's an aeroplane', the parents of a blind child must relate what they say to their child's experience: for example, 'Ooh, listen, that's an aeroplane'. In this way the content of her parents' language must be clear and relevant. It is no good the parent saying 'Put it here', they must specify things like location, for example, 'Put it on the table'.

As the blind child begins to talk further problems arise because there is less for her to talk about. She does not have sight of all the happenings which are going on around her. For the sighted child questions like 'What's that?' seem to follow on from pointing; verbal pointing, perhaps? In some sense the blind child will point through language, but only about things which she can and does experience. Unless her parents have realized fairly early on that she is listening to noises, her curiosity about things she does experience may not have been fostered. It may not have dawned on her that her parents experience these things too, and can be a source of information about her environment.

Thus, many of the problems that face the blind child in her acquisition of language rest on the fact that she and her parents do not experience the environment in the same way. They all feel, hear, smell and taste things, but much of her parents' experience and language is based on what they see, and this experience is not available to their child. How does this affect the blind child's own language?

### *In what ways is the language of blind children different from that of sighted children?*

The blind child, who is not otherwise handicapped, babbles in much the same way as a sighted child. She may babble less, presumably because she relies more on listening, and it is harder to listen if you are making a noise yourself. However, differences can be heard in the language of blind and sighted children. Relatively little attention had been paid to this aspect of the blind child's development until the late 1970s. It had been assumed, first, that sighted children follow a particular course of language development, and, second, that blind children's language development would follow much the same course as that of sighted children, bringing blind children a means of effective communication and a way of overcoming their other limitations. Both these assumptions have been questioned. There may be considerable variation in the pattern of development followed by individual sighted children (e.g. Lieven, 1982; Bancroft, 1985). There are a number of differences in the language acquired by blind children and sighted children and these differences may reflect differences in the process of acquisition (e.g. Urwin, 1981; Mills, 1983; Dunlea, 1984; Landau and Gleitman, 1985).

Some blind children, but not all, take longer than sighted children to say their first words, although the content of their earliest vocabularies are fairly similar to those of sighted children and the initial delays are usually made up quite quickly. However, there are differences in how blind children use the words in their vocabularies. They may not use them in communication, but rather in their own play or in direct imitation. Speaking almost seems to be an activity for its own sake (Burlingham, 1979). A further difference is that, whereas early on the sighted child uses function words, for example, 'allgone', 'there', 'more', 'up', these sorts of word seldom occur in the blind child's early vocabulary. If they are used they tend to be used to refer to the blind child's own actions (e.g. Dunlea, 1984). What the sighted child seems to be doing with these function words is to refer to aspects of her enviornment, for example, 'allgone milk' meaning that all the milk is finished, 'no ball here' meaning that her ball is out of reach. The blind child does not have these sorts of experience. However, she does have knowledge of her own body movements, and this is reflected in how she uses language, for example, saying 'up' as she gets up.

Thus, blind children use words early on to accompany what they are doing, or in direct imitation of their parents. Unlike sighted children they do not comment on objects, events or other people's actions. They use language for things they know about, just like sighted children; it is simply that their experiences are different. Dunlea (1984) concluded from her observations of four blind children and two sighted children that the blind children, in contrast to the sighted children, tended not to use their early words in contexts other than those in which the words were first learned. This also applied to their comprehension. Word meanings were not generalized from one situation to another. She argues, on the basis of this, that when blind children begin to talk they do not perceive the symbolic nature of words.

From the acquisition of the first few words the vocabularies of most blind children grow more slowly than those of sighted children (Burlingham, 1979). Again, this reflects their experience. The sighted child has plenty to see, she requests objects, labels are provided and she seems to take a delight in naming the objects around her. Blind children are slower to use language to ask for objects, or to ask about objects, and in fact this development may be a crucial step in their language (Wills, 1978). However, when the contents of the language of blind and sighted children at the one and two word stage are compared, blind children make more requests than sighted children (Dunlea, 1984). Once they realize that language can get them things, that it has a purpose and that it is useful, their vocabulary often takes off and expands rapidly. They begin to use language to their own advantage.

Children begin to combine words when their vocabularies contain around 50 words. When this stage is reached by a sighted child, much of what she has to say concerns, for example, the activities of other people, happenings she observes, demands for things she wants, comments on objects and where they are. Unlike the sighted child, the blind child still tends to use words to comment on her own activities, rather than on other people's. She will seldom refer to the locations of things which she cannot feel. She still may not use language to initiate an interaction, although she may have a stock of ready made phrases which she will produce as a way of attracting her parents' attention. For example, she may repeat 'Time for tea' over and over again until someone responds. Sighted children also pick up phrases from their parents, but the blind child's readiness to imitate and her attention to what is said seem to result in an abundance of such phrases, many of which may be used in isolation from any relevant context. Also her parents may inadvertently encourage her to imitate words and phrases without ensuring that she understands them.

As well as accumulating ready made phrases, the blind child may repeat whatever she hears other people say, a phenomenon called echolalia. She may have no idea of the meaning of what she is saying. Urwin (1981) suggests that she may do this to keep the channel open. Since the blind child cannot see her parents, she relies much more on being able to hear them, particularly when they are not touching her. It is important for her to keep her parents talking, and she may discover that they are more likely to carry on talking if she joins in and copies whatever they say. However, if the child persists in repeating what her parents say, but understands little or nothing, this may restrict her language development. Some parents and their blind children seem to enjoy these copying games, which after all introduce many of the basics of communication, for example, that you talk in turn and that turns are contingent, and the subsequent language development of these blind children does not seem to be adversely affected. In many ways this vocal imitation parallels what is going on for the sighted child: she sees something and names it; the blind child hears something and repeats it.

As the blind child gets older her language remains different in many ways from that of a sighted child. She may still tend to use sentences which she has heard her parents use, rather than producing her own. Many blind children have difficulties in using and understanding pronouns such as 'I' and 'you' correctly. The blind child will often refer to herself as 'you', referring to herself as someone else would. Her parent might say, 'Would you like a biscuit?', and the child may reply, 'You would like a biscuit', rather than 'I would like a biscuit'. Alternatively she may use her own name and reply, 'Jane would like a biscuit'. Thus, she fails to realize that the 'I' she talks about is the same as the 'you' that other people talk about. Urwin gives the example of Sam, who at 2 years 4 months said repeatedly, 'Sam go riding on a rocking horse? Sam go riding on a rocking horse?' until his mother responded. She reports the same child five months later as repeating 'Mummy watch you, Mummy watch you', whilst bouncing on a trampoline until his mother responded. Fraiberg (1977) has also noted that the blind child is delayed in representing herself in pretend play as distinct from others. She argues that the process underlying these two developments is the same and involves the child's realization, or lack of realization, that she is an individual, an 'I' in a world of individuals, a universe of 'I's. The blind child may also make mistakes in understanding to whom a pronoun refers: for example, if her parent asks 'Where's my mouth?', the child may point to her own, rather than to her parent's.

An alternative explanation is that the blind child's mistaken use of personal pronouns is due to the deictic nature of these pronouns: that is, their particular meaning in any situation relies upon the current discourse. For example, 'my' refers to me when I say it, but to you when you say it. It may be that vision helps the sighted child observe the transfer of pronouns from one user to another, and that the lack of this experience accounts for the blind child's confusion. If this explanation is correct, the blind child should also have difficulties with other deictic terms, for example, this/that, here/there.

Blind children may use certain words without having the same understanding as a sighted child as to what they mean, because they cannot experience the concept involved. This is an aspect of a phenomenon known as verbalism. For example, if blind children use colour terms which depend so much on vision, it has been argued that it is unlikely that they could understand them. Cutsforth (1951) argued that it was dangerous for blind people to use such words because they would come to undervalue their own experience. This seems a limited view for at least three reasons. First, even sighted people have words in their vocabularies of which they have no direct experience, yet we do not feel that this leads us to undervalue our experience and we do not prevent sighted children from learning such words, for example, all the words relating to outer space. Second, Cutsforth's argument assumes that words can only acquire meaning through direct experience, and yet it is quite clear that words often come to have meaning as a result of the speakers negotiating the meaning through communication (e.g. Searle, 1969). If we did not agree on word meaning in this way, we would all have to have exactly the same experiences to share the same meanings and in many cases this is impossible. A third reason is that Cutsforth seems to assume that certain word meanings can only be experienced visually. However, it is possible that the blind child may have an equivalent experience of even such visual concepts as colour. Urwin (1981) writes about a blind 4½ year old who did not want to go into the coal shed because, she said, 'It's dark in there'. She was asked what she meant by dark and said, 'Sort of still. And cold. Like when it's raining'. Surely this is as rich an understanding of darkness as a sighted person could have? Blind people may have a perfectly adequate understanding but one which is based on experience through a different modality, experience of which sighted people are less aware because of the dominance of the visual modality. The blind child may also interpret particular words differently. For example, Landau and Gleitman (1985) report that, when asked to look up, a blind 3 year old reached her arms above her head, whereas blindfolded sighted children tilted their heads back.

Most of the differences between the language of blind and sighted children reflect the blind children's reliance on experience through modalities other than vision. However, despite the fact that all blind children are deprived of visual experience to a marked degree, there is a great deal of variation between individual blind children in their acquisition of language. One factor which seems to be particularly critical in the blind child's acquisition of language is her parent's awareness of how she experiences the environment, and the extent to which they are able to make their language relevant and pertinent to this experience. This has implications for how parents can be helped to aid their blind child's entry into language.

### How does the blind child read?

Most blind children can see something. About three-quarters are estimated to have visual acuities of 2/60 or better on the Snellen chart. But for many this will not be sufficient for them to be able to read and write print. Over the years many other systems have been designed, the current one being braille. This is a punctiform code devised by Louis Braille and first published in a pamphlet in 1839, although it was not officially introduced as a teaching medium until 1850. Letters, common words and phrases are represented by various combinations of up to six raised points arranged in two columns, each containing up to three raised points.

It is much harder to read braille than ordinary print, and even fairly experienced braille readers can only manage to read at about half the speed at which average sighted people read print. Williams (1971) found that a group of 30 blind 16 year olds had an average reading speed for braille of 103 words per minute. Three of these adolescents had speeds of over 150 words per minute. In comparison, 21 out of 30 similarly aged sighted people read print at speeds in excess of 250 words per minute. Forty per cent of the 488 children seen by Williams aged 10–16 read braille at speeds below 40 words per minute.

Young braille readers make some errors due to the spatial arrangements of the raised dots which are equivalent to the visual errors of young sighted readers. Lorimer (1981) found that two-thirds of 7 and 8 year olds make reversal errors where the raised point pattern is rotated around the vertical axis like the printed letters b/d, confusing, for example, $\doteq \dot{\underline{\ }}$ with $\overline{\ }\dot{\ } \dot{=}$ and vertical alignment errors, confusing $\div \overline{\overline{\ }}$ with $\dot{=} \overline{\dot{\ }}$ (where . stands for a raised point which can be felt and − represents a location which is not raised). By 11 years of age about a quarter still show these problems. About a quarter of 7 and 8 year olds confuse inversions where the raised point pattern is rotated around the horizontal axis like the printed letters p/b, for example, $\dot{\underline{\ }}\dot{=}$ with $\dot{\underline{\ }}\overline{\dot{\ }}$ , where the raised dots are rotated around a horizontal axis between the top two lines. But almost no 11 year olds make this mistake. About a quarter of all the children confused signs which are only distinguished by the horizontal alignment of the dots, for example, ⠂⠂ with ⠒⠒. The most common error is from missing a raised point, for example, reading ⠤⠿ instead of ⠒⠿. This is particularly the case when the distinguishing raised point is in the bottom row, since the top two rows are used more often and therefore the braille reader will pay more attention to them. It is the way in which braille is constructed that leads to this large number of missed raised point confusions. The letters A to J consist of combinations of the top four raised points and these raised point combinations are repeated for the remaining letters, the only distinguishing feature being the presence of one or both of the raised points in the bottom row.

Since braille letters are more easily confused than printed letters they take longer to read. Another difference which contributes to the slower reading of braille is that braille letters are perceived sequentially by moving the fingers over the raised points. Sighted readers rely a great deal on scanning, and experienced sighted readers recognize some familiar words by their overall shape. The blind child cannot do this and has to integrate the separate letters before she knows what the word is. Millar (1981) presents evidence that the raised point combinations of braille letters are not necessarily coded as wholes, but as separate raised points in particular spatial positions, which then have to be interpreted. This will further slow the process down. However, it can be speeded up by encouraging the child to experiment with moving her fingers in different ways, and by making the child aware that she is reading slowly. Many blind people fail to realize they are reading slowly because they are unaware of the speed at which other people read (e.g. McBride, 1974; Lorimer and Tobin, 1980).

It is clear that reading braille is more demanding than sighted reading of print. Because of this it seems likely that the blind child will be ready to read at a later age than her sighted contemporaries. Her experiences will be limited and, as we have seen, she has problems relating her different experiences and in perceiving spatial relationships. Not surprisingly more able blind children read better and earlier than less able blind children (Lorimer, 1981).

## Social development

*How is interaction with others affected by blindness?*

One of the most important steps in initiating and maintaining inter-action is for the people concerned to look at one another and to make eye contact. Many social exchanges between sighted people are regulated by looking towards and away from the other's face, and by the expressions we see on the other person's face, for example, smiling, frowning, yawning, laughing. From such cues we can gauge aspects of the other person's attention, interest and understanding. We also rely on other cues, particularly what it is that is being said and the way in which it is spoken (e.g. Rutter, 1984). When we interact with a baby we do not have verbal cues and so visual cues are extremely important. Parents are found to hold their very young babies about a foot from their faces, a distance at which most babies' eyes focus easily, and parents will move the baby from side to side until their eyes meet. They will then hold the baby still and talk to her, trying to maintain eye contact (e.g. Stern, 1977). In this way parents work to get into eye contact with their babies. Parents are delighted when their baby smiles for the first time, and will work hard to elicit this facial expression. What will happen if the baby does not engage in eye contact, does not smile to the parents' smiling faces and only smiles fleeting and in response to her parents' voices or body play? How does blindness affect interaction with other people?

The blind baby's lack of eye contact can be particularly distressing for her parents. Blind babies do smile, but to the sound of their parents' voices and to their body play. The blind baby's smile tends to be more fleeting and harder to evoke than a sighted baby's. The continuous sight of a smiling face and the eye contact which occurs between parent and sighted baby seem to be particularly powerful elicitors and maintainers of the sighted baby's smile. The cues available to the blind baby are more intermittent than the visual cues which bombard the sighted baby, apart from fairly vigorous games involving tickling. It is interesting that it is these sorts of game which most easily elicit smiles in blind babies.

The faces of blind children give little away; they are often blank and expressionless. This blankness tends to be mirrored on the faces of those with whom the blind child is interacting (Fraiberg, 1977), unlike when the baby is sighted. If we saw this sort of immobility of the facial muscles and the vacancy of the eyes in a sighted child, we would assume a lack of interest or boredom, or even that the child was mentally handicapped. Yet a blind child may be interested, despite the lack of evidence for it on her face. She shows her interest in other ways, as Fraiberg (1977) has pointed out so clearly. She noticed that although the blind child's face may give nothing away, her hands often reflect her interest in a particular toy, searching for a toy she has dropped, casting away a toy she is not interested in, recognizing her parent's face by touching it, her awareness of her parent's departure. Her hands, rather than her face, are her means of expression. As part of her intervention work with parents of blind babies, Fraiberg directs their attention away from their baby's face and towards their baby's hands. She reports that once it is pointed out to parents that their baby is expressing herself, they become aware of and receptive to their baby's hand language. They then find it much easier and more rewarding to interact with their baby. The blind baby can express with her hands many of the basics of successful interaction, but the absence of vision cannot be compensated for entirely. The sighted baby and her parent have plenty to talk about from the earliest months, and the lack of visual regard in the blind baby will limit her interactions. She cannot indicate successfully what she wants until she knows that it exists and where it is to be found. This will not occur until around the end of the first year at the earliest, by which time the sighted child will have been making requests for about three months. The blind child will initiate far fewer interactions in her first year than the sighted child because she does not realize that there is someone to interact with unless she can touch or hear that person. She has fewer reasons for interaction.

Interaction with a blind baby is very different from interaction with a sighted baby. Her lack of eye contact and facial expression, and a restricted understanding of her surroundings, all contribute to make her appear less interested in interaction, and lacking interest when it occurs. This lack of interest is more apparent than real, for the blind baby shows her interest in other ways, often by her hand movements. As Fraiberg has ably demonstrated, it is crucial for successful interaction that parents are guided towards understanding their blind baby's ways of expressing herself. Without this awareness there is a possibility that adequate interaction may never get off the ground, and this may result in a child who presents the sort of profile seen in Peter.

### *Does the blind child adjust successfully to her handicap?*

It is quite clear in the literature that a significant proportion of blind children show behaviours which are characteristic of some sort of personality disorder. Cruickshank (1964) put the proportion as high as one-third. The corresponding figure for today should be much lower given our greater awareness of the problems facing the blind child and her parents, due to the work of pioneers such as Fraiberg. In fact, the personality problems of blind children led Fraiberg into her work with blind babies. She was referred a number of blind children who presented quite marked behavioural abnormalities which shared many features of the autistic syndrome. However, these children were not autistic. Unlike sighted autistic children, the perception of these blind children tended to remain mouth-centred, and perception by touching was minimal. Fraiberg concluded that the deviant behaviours of many of these blind children were a consequence of the blindness itself. It is hard to eliminate the possibility that those children with particularly deviant behaviours have some brain damage. Indeed, for a while it was held that emotional disturbance was more prevalent amongst retrolental fibroplasial blinded children who, because they are often premature, have a greater chance of being brain damaged. A number of reports have failed to support this claim (e.g. Norris et al., 1957; Keeler, 1958). Keeler's study is interesting because it shows that what seems to be critical for deviant development is total or near total congenital blindness plus a history of poor emotional stimulation in the first few months. This can explain the apparently raised incidence amongst retrolental fibroplasial children. These children commonly spend their first few days or weeks in incubators. This will further limit the amount of contact and interaction they have with their parents. Also the parents' knowledge in many cases that their child has been blinded by some medical intervention may influence the nature of their subsequent interactions.

By no means all blind children present such deviant behaviours, although the majority will exhibit at least one. For example, although Toni seemed to have adjusted well, she had a couple of slightly odd behaviours: her phase of lying prone on the floor smiling to herself, and later falling into a deep sleep when she was anxious.

When does the blind child realize that she is different? This awareness seems to come at around 5 or 6 years when she will begin to use sighted people to do things that she cannot (Burlingham, 1979). This in itself may present problems for the blind child who may want to do things for herself and yet cannot without the support of a sighted person. This dependence on others may account for the relative absence of aggressive behaviour in blind children. It may be that blind children are less aggressive, but an alternative view is that they fear showing aggression towards those people upon whom they depend so much, fearing that they may lose their support. A corollary of this lack of aggression is an apparent compliance with what others want of them. Burlingham (1979) talks of this compliance as 'a thin disguise which hides the revolt against dependency'. This conveys the feeling held by others that the phase of conflict between dependence and independence can be particularly difficult for the blind child. This phase occurs in many sighted children, but is usually resolved easily and quickly.

For individual blind children there may be particular episodes in their lives which are especially disturbing. The child who becomes blind after a period of sight, particularly if she becomes blind fairly late on in childhood, may have many problems and fears. These may range from a fear of not being able to read to despair at never seeing people again. However, with support and assurances these difficulties may be overcome, and the child will gradually learn how to experience the environment through her intact senses. If she is able to overcome the initial despair and adjust to her sightless life she will be able to benefit from the visual experiences she had, and her knowledge of people, objects and space in particular.

Blind children often go to residential schools, many from the age of 5. This may be particularly disruptive, since up until this age the child may have experienced few separations from her parents, and separations can be especially traumatic for the blind child who is so reliant on familiarity. Wills (1981b) talks about how blind children can be prepared for this major change.

Many sighted children talk about things they will be able to do when they are older. Blind children are no exception, and some think that one of the things they will be able to do when they are older is to see (Burlingham, 1979). This is not so far fetched when we remember that around the age of 5 years blind children come to realize that they are different and that other people can do things which they cannot. Most of these people will be older, their parents or older siblings, and the blind child may think that when she reaches their age she will be able to see to do all the things she is presently dependent on others to do for her. This belief is understandable, but the gradual realization that she is different, and will always be different, must be particularly distressing.

As the blind child approaches adolescence further problems of adjustment may arise. Throughout childhood she will have come to realize that some people are male, and others are female, but she may have a very unclear idea about what it is that distinguishes them. Adolescence, with its growing awareness of sexuality often accompanied by taboos on touching other people's bodies, may be a period of great confusion and anxiety about her own and other people's bodies, and about her feelings.

Some blind children seem to adjust more easily and successfully than others. Why should this be so? Keeler's (1958) study points to the role of the early environment and the time of onset and extent of the child's blindness. Many researchers emphasize this role of the blind child's environment and believe it to be far more important than the nature of the child's blindness. However, the two can be seen to be related. The child who has even minimal vision is more likely to show an interest in her environment, to make some visual contact with her parents, and may even reach and become mobile using visual cues. This may be of great encouragement to her parents, and make it easier for them to interact successfully with her. Some of the factors which seem to be predictive of the blind child's adjustment to her handicap, and of her development in general, are her parents' acceptance of her handicap, their awareness of her signals and ability to read them, and their confidence in their role as parents. Factors like the parents' intelligence or social status seem to be relatively unimportant.

# 3

# How do deaf children develop?

## Introduction

I have chosen to look at deafness as the second handicap because hearing is one of our main senses, and because it has been argued that deaf people provide an ideal opportunity to examine the role of sound in development. The argument goes like this: deaf people cannot hear; hearing people can hear; any differences in the development of deaf and hearing people are due to their different hearing status; from this we can infer the role of hearing in normal development. In practice, the situation is much more complex than this suggests. In the first chapter it was seen that there is tremendous variation in the nature and extent of deafness within the hard-of-hearing population. Also, these children are individuals subject to particular experiences and environments. All of this makes for a reality which is extremely complicated but fascinating from the point of view of attempting to elucidate how development occurs.

## Motor development

Deaf children who are not handicapped in any other way are likely to reach the early major motor milestones, for example, sitting up, standing unaided and walking, at about the same time as hearing children. However, several studies indicate that deaf children have difficulties on some tests of balance and general coordination (e.g. Wiegersma and Van der Velde, 1983).

Some of the tasks on which Wiegersma and Van der Velde found that 6-10 year old deaf children were less competent than hearing children involved dynamic coordination, for example, walking backwards and forwards along a narrow board, skipping and jumping, and hopping to and fro over a line. The deaf children were also less competent than hearing children on some tests of visual-motor coordination, for example, lacing a shoe-lace through holes in a board. However, there were no differences between the performances of the deaf and hearing children on some other visual-motor tasks. A further finding was that deaf 8–10 year olds, when the task required a movement, executed this movement more slowly than hearing children. Wiegersma and Van der Velde examined a number of possible explanations of these findings: vestibular defects; neurological defects; the deprivation of sound as an incentive and guide to movement; the lack of a verbal account of the movement; and overprotection by the parents. The authors reached no conclusions except that more research is necessary to explain the results.

## Perceptual development

### *Is the acuity of the other senses heightened?*

Blind children and deaf children provide an ideal opportunity for testing the so called sensory-compensation hypothesis, the idea that the loss of one sense may be compensated for by an increase in the sensitivity of the remaining senses. In the last chapter we saw that this does not seem to be the case for the blind child, and the evidence for compensation in the deaf is inconclusive. Using animals, MacDougall and Rabinovitch (1971) report that deafened animals are no better at visual discrimination of patterns than are animals who can hear. This does not rule out the possibility that deaf people will not show a heightened sensitivity in this or some other modality compared to their hearing contemporaries, although there are several reports which indicate that the visual abilities of deaf children are certainly no better and possibly even worse than those of hearing children (e.g. Sterritt et al., 1966). The deaf person's sense of touch has also been examined, and again the results are inconclusive, with some reports demonstrating superior tactual skills in deaf children (e.g. Blank and Bridger, 1966), others no difference (e.g. Schiff and Dytell, 1971), and yet others report that deaf children are actually worse than hearing children at tasks involving touch (e.g. Herren and Dietrich, 1977). Can we draw any conclusions from all this? One problem is that the tasks were all different. For example, Schiff and Dytell (1971) presented letters tactually to deaf and hearing children and adolescents who then either identified the letters by matching from memory or selected the matching letter from a visual display. In Herren and Dietrich's study 5–9 year old deaf and hearing children had to identify visually drawings of shapes they had previously explored tactually. Blank and Bridger studied 3–6 year olds' performance on several visual and tactual tasks exploring their concepts of the presence or absence of something and their concepts of the numbers one and two. Given the lack of consistency in the methods and findings it cannot be concluded that the deaf child's lack of the auditory modality is or is not compensated by an increased sensitivity in either the visual or the tactual modality.

Another way to examine this question of compensation is to look at the deaf child's awareness of her environment. Very often it is a sound which first of all directs our attention towards some change in the environment: approaching footsteps, the front door bell, the kettle whistling. We may act on the information we hear before we have any other sensory indication: call out to the approaching person, go to the front door or into the kitchen. All of this will be difficult, if not impossible, for the deaf person, especially the profoundly deaf person. It might be reasonable therefore to expect that deafness would reduce a person's awareness of her surroundings. If the deaf child is less aware of things that are going on around her and if this matters, it seems likely that her knowledge of her environment will differ from that of her hearing contemporaries. This possibility can be considered by examining the cognitive development of the deaf child.

## Cognitive development

A great deal of interest has centred on the deaf child's ability to think and understand. Much of this interest has stemmed from the controversy surrounding the role of language in cognitive development. For many years philosophers and psychologists have debated whether or not language and thought are related and, if they are, what is the nature of the relationship. Before examining the deaf child's role in this controversy, let us consider the main views concerning the relationship between language and thought, or cognition.

Two extreme positions have been held by Watson (1913) and Chomsky (1975). Watson proposed that 'thought processes are really motor habits in the larynx'. In this view, thought, particularly verbal thought, and spoken language are the same process. By contrast, Chomsky has argued that language is separate from cognition and develops independently from it. He has proposed that language structures exist in the brain at birth, and that, provided the child experiences language, language will develop.

Both of these extreme viewpoints have attracted a great deal of criticism. Other theorists have proposed that thought and language are related, although there is disagreement about the nature of the relationship, specifically whether thought determines language (Piaget, 1967), or language determines thought (e.g. Sapir, 1912). Between these two positions is the view of Vygotsky (1962), who proposed that language and thought can influence each other.

Piaget (1967) argued that in order to develop intelligence it is necessary for the child to act on the environment and to take account of the consequences of her actions. Through this, the child constructs an understanding of the environment which is reflected in her intelligence. The language of the child is dependent, in Piaget's view, on the structure of her intelligence. Thus, as knowledge or cognition develops, the child's language will develop to reflect changes in her understanding of the environment. In this view, language reflects thought, although Piaget acknowledged that the acquisition of language enables the separation of thought from action.

Sapir's view was developed by Whorf (1940) who argued that an individual's perception and understanding of the world is dependent upon the language to which she is exposed. If the language she acquires ascribes an attribute to a phenomenon, or expresses a concept, the child will experience and have an understanding of that attribute or concept. If the attribute or concept is not expressed in the language, the child will have no experience or understanding of that attribute or concept. This is the strong version of the hypothesis. A weaker form proposes that certain aspects of language predispose the individual to think in a particular way.

Vygotsky's view can be seen as embodying several aspects of these different accounts. He proposed that thought and language are initially separate and develop in parallel until about the age of 2 years. At this point language and thought begin to merge and influence one another, with the eventual result that language can be used to help thinking and thought can be reflected in language. In other words, the relationship between thought and language is in both directions. This view can account for much of the research carried out in this field.

The study of deaf children was considered to provide a way of examining the relationship between language and cognition. If the deaf person has no language, and if language is a prerequisite of cognition, then the deaf person's ability to reason and think should be impaired or even absent. Conversely, if language is dependent upon cognition, then the deaf person's knowledge and understanding should be equivalent to that of the hearing person's.

All this presupposes that deaf people have no language. However, none of the theoretical viewpoints require that the language is spoken language. Gradually it is becoming recognized that the sign languages of the deaf, for example, American Sign Language (ASL) and British Sign Language (BSL), are languages in their own right (e.g. Bellugi, 1980; Kyle and Woll, 1985). These sign languages are naturally occurring languages, in the same sense that French and English are naturally occurring languages. As in spoken languages, there are regional variations in each sign language and each has its own distinct grammatical features. Sign languages such as ASL and BSL do not follow the same grammatical rules as one another, nor do their grammars match those of spoken American or English. This is in contrast to artificial sign languages, for example, Signed Exact English and Paget-Gorman, which follow the grammatical rules of English.

Thus, although a deaf person may have unintelligible speech, they may possess a sign language of comparable complexity and sophistication to any naturally occurring spoken language. In this very important sense, deaf people who can communicate by sign language cannot be said to be without language. For this reason, study of the intellectual development of the deaf has turned out to be an unsatisfactory way of examining the nature of the relationship between language and cognition. However, the study of their cognitive development is still of great interest.

### How intelligent is the deaf child?

We hear too much about the deaf through the media to continue to equate being deaf with being dumb in the sense of stupid. But the change in our attitude towards regarding the deaf as intelligent and able members of our society is recent and certainly incomplete. Linguistic skills are still rated very highly and we may all be guilty of misjudging a person's intellectual capabilities because we have paid too much attention to their spoken language. Here the deaf person is obviously at a severe disadvantage. Conrad (1979) found that over 60 per cent of profoundly deaf school leavers had speech which was unintelligible or very difficult to understand, except by people involved in deaf education.

In fact, the IQs of deaf children, as assessed, for example, on the Performance Scale of the WISC (Wechsler, 1974) are typically found to fall within the normal range, although the mean scores may fall below the average for hearing children (e.g. Vernon, 1967). However, this test may not do justice to the deaf child. The intelligence of hearing children is usually based on their scores on both the Verbal and Performance Scales of the WISC but, because of the deaf child's limited language skills, the deaf child's intelligence is based on the Performance Scale. This raises two problems: how do the Verbal and Performance IQs compare, and, more importantly, how non-verbal is the Performance Scale? A study by Graham and Shapiro (1953) suggests that deaf children's actual intelligence may have been underrated. They showed that, when the Performance Scale of the WISC was given to hearing and deaf children using pantomime instructions, all the children obtained lower scores than hearing children who were given verbal instructions. There were some differences between the hearing and deaf groups given pantomime instructions, with the deaf children being superior on one subtest. These findings point to at least one influence of language on intelligence: it helps performance on intelligence tests! But it is also quite clear that spoken language is not a prerequisite for cognition.

Interestingly, it has been reported that children with some form of hereditary deafness tend to have higher non-verbal IQs than children who are deaf for other reasons. The former children have an average IQ of 100, whereas the latter group has an average IQ of 95. Not surprisingly, deaf children with additional handicaps have an average IQ about 10 points below this. If those children who have some form of hereditary deafness are examined more closely, it has been found that, if both of the child's parents are also deaf, then the child's IQ will be higher than if her parents can hear (e.g. Conrad, 1979; Sisco and Anderson, 1980). There are a number of possible explanations for this observation, but the one which Conrad favoured was that those deaf children who have deaf parents are more likely to have been exposed to a sign language from an early age. Deaf and hearing children exposed to a sign language begin to produce signs three to four months earlier than hearing children produce spoken words (see p. 71). Perhaps this early exposure to some form of signing has real advantages for the deaf child's intellectual development. However, in a carefully controlled study, Conrad and Weiskrantz (1981) found no differences in intelligence between deaf children with deaf parents, deaf children with hearing parents and hearing children of hearing parents. The earlier proposal, that early signing may have a beneficial effect on intelligence as measured by IQ tests, appears to be a myth.

It is certainly wrong to think of the deaf person as being dumb, in the figurative sense of being intellectually inferior to the speaking members of the population. In terms of how they perform on non-verbal intelligence scales they are within the normal range. Cognitive development can occur and does occur in the presence of poor spoken language skills.

So far I have only looked at cognitive development from the point of view of intelligence test scores. In order to look more closely at the processes involved I want to examine three areas of cognitive development in the deaf person to see whether being able to hear and to acquire spoken language plays any part.

### *What do young deaf children understand about objects and people?*

Unfortunately, we know relatively little about the very early development of deaf children for the simple reason that they are rarely identified early enough. However, we do know a little more about their development later on. When deaf children begin to communicate they do not appear to have an impaired understanding of people, objects or the relationships which can exist between people and objects. They seem to know a great deal about objects even if they are not given a formal sign system but rely on gestures (Feldman et al., 1978). They seem to engage in similar types of pretend play to hearing children (Gregory, 1976) which we would not expect if their early cognitive development was hampered by their not being able to hear. Of course, there are some things which the deaf child will not know, at least not in the same way as a hearing child, for example, that hens cluck and that balloons go bang.

Sound is clearly of importance in the development of the hearing child. However, deaf children appear to know almost as much about objects and people as their hearing contemporaries, although their understanding may be qualitatively different. This suggests that sound is not essential, nor is the ability to hear a prerequisite for these sorts of developments. There may be different routes by which these developments can occur. Is the same true of later cognitive development?

### What do deaf children understand about quantity and other concepts?

Much of the research on deaf children's understanding of quantity and various other concepts was initiated by Furth in the 1960s. He found, for example, that 7-12 year old deaf children were just as competent as hearing children of a similar age on tasks requiring judgements of sameness and similarity, but that the deaf children were not as competent at choosing opposites (Furth, 1966). Why? Is this something for which we need spoken language? It has been suggested that it is hard to explain the concept of opposites using gestures (Blank, 1974), and if deaf children are trained they do much better. An interesting account of their difficulty is that sign languages of the deaf may not express opposites like big and small as distinctly as spoken languages. For example, in BSL, big is signed by positioning the hands apart, palms facing, fingers pointing upwards and moving the hands outwards. In contrast, small is signed by a narrow gap between the thumb and first finger. These signs bear a close resemblance to the meaning they stand for. In spoken English the words bear no relationship to the meaning they convey. Other contrasting terms bear much more resemblance to one another in sign than in words (Furth, 1973). It may be that the lack of difference between signs signifying opposites makes it harder to perceive or comprehend the differences which are being referred to. If this is correct, then it suggests that the nature of a language can influence cognition.

There is other evidence which supports the idea that our language influences our understanding. Schwam (1980) asked young deaf and hearing children about the quantities of liquid in two containers. All the deaf children were learning ASL, whereas none of the hearing children had learned any sign language. When both hearing and deaf children were asked, in ASL, which glass had least in they chose the correct one. But they also chose the one with least in when they were asked which glass had most in! On the other hand, most of the hearing children, when they were asked verbally, chose the glass with most in it regardless of the question. The explanation offered by Schwam is based on the relative similarity of the signs for more and less to the meanings they stand for. In ASL, the sign for less is made by positioning the palm of one hand above and facing the palm of the other hand, and moving the top hand down towards the lower hand. In contrast, the sign for more is not similar to its meaning, the sign involves moving the finger tips of each hand together, the palms facing the signer. The sign for less could be related visually to the lower water level in one of the containers, whereas the sign for more cannot be related visually. The sign for more is one of the earliest signs produced by deaf children, but what is relevant here is the context in which it is likely to have been learned. The sign for more is often used in situations when there is a lack of something, such as 'want more milk', so the deaf child may understand the sign to mean which container should have more water added, and so choose the one which contains the least, not the most.

Other tasks which have been used to examine the cognitive development of deaf children are Piaget's classic conservation tasks. In these tasks the child has to judge the equivalence of two identical quantities after one has been changed perceptually. For example, the child is first shown two identical balls of plasticine, and agrees that they are the same. One ball is then rolled into a sausage shape, and the child is asked if the ball and sausage contain the same amount of plasticine. The child is judged as conserving if she says the two amounts are the same. The results of the performance of deaf children on such tasks indicate a delay in the age at which deaf children conserve, compared to hearing children, though there is disagreement about the extent of the delay. For example, on conservation of weight and volume, which hearing children typically achieve at about 7-8 years, Oléron and Herren (1961) reported deaf children to be about six years behind hearing children. Furth (1966), using weight conservation, found that the performances of deaf children of about 8½ years were equivalent to those of hearing children of just under 7 years old. Templin (1967) found that on an initial test of weight conservation 12 and 14 year old deaf children were retarded by two years, and 11 year olds by five years; however, when the task was given to the children on a second occasion the 14 year olds were retarded by six years!

It is not immediately obvious how these disparate results can be reconciled. However, research with young hearing children suggests a possible explanation. Piaget's original proposals, that children are unable to achieve certain tasks, including conservation, before they reach the age of 6 or 7, have been criticized (e.g. Donaldson, 1978). It has been demonstrated that children as young as 3 and 4 can exhibit these and related abilities provided that the experiment makes sense to them. The way in which the task is presented and questions are phrased are crucial. In the experiments reporting delays in deaf children's ability to conserve, the tasks were administered in different ways. This could account for some of the discrepancies in the amount of delay. In addition, it seems very likely that the deaf children's comprehension of what was required of them would have been inferior to that of hearing children in the same situation. Also, the deaf children's comprehension may have been better in some of the experiments than in others.

Another important point is made by Furth and this is that the deaf child may be living in a somewhat impoverished environment. If the deaf child's experience in concrete situations is limited, for whatever reason, then perhaps we should expect her to perform less well on the conservation type of task. However, this should not be interpreted to mean that the deaf child is less intelligent than a hearing child of a similar age.

### Can older deaf children reason abstractly?

Furth's position, following Piagetian theory, is that any developmental lag in the deaf child's cognitive skills is not due to any lack of intelligence or linguistic skill, but rather to lack of experience and training. Working with deaf adolescents, Furth (1973) reports that although some of them show that they are able to understand symbolic logic and permutations despite very poor language skills, about half of them cannot. What should we make of this? Since some of the adolescents can think and reason in this abstract way, deafness itself cannot preclude this capability. However, we still need to explain why it is that some adolescents have more difficulty than others.

The position held by Furth is that an appropriate environment is needed to foster this sort of development. If we look a little further afield to cross cultural studies of abstract thought, a very similar argument has been made by researchers such as Cole and Scribner (1974). They report that adolescents and young adults who have received little formal education perform poorly on abstract reasoning tasks, whereas individuals from a similar background, but who have had some formal education, perform fairly well. Their argument is that development beyond the concrete operational stage is a function of the formal educational system. Returning to the deaf adolescent, it is not the case that the deaf adolescent receives no formal education. After all, they attend school. But as we shall see in later sections, despite apparently being of average intelligence, their educational achievement is often poor. So perhaps it is not so far fetched to draw a parallel between these deaf adolescents and Cole and Scribner's uneducated adolescents. What they both seem to have in common is a relative lack of formal education, either because they do not attend school or because their handicap seems to prevent them from benefiting from it.

What can be concluded about the deaf child's cognitive development? It seems likely that the process of development in the first two years may be very different for deaf children and hearing children, although they seem to reach a similar end point. Sound and spoken language are obviously not necessary for early cognitive development. However, there do seem to be some benefits of having a language which is shared by others. It seems feasible to explain the differences between the cognitive abilities of deaf and hearing children and adolescents by recourse to the way in which the deaf child's limited spoken language skills restrict her environment, both in and out of the educational system. Language seems to afford possibilities for development through its influence on the child's environment. If this is true, then it raises implications for the education of the deaf, in particular the provision of a language they can acquire and through which they can share knowledge and information with others.

## The development of communication

This is the area of research with the deaf which has been particularly prolific. The early work tended to concentrate on the problems facing the deaf child who was trying to acquire spoken language. These researchers were concerned with the nature of the deaf child's spoken language and related skills like reading and writing. More recently questions have been asked about the status of sign systems as languages in their own right, and about the sort of early communication which develops between the deaf child and her parents.

### Can the young deaf child and her parents communicate without spoken language?

In the 1970s there was a major shift in emphasis in the study of child language away from the child's actual acquisition of spoken language and towards the nature of the communication which occurred between her and her caretakers before spoken language emerged (e.g. Golinkoff, 1983). This research has demonstrated that there is a rich communication network which is apparent long before formal spoken language is used. For the hearing child this preverbal communication is by gestures, non-verbal noises and significant looks. What impact will deafness have on these early sorts of communication? Is being able to hear necessary for non-verbal communications and for emerging verbal communications?

A study by Feldman et al. (1978) provides some of the answers. They studied six congenitally deaf children whose parents were committed to just using spoken language, the oral only approach. The children were seen first at between 1½ and 4 years of age. These children began to communicate by pointing to things around them and by using eye contact, just like hearing children. In hearing children gesturing tends to decline as speech emerges, but Feldman et al. found that as the deaf children got older, rather than their gestures declining, they began to combine gestures, and to devise new gestures which were iconic, that is, the gestures bore some visual similarity to the meaning being conveyed, rather like pantomime gestures. These gestures were used both singly, and later in combination, to convey things to others. Very similar findings were reported for two deaf children of hearing parents by Mohay (1982), although a longitudinal study of eight prelingually deaf children of hearing parents carried out by Gregory and Mogford (1981) found no evidence of the children using gestures, apart from pointing. The primary concern of Gregory and Mogford was with the children's acquisition of spoken language, and this difference in focus between this and the other studies may, at least in part, explain the discrepancy in the results.

These important studies reporting the development of gesturing by young deaf children answer some of our questions. It is clear that young deaf children want to communicate and in many ways the systems they individually devise reflect many of the changes seen in the early verbal communication attempts of hearing children. However, late on, differences may appear. In the study by Feldman et al. the gestured utterances of the deaf children were shorter and less complex than the verbal utterances of hearing children even though they may have had as much to communicate about.

An interesting question arises as to the origins of the gestures used by the deaf children. In Feldman et al.'s study, although the parents were committed to an oral only approach, they did use gestures but only about a quarter of their gestures were the same as their child's. And, more importantly, the mothers lagged behind their children in combining signs. The parents also relied more heavily on objects as props. This particular study suggests that children do not need to be set an example from a sophisticated communicator; they will find a way of communicating what they want with little outside help except someone to communicate with and something to communicate about.

However, two other studies argue that exposure to a sophisticated communicator may be important for the development of certain aspects of language. On the basis of her observations, Mohay (1982) proposes that the development of ways of conveying meaning, or semantic processes, probably occurs independently of an adult model. On the other hand, phonological processes, which for spoken language would be the sounds and for sign language would be the form of the signs, are, according to Mohay, dependent upon an adult model.

The second study (Volterra, 1983) examined the acquisition of gestures by both hearing children and a deaf child. The deaf child had deaf parents, who were fluent signers, and this child was therefore exposed to a sign language model. In contrast, the parents of the hearing children could hear, and these children had no sign language model. All the children developed gestures for referring to objects and actions (referential gestures), and they used pointing to indicate particular instances of an object, location or person (deictic gestures, for example, referring to that, there, you). Combinations of gestures were produced by these children. However, a difference was found between the combinations produced by the deaf child and those produced by the hearing children. All the children combined deictic gestures, for example, 'there that', and deictic and referential gestures, for example, 'that drink'. However, only the deaf child produced combinations of two referential gestures, for example, 'fish eat'. When the hearing children reached this stage they used words rather than gestures. Volterra argues that the development, use and combining of gestures is not dependent upon the child having access to an appropriate language model, but that the ability to combine referential gestures is dependent upon access to such a model.

With the exception of the parents of the deaf child in Volterra's study, none of the parents of the deaf children involved in the studies described in this section used a sign language. In the next section I shall examine the development of sign language in deaf children whose parents use signing, commonly parents who are deaf themselves.

## *Is learning to sign like learning to speak?*

There are many reports of the stages through which hearing children progress in their acquisition of language (e.g. Nelson, 1973). Not surprisingly, there are relatively few reports of the progressive acquisition of signs by deaf children (e.g. Schlesinger and Meadow, 1972; McIntire, 1977; Bonvillian et al., 1983). Schlesinger and Meadow followed the development of a deaf girl, Ann, from 8 to 22 months. Ann's parents were also deaf and they used ASL. Ann first attempted to produce a recognizable sign at the age of 10 months. Her first combination (bye sleep) appeared at 14 months. By 19.5 months she had a vocabulary of 142 signs and 14 manual letters of the alphabet. By contrast a hearing child of this age might be saying 50 words.

Bonvillian et al. (1983) and McIntire (1977) also report that signs are acquired at an earlier age than spoken words. Bonvillian et al. studied 11 children from the age of 7 months. Only one of the children was deaf, but all the children had at least one parent who was deaf and all the children experienced ASL at home. The first signs appeared at a mean age of 8.6 months, and signs were combined first at an average age of 17 months. McIntire recorded 85 signs from a 13 month old child with a borderline hearing loss, whose parents were hearing impaired. This child combined signs by 10 months, and by 21 months had over 200 signs.

From these studies it appears that deaf and hearing children, exposed to a sign language, produce signs earlier and add to their vocabularies more quickly than hearing children do using words. However, it might be more interesting to examine how these early words and signs are used by hearing and deaf children. Are the early signs of deaf children used in the same way as the early words of hearing children, or is their use more similar to the way in which hearing children use gestures?

It has been suggested that signs are acquired earlier than words because signs follow on from gestures, whereas words require the child to switch from gesturing to speaking. An interesting study by Petitto (1983) suggests that the continuity between gestures and signs which is implied may not be correct. Petitto studied a deaf child learning ASL. If there is continuity between gesture and sign, then the deaf child's acquisition of deictic pronouns, for example, 'I' and 'you', should proceed smoothly. The correct use of these pronouns depends upon the context in which they occur. For example, 'I' is correct when I am referring to myself, and is also correct when you are referring to yourself. 'I' is not correct when you are referring to me, or I to you. The pronouns are never confused when children use pointing, since they will point towards themselves or towards the other person as and when appropriate. Hearing children have difficulties when they first start to use the spoken forms, often confusing personal pronouns. If signing is continuous with gesture, then deaf children should not exhibit this confusion in their signing. However, the child studied by Pettito used the sign for 'you' when she meant 'me'. This suggests that there may be no more continuity between gesture and signing than between gesture and speaking.

By examining the acquisition of a sign language we can also find out whether the stages through which a hearing child progresses in her spoken language development are peculiar to the oral–aural modalities or a characteristic of language acquisition in general. For example, do the early signs have some equivalence to whole phrases? The evidence indicates they do. At 15 months, Ann, in Schlesinger and Meadow's study, used the sign for smell to mean a number of different things: 'I want to go to the bathroom'; 'I'm soiled, please change me'; 'I want the pretty smelling flower'. In this respect signing and speaking may be similar.

Schlesinger and Meadow also report that some of Ann's signs were variants on the adult form, rather like the baby talk of young hearing children. Other reports (e.g. Bellugi and Klima, 1972) provide evidence of further similarities in learning to sign and learning to speak. The concept and semantic relations which were expressed by one of their deaf children, Pola, matched those of hearing children. Linguistic rules tended to be overgeneralized initially and only later were they applied appropriately. The increase in the number of combinations of signs seemed to parallel that found for hearing children combining words.

However, similarities at this sort of level may mask important differences. Lieven (1982) makes this point in discussing conversations between adults and children, and indicates the need for closer examination of the use to which language is put.

Learning to sign, at least in the early stages, seems to be fairly similar structurally to learning to speak. However, because different languages are involved there will be differences. Some of the differences will arise because the two languages involve different modalities. For example, two words cannot be spoken at the same time, but two signs can be produced simultaneously using both hands, and this is something deaf children have been observed to do (e.g. Schlesinger, 1978). Other differences will arise simply because a sign language and a spoken language are different languages. For example, hearing children learning English or American usually start using the present progressive ending '-ing' before they use the accompanying auxiliary verb. So a hearing child might say 'boy listening' before saying 'boy is listening'. They seem to pay more attention to the word ending '-ing' than to the auxiliary 'is'. In ASL the ending '-ing' used not to exist, although it has been added recently. Schlesinger and Meadow (1972) found that deaf children who received both spoken American and ASL varied in their acquisition of the ending '-ing'. Two things seemed to be crucial: first, how much residual hearing the child had: the less they could hear the more likely they were to acquire the auxiliary 'is' before the ending '-ing'. The second influential factor was the use of the '-ing' sign by the parents: the more precisely and frequently the parents used it the more likely the child was to use the '-ing' ending before the auxiliary.

This last study examined the development of deaf children who received both spoken and signed input, but these children are relatively few in number. By far the largest group of deaf children are those who are initially exposed to spoken language only. These are mainly children whose parents can hear and the majority of these parents will hope that their child will eventually be able to communicate using spoken language. Kyle and Allsop (1982a) found that 26 per cent of the deaf adults they interviewed began learning a sign language before the age of 4 years; a further 40 per cent began to learn between the ages of 5 and 7 years. The remaining 34 per cent began to learn after the age of 8. A crucial question to be answered for those children initially exposed to spoken language only concerns the amount and quality of spoken language that they will be able to acquire.

### How much spoken language can a deaf child acquire?

The amount of spoken language that a deaf child can acquire depends on many factors. For example, how much can she hear; is what she hears clear and not distorted; how much use does she make of any residual hearing; do the adults around her talk clearly and often?

The deaf child can usually make some use of her residual hearing if her hearing loss is less than 60 dB. With such losses she may be able to distinguish speech sounds even though this ability may be based on different acoustic cues from those used by hearing people. Unfortunately, the parents of a deaf child may not be as helpful as they could be; they tend to talk less than parents do to hearing children, and they are inclined to give the child facts and answers rather than ask the child questions, for obvious reasons. This also seems to happen at school with teachers (Wood, 1981), although Wood et al. (1986) have shown that, at least over short periods of time, teachers can change how they talk to 11 year old deaf children. When the teachers asked fewer questions and focused more on what the children were trying to communicate, the children made longer and more frequent contributions. In addition to being exposed to rather different conversations from children who can hear, the majority of deaf children will also be denied access to conversations between other people, an experience which may be important for the hearing child's acquisition of language.

A deaf baby usually starts to babble just like a hearing baby but is likely to stop making these noises at around 9 months (e.g. Meadow, 1980). It is unclear why deaf babies stop making these noises. It may be because being able to hear the sounds you make is necessary to maintain babbling. Alternatively, it may be that the early babbling sounds are unrelated to the word-like sounds which, in hearing children, replace them.

For the deaf child the acquisition of words is a laborious business and only the unusually bright deaf child will have as many as 200 words by the time she is 4 or 5 years old. By this age a hearing child has a vocabulary of around 2,000 words. Schlesinger and Meadow (1972) found that three-quarters of a group of deaf children, with a mean age of 44 months, had spoken language abilities characteristic of hearing children of 28 months or younger. The speech of the deaf child is often unintelligible to strangers and any proficiency that the child gains in spoken language will soon disappear without constant spoken language tuition. Kyle (1981) asked teachers of 6-11 year old deaf children to rate their speech over three years. No significant improvements occurred over that time. Kyle also reports that differences between the speech of the children were due to variations in the extent of their hearing loss, and were independent of the amount or type of speech training they received.

The study by Gregory and Mogford (1981) is a useful source of information about the early words of young deaf children. They report that the average age at which six of the eight deaf children they studied said their first word was 16 months, compared to reports of hearing children saying their first words at about 11 months. There are several relevant points to be noted in this study. Not surprisingly it was found that the more deaf the child, the later the appearance of the first word. In fact the two most profoundly deaf children were saying less than ten words by the time they were 4 years old. The other six children reached the ten word stage at an average age of 23 months, compared to 12 months for hearing children. The rate at which words were acquired also differed for the deaf and hearing children. Hearing children took one month to get from the one word to the ten word stage, but for the deaf children this took seven months. However, the rate of acquisition between ten and 50 words was similar at about six to seven words per month. But a difference shows up again when we look at the rate at which the next 50 words are acquired. For the deaf children the acquisition rate increases to around ten words a month, but hearing children only take one month to acquire their second 50 words.

One of the difficulties for researchers working on the emergence of the hearing child's first word is how to define what constitutes a word. However, this does not seem to be such a problem in research with the deaf. The hearing child is commonly reported as attempting to utter words for several months before the utterance can strictly be called a word. This does not seem to happen with deaf children. Their first words are sounds which the parent has trained and worked on with the child. They are consciously elicited, rather than emerging gradually, and it is much more obvious when the deaf child has a word.

Both deaf and hearing children begin to combine words when their vocabularies have reached about 50 words, at about 30 and 18 months respectively. This is followed by a rapid increase in vocabulary size for the hearing child, but not for the deaf child. Obviously further study of the two word stage is necessary. It seems quite possible that the nature of the two word stage will be different for deaf children. Gregory and Mogford cite the example of a deaf boy who was producing several two word utterances at 30 months, including 'not hot' and 'hot tea'. Two months later he said 'not hot hot tea' meaning cold tea. This may reflect different processes underlying the way in which deaf children and hearing children combine words.

What sort of words do deaf children acquire first? Gregory and Mogford report that at vocabulary sizes of both 50 and 100 words the deaf children, compared to hearing children, had fewer words that name objects and events, and more words that are used within a social relationship like 'thank you', or describe affective states like 'ouch'. At the 50 word stage the deaf children had more words to describe or demand an action and at the 100 word stage they had more words to describe the attributes of objects.

These differences are interesting. The deaf child is not just being taught the names of objects, although these form the largest group of words for both hearing and deaf children at this stage. In her early vocabulary the deaf child has more words than the hearing child that will enable her to control what is happening. However, as Gregory and Mogford point out, these deaf children are older than the hearing children when they reach each of these stages. This may be the reason why they are saying different things. It would be interesting to compare the proportions of the different categories of words for deaf and hearing children of similar chronological age to see if they are saying more similar things than deaf and hearing children who are matched for vocabulary size.

Quite clearly the majority of profoundly deaf children face considerable difficulties in acquiring spoken language. It is also clear that their understanding of spoken language is limited. For example, Bishop (1983) reports 8–12 year old deaf children as having less understanding of spoken language than 4 year old hearing children. They may also have difficulties interpreting the meaning of what they hear. For example, the instruction to give the doll a bath may be interpreted literally, and a bath passed to the doll.

### Does the deaf child have problems reading and writing?

As well as having problems producing and understanding spoken language, the deaf child also has difficulties with reading and writing. The writing of deaf children is different from the writing of younger hearing children (e.g. Swisher, 1976). They make some errors which hearing children would seldom make, like omitting words, for example 'is'. This is not surprising as this is often omitted in ASL. Other differences are that they tend to use more nouns and verbs when they write, and the content of their sentences is more concrete. They use pronouns and prepositions far less than hearing children and use virtually no adverbs. The sentences they do write are much shorter and simpler than hearing children's written sentences. Kyle and Woll (1985) point out that the written work of deaf people often reflects the grammatical structure of the sign language they use and that, until this is realized, their writing may seem unintelligible.

It seems likely that this picture will vary depending on the extent of the deaf child's hearing loss. This is certainly true for reading. Conrad (1979) examined the reading comprehension of most deaf school leavers in England over a two year period. They were aged 15–16.5 years. About 50 per cent of hearing children have a reading age of 15 years when they leave school. Compared to this, Conrad found that 2.5 per cent of profoundly deaf school leavers with hearing losses of 85 dB or more could read at this level. In other words, five children from a group of 202 profoundly deaf children had a reading age of 15. More than 50 per cent of these deaf school leavers had reading ages below 7 years 10 months. Conrad examined two factors which affected this. One was the child's hearing loss: the greater the loss the worse the child read. The other factor was the child's intelligence: deaf children of above average intelligence read better than those of below average intelligence. Neither of these findings is at all surprising. What is surprising, if not frightening, is how poorly the majority of these children read. It is a severe handicap to them. It is so severe that many of them will be unable as adults to read and comprehend the subtitles that are provided on some television programmes, not to mention newspapers, official forms and so on. Of the deaf adults interviewed by Kyle and Allsop (1982b), 77 per cent said that they read a daily newspaper. However, 74 per cent of those interviewed said that daily newspapers were too difficult for deaf people. The average deaf adolescent has a reading age of 9 years. What that means is that 50 per cent of deaf school leavers read at levels below that of a hearing 9 year old, with many of them being unable to read at all by the time they leave school.

We have already seen that the nature of the deaf child's early language differs from that of a hearing child's, so it seems reasonable to ask if her reading skills are similar. It appears that although the average deaf adolescent achieves a reading age of 9 years, she is actually gaining that score in a different manner from that of a hearing 9 year old. The deaf adolescent seems to adopt various strategies to compensate for her limited understanding of grammar (Wood, 1981). We need to find out more about these different strategies to be in a position to understand better the processes underlying reading and the problems facing the deaf child and adolescent. In addition, Wood et al. (1986) point to the probable importance of the teacher's approach to teaching reading. They suggest that focusing on what the child understands when she reads, rather than on the intelligibility of her reading aloud, may be a more successful approach.

## Social development

### *How is interaction with others affected by deafness?*

Most of us take social interaction for granted and pay relatively little attention to the underlying processes. Deafness provides a way of examining the importance of being able to hear for interaction with others. Being deaf does not just mean that you cannot hear: it can lead to severe communication problems in the absence of sign language. It seems likely that deafness will affect interaction in other ways: the deaf person failing to turn to the sound of another person's approach and the resulting delay in beginning to interact with that person; a lack of awareness of turn taking in spoken conversation and subsequent vocal clashes early on; a greater dependence by the child on her parents; problems in understanding the speech of others; limited spoken language skills; frustration for the parents in managing the child, and inference by strangers that the deaf child is mentally handicapped.

The relatively late age of usual diagnosis prevents us from finding out whether or not deafness does result in many of these difficulties. However, a study by Gregory (1976), based on interviews with parents who had a deaf child, suggests that a number of these problems exists. Three-quarters of the 122 families felt that their greatest problem concerned difficulties with communication: for example, one child only realized that the family was going on holiday when the suitcase was being packed; many of the children failed to understand why they were not allowed to do certain things, and it was hard to capture the child's attention (one parent successfully resorted to having a ready supply of soft balls that she could throw at the child to get her to look round). The deaf children had more temper tantrums than hearing children. Many of the parents found bringing up their child frustrating and felt that strangers did not understand. In several cases comments from strangers implied that they thought that the deaf child was mentally handicapped. It is clear that these problems do exist but we do not know how they affect the interaction between the child and her parents, although it seems likely that it will run much less smoothly and be more frustrating than the interaction between a hearing child and her parents. Certainly, deaf children engage in more solitary play than hearing children of a similar age: unless you can talk to another person about what you or they are doing, it is much harder to play together.

In general agreement with Gregory, Denmark et al. (1979) report that more than 85 per cent of the parents of 75 deaf adolescents reported having had behaviour problems with their children when they were of pre-school age. The parents attributed these problems to the children's deafness. At school age, over 60 per cent of the parents reported difficulties with the children's behaviour, and more than 70 per cent had difficulties with behaviour problems after the children left school.

Deafness in a child affects the way in which the parents talk to that child. One of the most obvious outcomes is that the parents talk less than parents do to hearing children. Gregory (1976) found that, when the child was deaf, the amount of interaction between child and caregiver decreased after the child reached the age of 2 years, whereas the amount increases if the child can hear. The content of parents' speech to their child is also different if their child cannot hear. A study by Goss (1970) reports that the speech of mothers of deaf children is more likely than the speech of parents of hearing children to contain directions for what the child should be doing, rather than leaving it up to the child. The parents are less inclined to ask for information and opinions from the child. Similar findings are reported by Schlesinger and Meadow (1972) who interviewed parents of deaf children of pre-school age.

These parents were more intrusive than parents of children who can hear and were more likely to supervise what the child was doing. These interviews also indicated that the parents were concerned about whether they were expecting enough or too much from their child. The parents were less permissive than parents of hearing children, and were much more likely to use physical punishment for disciplining the child. Not only did these parents spank their children more than parents spank hearing children, but almost three-quarters of the parents of the deaf children felt comfortable with this method of discipline, whereas only a quarter of parents of hearing children felt happy using this method. Meadow (1980) found that whereas 69 per cent of parents of hearing 4 year olds would deprive the children of sweets or television as a punishment, only 5 per cent of the parents of deaf 4 year olds used this sort of punishment.

It is not at all surprising that the parents of deaf children are more likely than parents of hearing children to use some form of physical punishment to discipline their children. If the child is unable to hear and understand what the parents say then verbal reprimand is only going to lead to frustration. Schlesinger and Meadow also report that, compared to hearing children, the deaf children seemed less happy and less compliant, but similarly curious about their environment although they were less imaginative. Of course, all this depends upon the deaf child's own language capability and comprehension. If her spoken language skills are good, or she and her parents can communicate in sign language, the more normal the interaction between her and her parents will be.

Thus interaction with a deaf child can be difficult and frustrating. How does it affect her?

### *Does the deaf child adjust successfully to her handicap?*

There is no simple answer to this question. However, it is important, since if we find that some deaf children are better adjusted than others, and if we can identify some of the factors which differentiate deaf children who manage to overcome their handicap from those deaf children who have many problems, then we may be in a position to make practical suggestions as to how to help the deaf child and her family. Obviously some of the factors may be fixed for an individual child and we may not be able to change the situation directly, but awareness of the factors involved may provide a useful starting point.

There are many reports suggesting that deaf children are not as socially mature as hearing children (e.g. Myklebust, 1964; Bradford and Hardy, 1979). However, there are differences between deaf children. Schlesinger and Meadow (1972) report that, of deaf children who were attending a residential school, those whose parents were also deaf were more mature, independent and able to take responsibility than those who had hearing parents. Deaf children whose parents were able to hear, and who were attending a day school, had ratings which were intermediate. So, at least part of the answer to the original question depends on the hearing status of the deaf child's parents and the type of school. Presumably the hearing status of the parents will affect their attitude to their child's deafness. For a deaf parent who has already coped with a hearing loss, the birth of a deaf child will not be such a disaster, indeed the handicap may even be expected. These parents are likely to have a more positive attitude to deafness than parents who have had no prior experience of deafness. Deaf parents are more likely to use a sign language than are hearing parents, and so from the beginning will have a communication system which they will be able to share with their child. Even if the deaf parents do not use any sign language they will probably still be at an advantage over hearing parents, because they will be more tuned in to non-verbal cues and will be experienced at adjusting their behaviour for the deaf. The deaf child born to deaf parents will be entering a particular subculture which she can come to share with her parents. This will not be so for the deaf child born to hearing parents. It seems likely that these differences between the parents will contribute to the relatively successful adjustment of the deaf child of deaf parents.

For deaf children of hearing parents the type of schooling may be crucial. Those children who attend a day school seem to be better adjusted than those attending a residential school. Of course the decision to send a deaf child to a residential school is likely to be determined partly by their behaviour prior to their going to the school. Also parental factors cannot be eliminated, since parents who agree to send their child to a residential school may have very different attitudes from parents who send their child to a day school. Indeed it seems possible that parents who keep their deaf child at home during term time may have a more positive attitude towards deafness than parents who send their child away to school. If this line of argument is correct then deaf children of deaf parents attending day schools for the deaf should be the best adjusted of all deaf children. However, they are such a small group that such comparisons have not been made.

There are a number of other factors which are relevant to the deaf child's adjustment to her handicap. The cause of the child's deafness clearly cannot be changed, but it may be a crucial indicator of how well the child will adjust to her handicap. The child whose deafness is due to some genetic defect is least likely to have any additional handicap, whereas other causes of deafness are commonly associated with other handicaps of varying severity. The genetically deafened child is also likely to have at least one parent who is deaf. Also, knowing what caused a handicap, whether the handicap is deafness or some other, seems to result in the parents feeling less guilty (Meadow, 1968).

Since communication is seen as the biggest problem for both the parents and the deaf child, one factor which will be crucial in the deaf child's adjustment will be the nature and extent of her deafness: for example, when did it occur; how much can she hear; can she hear high frequencies as well as low frequencies; will a hearing aid help; was she born deaf or did she become deaf after she had started to talk? All these questions have been considered in earlier sections. However, it does not follow necessarily that the profoundly deaf child will not adjust as well as the moderately deaf child. The most common cause of sensorineural deafness is genetic, and this sort of damage is more severe than conductive deafness. Therefore a sizeable proportion of children with sensorineural damage will have at least one deaf parent. Thus, although these children will have a severe loss and so be at a disadvantage, they will in fact also be at an advantage by having one or two deaf parents. This sort of consideration indicates that we should not think of the deaf as a homogeneous population, but as individuals.

Initially the deaf child of deaf parents is likely to get more help from the available services, in that she will be identified as being deaf early because her deafness will be anticipated. Amplification may be appropriate and provided early, and this may have benefits. Pre-school teaching will also be started if this is available. On the other hand, although the diagnosis of deafness in a child born to hearing parents may be delayed, once it is made the child may be at an advantage in that her parents may be in a better position to fight for services for their child. Unfortunately, hearing parents may have expectations for their child's development and achievement which the child will have difficulty in meeting.

Another difference is that hearing parents are much more likely to be overprotective of a deaf child. Meadow (1967) looked at the attitudes of deaf and hearing parents to allowing pre-school deaf children out to play near by. Half of the deaf parents said that they would allow a deaf child of under 5 years old to play independently nearby, but only 15 per cent of hearing parents felt that they would. Again it seems as though deaf parents tend not to perceive a deaf child as having any particular problem, whereas this is not the case for hearing parents.

# 4

# How do children with motor
# handicaps develop?

## Introduction

In this chapter I shall consider children with spina bifida, cerebral palsy and damage as a result of the drug thalidomide. This covers a vast area in terms of the nature and extent of the motor difficulties and other difficulties which face these children. As a result it has been necessary to be selective, concentrating on those studies which have particular implications for our understanding of developmental processes.

A child with a motor handicap is likely to be restricted in how she is able to interact with the environment. Obviously, the extent of this restriction will vary with the extent of the handicap. Our theoretical interest in these children resides in the question of whether the ways in which their interaction is restricted have any effect on how they develop. Different accounts of how development occurs lead to different predictions as to the consequences of motor handicap for development. This can be illustrated by considering the views of the nativist, the empiricist and the interactionist.

The nativist position (e.g. Bower, 1974) holds either that knowledge is present at birth or that the structures necessary to obtain knowledge are present at birth and that all that is necessary is for the child to be exposed to the relevant information. If this view is correct, in particular the former version, and provided that the motor handicap is not associated with any sort of brain damage, then the child with a motor handicap should have similar knowledge and understanding to that of a non-handicapped child.

The empiricist view (e.g. Watson, 1919) proposes that babies are born without any understanding and acquire knowledge from experiences in the environment. In this view the child need not be active, but can be a passive recipient of experience. The analogy of this view which is sometimes used is of an empty vessel into which information and knowledge are poured. If this view is correct, then the understanding of the child with a motor handicap will extend to experiences she has had, regardless of whether she has been actively involved in the experiences.

This is in contrast to the view of those arguing for the importance of the child interacting with the environment and constructing an understanding for herself (e.g. Piaget and Inhelder, 1969). The prediction from this view would be that the child with a motor handicap would lack understanding of situations in which she has been unable actively to participate.

## Motor development

### *What motor skills can children with motor handicaps acquire?*

There is a great deal of variation in the sort of motor skills that these children can develop depending on the nature and severity of their handicap. In children with cerebral palsy all the motor milestones seem to be delayed. Denhoff and Holden (1951) reported considerable delays in the development of early motor milestones: the average age at which 74 children with cerebral palsy held up their heads was 12.4 months, and 86 per cent of a group of 28 children started to reach much later than the usual age of 5 months. Hewett (1970) found that by the age of 5 years or more, 38 per cent of the 125 cerebral palsied children she studied could not sit unsupported, 10 per cent had some balance when they sat but were unable to stand without support, and a further 10.4 per cent could sit and stand but not walk. This means that less than half of these children could walk by the age of 5. In addition, when the cerebral palsied child does walk, the nature of her handicap may leave her with a very odd gait.

Usually the main motor problem facing spina bifida children is paralysis of the legs. We might therefore expect their motor difficulties to be in areas which require the use of legs. Not surprisingly, these children are often delayed in standing and walking and some never manage to do either. Anderson and Spain's study (1977) found that by the age of 3 years 40 per cent were still not able to walk or could only walk a few steps and by 6 years just under half were able to get around the house easily. But what is more surprising is that these children often have problems using their hands. They are less skilled than non-handicapped children at tasks requiring fine motor control like picking up small objects, putting pegs into holes in a peg board, or tracing a picture. Interestingly this difficulty has been related to their paraplegia, in that they find it harder to keep their balance when they are sitting down and tend to support themselves with one hand. Thus it will be difficult for them to gain experience in fine motor tasks and they will have fewer opportunities of using both hands together.

In a fascinating study, Gouin Décarie (1969) administered the Griffiths Mental Development Scale (Griffiths, 1954) to 22 children damaged by thalidomide aged 17–44 months. Although this scale provides an overall developmental quotient, the test items are divided between five subscales. Interestingly, these physically handicapped children did particularly well on the subscales of locomotor, eye and hand, and performance, especially on the last two. Admittedly their mean quotients fell below the norm of 100 but only by 5, 8 and 18 points for the eye and hand, the performance and the locomotor scales respectively. This suggests that the motor skills of thalidomide damaged children are reasonably similar to those of non-handicapped children. However, at a later assessment, when the children were about 4 years old, a rather different picture appeared (Gouin Décarie and O'Neill, 1973/4). About half of the children had their lowest score on the locomotor scale, making this their most backward area of development, whereas at the earlier assessment it was in the middle of the five scores on average. No child at the second assessment had their highest score on this scale. Unfortunately Gouin Décarie and O'Neill do not give any more information about the other motor scales at this assessment.

There are several things to notice about Gouin Décarie's method: first, she credited the child with passing an item if the normal age of achievement of that item fell below the child's chronological age, and if it was physically impossible for the child to perform it; second, the child was credited with the item regardless of whether or not she did it in the conventional way. For example, she would pass the item of holding a pencil as if to mark the paper if she did this successfully while holding the pencil with her toes or in her mouth. The point may have artifically raised these children's scores. The second indicates that the ways by which the children achieved the different items was varied, and demonstrates that they may compensate for their disability by adopting a different approach: they do similar sorts of things to normal children in whatever way they can. Such compensation is supported by Pringle and Fiddes's (1970) description of a thalidomide damaged girl, Fiona, who was born without arms and with severely dislocated hips. She was in plaster from her knees up to her shoulders for the first 18 months of her life. According to her mother, as soon as the plaster was removed, Fiona began to use her feet for all sorts of activities.

Another fascinating case was reported by Kopp and Shaperman (1973). This boy was not damaged by thalidomide but is similar in many ways. He was born with no limbs except for a 6 cm long digit on his hip, which was non-functional. He spent his first three months in hospital and at 4 months was fostered. By 5 months he was able to roll over, at 6 months he could hold his trunk upright with some side support, and he had good head control. Around this time he was fitted with a bucket arrangement so that he could keep upright. By the age of a year he was able to push a ball around with his head and trunk, and, interestingly, although he had no way of manipulating objects except by mouthing them, he refused to use his mouth to hold objects.

This last case and the studies of thalidomide damaged children demonstrate that even without the normal complement of limbs these children discover ways of doing motor tasks using whatever they have. Nevertheless, mobility will be limited if a child's legs and hips are malformed or absent, and the severely physically handicapped child will not be able to develop the same motor skills as a normal child. Does this have any effect on how they perceive and understand the world? Are the sort of motor developments seen in normal children necessary for development in other areas?

## Perceptual development

If action is important for perception (e.g. Piaget and Inhelder, 1969) then the child with a motor handicap should have difficulties in this area. And indeed some of the children do have problems, especially in areas which involve an awareness of spatial relationships. For example, many children with spina bifida, especially those with associated hydrocephalus, find the following sorts of task difficult: geometry; science subjects; geography; copying designs and letters (e.g. Anderson and Spain, 1977). This could be due to their limited motor control, but this seems unlikely since they are just as poor at copying designs by arranging matches appropriately. Their writing of individual letters is reasonable, but the spatial qualities of what they write is poor: the letters within each word tend not to be spaced evenly, or to lie on a straight line, and the same goes for the words within a sentence. A similar proportion to non-handicapped children of the same age and intelligence make reversal errors when they write, but the nature of the errors is quite different. Whereas the non-handicapped children might write a 'd' for a 'b', or a 'p' for a 'g', spina bifida children with hydrocephalus are more likely to confuse letters which involve a diagonal, for example writing 'z' instead of 's' (Anderson and Spain, 1977).

A problem with mirror images or reversals is common amongst children with cerebral palsy, in particular those with spastic damage, where as many as one in six is found to have difficulties: they may write letters upside down or back to front. They seem to find it particularly difficult to copy designs, tending to orient sloping lines incorrectly, and to make mistakes at points where two lines make an angle: this is especially clear in their attempts to copy a diamond, their end product often bearing no relationship to the original (Abercrombie, 1964). Like children with spina bifida, spastic cerebral palsied children have spatial problems so that they will tend to fail to place parts of a figure in correct relation to each other part. This particular difficulty is apparent in their attempts to draw people.

Amongst children with cerebral palsy it is those who are spastic who tend to have these sorts of problem. They may also have problems judging distances and directions. They may find getting dressed difficult, for example, not knowing which sleeve to put an arm into. These children may also have some tactual perceptual difficulties. For instance, they may not know which finger has been touched if they are blindfolded. In general, their tactual sensitivity is poor.

Although many children with spina bifida and cerebral palsy show these perceptual problems they do not seem to be a necessary consequence of physical handicap since by no means all the children handicapped in either of these ways exhibit these problems. This variation is also found in children damaged by thalidomide. Pringle and Fiddes (1970) describe six cases in some detail and it is clear that although several of these children have perceptual difficulties which seem similar to those found in some spina bifida and cerebral palsied children, the difficulties are not characteristic of all the children.

This raises the question as to whether or not these difficulties are due to a particular sort of motor handicap. The differences between the three groups of cerebral palsied children suggests that being unable to control movement, as in athetosis, or having poor coordination, as in ataxia, have less effect on spatial awareness than if movements are stiff and jerky because of spasticity. This ties in to some extent with the findings for spina bifida and thalidomide damaged children. A person with spina bifida is likely to have legs which are paralysed, whereas the thalidomide damaged person will usually be able to move her unaffected limbs normally. Perhaps it is the sort of movement that a person is capable of which is important for an understanding of spatial relationships. It is obviously not straightforward as we can see from the cases cited by Pringle and Fiddes. One child, who had a particularly good understanding of spatial relationships, had no arms and such severely dislocated hips that she could not walk. Another had almost normal hands and no legs (although he could use artificial ones) and yet he had problems with spatial relationships. Thus it is not at all clear whether or not a particular motor ability is necessary for the development of spatial awareness. Pringle and Fiddes point to a further factor, that of how well adjusted the child is. They found that the children who were coping most satisfactorily with their handicap were also those who showed few perceptual problems. It has also been suggested (Cruickshank, 1976) that some perceptual errors made by cerebral palsied children are related to intellectual level.

## Cognitive development

### *How intelligent are these children?*

In assessing how far physical handicap affects intelligence, additional handicaps present a problem since many of the children are also brain damaged. This damage may affect their cognitive functioning, and such an influence needs to be ruled out before the question can be answered. One way to do this would be to look at children who have varying degrees of brain damage and physical handicap and see which is related most closely to intelligence. Unfortunately, the extent of brain damage is usually unknown - indeed it is normally inferred from the intelligence level of the child. However, children with spina bifida do provide one way of looking at this question. Three groups of spina bifida children can be identified: those without hydrocephalus; those with hydrocephalus and no shunt; and those with hydrocephalus and a shunt (see p. 16). The first group of children are those least likely to have any brain damage. The hydrocephalus in the second group of children is presumably mild or self-arresting, and so we can assume that if these children have any brain damage it is probably slight. The third group of children are most likely to have suffered some brain damage because of severe hydrocephalus.

When the intelligence levels of these three groups of children were examined by Lorber (1971) it was found that the children with shunts tended to have the lowest intelligence. From table 4.1 it can be seen that of the 16 spina bifida children with an IQ below 60, 13 (81 per cent) of them have a shunt controlled hydrocephalus. In the intelligence range of 61-79, 21 (75 per cent) of the 28 children are hydrocephalic and have shunts. The numbers in each of the three groups who have an IQ between 61 and 79 are 2 (6 per cent) of the no hydrocephalus group; 5 (18 per cent) of the hydrocephalic but no shunt group; 21 (28 per cent) of the hydrocephalic and shunt group. In other words it is those children who are likely to have brain damage who are found to have the lower IQs. However, is this independent of physical handicap?

Unfortunately, it is those children with the most severe form of spina bifida, myelomeningocele, who are most affected physically and most likely to have hydrocephalus. However, if we examine the children who have IQs

**Table 4.1** Relationship between intelligence, hydrocephalus and physical handicap

| Physical handicap | No hydrocephalus | Hydrocephalus No shunt | Shunt |
|---|---|---|---|
| No handicap | 3 | 1 | 0 |
| Moderate handicap[a] | 9 | 6 | 5 |
| Severe handicap IQ 80+ | 15 | 15 | 36 |
| Severe handicap IQ 61-79 | 2 | 5 | 21 |
| Extreme handicap IQ <60 | 2 | 1 | 13 |

[a]Five of the 20 children in this group had IQs 75-9, the others 80+.
*Source*: after Lorber, 1971

below 80, with the exception of the five children with moderate physical handicaps and IQs of 75-9, we find that they are all severely handicapped physically regardless of which of the three groups they fall into (no hydrocephalus; hydrocephalus and no shunt; hydrocephelus plus shunt). This suggests that their physical handicap may determine their low IQ. But to conclude this we need to be certain that those children who have no hydrocephalus, who are severely handicapped physically and who have an IQ below 80 really have no brain damage. Obviously it is impossible to rule out brain damage in these children. A further reason for questioning the primacy of physical handicap rather than brain damage is that some spina bifida children are severely handicapped physically and yet are of normal intelligence. Interestingly, these children are very unlikely to be hydrocephalic. So can a physical handicap result in cognitive impairment? From the evidence discussed so far, it seems that a physical handicap alone is not sufficient to cause cognitive impairment.

Cerebral palsied children tend to be of below average intelligence with only about 20 per cent achieving normal levels. However, once again we have the problem of separating the relative contributions of physical handicap and brain damage. If those children with a spastic type of cerebral palsy are examined, it is found that in general the more limbs that are affected the greater the likelihood of below average intelligence. This suggests that the physical handicap does affect intelligence. Yet this is obviously not necessarily true as is shown by looking at the athetoid group of cerebral palsied children. These children are often of average or above average intelligence. Also, since it is particularly difficult to assess the intelligence of children who have relatively little control over their movements and who may speak incoherently, it seems likely that these children's intelligence may have been underestimated.

It seems quite clear that a physical handicap, even if it is severe, does not necessarily restrict intellectual development. The same sort of picture emerges from studies of thalidomide damaged children. In her study, Gouin Décarie found no relationship between the severity of each child's handicap and their developmental quotient on the Griffiths Scale, although the mean quotient was 90, 10 points below average. This mean may be inflated because of her method of scoring. Nevertheless three of the 22 children had quotients of 110 or more, and only three had quotients below 73.

All of this points strongly to the conclusion that a physical handicap is not necessarily a recipe for cognitive impairment. Why then are some physically handicapped children of below average intelligence? Brain damage may be one factor, but this cannot account for why some of Gouin Décarie's thalidomide damaged children were functioning below the norm. To explain this Gouin Décarie points out that the children's scores were related to the length of time they had spent in an institution since they had been born. There were some obvious exceptions: three of the children with some of the lowest quotients had spent very little time away from home. But generally the relationship held true. Also Gouin Décarie points out that these three children had problems additional to their physical handicap.

This finding immediately suggests that although a physical handicap itself may not be particularly restricting intellectually, it may have environmental consequences which are. The physical handicap may seriously limit the child's experience, and it may be that it is the extent of this limitation which is crucial, rather than the severity of the handicap that brought it about.

The later paper by Gouin Décarie and O'Neill (1973/4) sheds some more light on this question. They report that at a second assessment 20 months later, when the children were around 4 years old, the mean quotient had increased significantly to 98. Six children had quotients above 110. Since the physical handicaps of these children can hardly have changed, this improvement is further support for the case that a low IQ does not necessarily follow from a motor handicap. The greatest improvements were found in the children who were the youngest at the first assessment, and in those children who had spent least time in hospital. The changes did not appear to have been influenced by the extent of the child's handicap. Gouin Décarie and O'Neill point to two factors. First, all the children were now able to stand upright and walk. Second, the children had turned to other fields of activity, in particular language. On the previous assessment the lowest mean score was for the language scale, and for the majority this was the most backward area. At the second assessment this was still the most backward area for nine of the children, but for another nine out of the 22 it was the most developed area.

These improvements were not always maintained. At a third assessment some 30 months later when the children were about 6 years old, the mean overall quotient had fallen to 94 although it is not stated whether this fall was significant. Four children had a higher IQ than before, but for six it was lower than at the second assessment. Why should this decline occur? Three had had a low IQ earlier and had fallen further, and three were amongst the most able. The latter children had become very aware of their disabilities and Gouin Décarie and O'Neill argue that their poorer performance reflects emotional difficulties. In particular, these children had a number of family problems: the parents of one had divorced; the mother of another had become alcoholic; and the third child had withdrawn into a world of fantasy and had given up competing with his classmates. For the four children who showed an improvement, Gouin Décarie points to the school environment as an explanation. This environment was a great deal more stimulating than their home environment for two of the children in particular.

Pringle and Fiddes's (1970) study of children damaged by thalidomide and children with similar handicaps provides some support for the importance of the environment surrounding the child rather than the degree of physical handicap. They found significant relationships between each of these factors and intellectual ability, but the relationship with the environment was stronger. It is obviously hard to distinguish these two factors. The children in Pringle and Fiddes's study were older than Gouin Décarie's and, on average, their Terman-Merrill IQs were only just below normal, at 97 points. Pringle and Fiddes also point to deafness as a contributory problem. They divided the 60 children definitely damaged by thalidomide into those who were profoundly deaf and those who were not. When the deaf children were excluded the mean IQ for the remaining 53 children was 101.5, whilst that for the seven profoundly deaf children was 66. For these children then, deafness seems to be by far their greatest problem, certainly as regards performance on a standard intelligence test, and their physical difficulties alone seem to have little or no adverse effects on intelligence. Pringle and Fiddes report the average IQs for the 53 hearing thalidomide damaged children according to the degree of their physical impairment as: mild, 109; moderate, 98; and severe, 97.

The findings of Pringle and Fiddes suggest why Gouin Décarie's children seemed to do less well intellectually on the first assessment. One of the subscales on the Griffiths test assesses hearing and speech, and this was the scale on which the children performed least well, with a mean quotient of 73. If this particularly low score can be explained by some of the children having impaired hearing, their exclusion should leave a raised overall quotient for the remaining children. Although Gouin Décarie mentions two cases of hearing difficulty it may be that some of the children were too young to assess accurately. By the second and third assessments these children may have found ways of coping with any hearing problems, and hence the higher IQs.

On balance there is very little evidence to show that a physical handicap necessarily has an adverse direct effect on intelligence. A number of physically handicapped children, even some of the most severely handicapped, function at a normal or even above average intellectual level. On the other hand many physically handicapped children do not. There are a number of possible reasons for this: brain damage; deafness; some other handicap; or an impoverished environment as a consequence of the physical or additional handicap. Whatever the reason, and it is likely to be different for each individual child, the fact that intellectual development is not solely dependent on physical action has important theoretical and practical implications.

### What do children with motor handicaps understand about objects?

According to Piaget (1953), an important development during the first two years of life is the growing understanding that objects exist independently of other objects and people, including oneself, and that objects continue to exist even when they are out of sight. He called this the sensorimotor stage of development, and the development of this understanding he called object permanence. For Piaget, full comprehension of object permanence by the child is a necessary prerequisite for, and marks the beginning of, the next period of development: the pre-operational stage. According to Piaget, this development depends upon the child actively manipulating the environment. Through this activity the child constructs increasingly appropriate beliefs about objects.

One of the main methods Piaget devised to investigate young children's understanding of object permanence was to examine how they searched for objects which had been hidden in a variety of ways. A child has a complete understanding of object permanence when she is able to retrieve successfully an object which has been moved, under cover of another object, from the place where the child originally saw it being hidden, through a series of hiding places, to a final hiding place. For example, a toy car is hidden under a beaker in front of the child, then this beaker, still concealing the car, is hidden first under a cloth, then under a box. Finally the beaker is removed from under the box, leaving the car behind. A child who successfully finds the car after watching this series of invisible displacements has reached the end of the sensorimotor period.

The study of physically handicapped children should provide an opportunity to examine whether or not an understanding of objects is dependent upon their being actively manipulated. Alternatively, is the opportunity to view objects and their manipulation by others sufficient? For the majority of physically handicapped children their handicap will not prevent them from manipulating objects entirely. Some may substitute the use of their mouths or feet for their hands, and others may have some use of their hands. However, the physically handicapped child's understanding of objects may tell us something about what sorts of experience of objects are necessary for an understanding of object permanence.

Gouin Décarie (1969) examined her thalidomide damaged chidren's understanding of objects by looking at how they behaved towards hidden objects. Of the 21 children aged 17-44 months who would cooperate, all but two 17 month olds had reached the end of Piaget's sensorimotor period in that they were able to cope with a series of invisible displacements. Thus the thalidomide damaged children aged 18 months and over, with the exception of the non-cooperative child, had achieved the final stage of object permanence. How did they reach this level of understanding?

All 19 successful children could bring their hands together, although it was difficult for eight of them. None of the others – the two who had not reached the final stage and the child who would not cooperate – could bring their hands together, nor could they get either hand up to their mouths. Gouin Décarie does not say if any of these children could get their feet to their mouths. Perhaps hand–hand and hand–mouth coordination is necessary for a satisfactory understanding of object permanence? But the two children who had not yet reached the final stage of the sensorimotor period, and who had these severe limitations, were younger than the age at which object permanence is normally achieved. We really need to know whether these children's understanding of objects developed further over the next few months, and this information is not available. It is interesting that one of the children could cope with a single invisible displacement, and so had almost reached the final stage. The other failed with a visible displacement. This suggests that mouth–hand and hand–hand coordination may not be essential, although it obviously helps. Again it would be useful to know whether or not either of these two children had functional feet which they could use to manipulate objects, and bring them to their mouths.

Further evidence that object manipulation is not necessary for the understanding of object permanence is provided by Kopp and Shaperman's (1973) case study, although unfortunately there are problems of interpretation here as well. The child's comprehension of objects was first examined when he was 2¾. For the previous three months he had been fitted with an artificial arm. Admittedly the report states that he needed very little training in how to manipulate objects with this limb. This adds weight to the view that he already knew a lot about objects, how they related to one another and how people, including himself, could act on them. Certainly by the time any formal testing was done he had reached the end of the sensorimotor period in terms of his understanding of object permanence.

What is clear from these reports is that children can have very limited opportunities for manipulating objects, and still develop an understanding of their permanence by about the same age as a child who has many more opportunities for manipulation. If it is assumed that Kopp and Shaperman's child had reached the end of the sensorimotor period before he was provided with the artificial limb, then it seems unlikely that the reason why Gouin Décarie's 17 month olds were at an earlier stage was because their handicap prevented them from bringing their hands together or up to their mouths. A more reasonable explanation seems to be that they were too young.

If manipulation of objects is not necessary for an understanding of object permanence, can we point to any experience that is? It is clear from Kopp and

Shaperman's report that this child was able to move himself around by rolling from about 5 months of age, and by a year he was pushing a ball along the ground with his head and trunk. From Gouin Décarie's report it also seems as though even the most handicapped of her thalidomide damaged children found a way of moving themselves around, and presumably whilst doing this they would have come into contact with various objects, and by this means could discover a great deal about acting on objects. Contrast this with a child severely handicapped by cerebral palsy. Such a child, especially if all four limbs are affected, may be relatively immobile, and there may be no way in which she can move any part of her body to contact objects intentionally. All that such children may be able to do is to observe the actions of other people. As we have already seen such children are often particularly handicapped intellectually, and it seems likely that their understanding of object permanence would be impaired.

The additional problems facing these children - possible brain damage and a restricted environment - have been emphasized as factors which limit the opportunities the children have for intellectual development. Nevertheless it seems probable that if a child's physical handicap prevents her from moving her body or any part of herself to make contact with her environment, then this will be a real handicap to her development. Cognitive development can proceed provided that the child is capable of acting on her environment in some way, even if the action is extremely limited.

### *What do children with motor handicaps understand about people?*

Gouin Décarie (1969) examined the ways in which her thalidomide damaged children responded to people and found a great deal of variation between the children. She was looking for instances of 16 behaviours which included: smiling; responding to 'No'; distress when a parent leaves; and using gestures. The results are not reported in any detail but she does make the crucial point that there was no relationship between the children's handicap and how they responded to people. A child who was severely handicapped might show a fairly sophisticated response to people, and yet another child with a relatively minor disability might show little response to people. It is unfortunate that Gouin Décarie does not give many details about how the children responded. This makes it difficult to compare these children's reactions to people with the reactions of non-handicapped children. Without more details it is not possible to specify what these children understood about people.

What is clear is that some of the children were delayed in this area of development, since the youngest child was 17 months old, and Gouin Décarie states that one child exhibited only three of the 16 behaviours. If this delay cannot be explained solely by the physical deformity of the child, what can account for it? Many of these children had spent a substantial proportion of their lives in hospital or institutional care. It is known that interaction with a few familiar people over the first few years is necessary for the development of normal responses to people. In hospitals or institutions this interaction may be lacking.

In her article Gouin Décarie examines the specific behaviours of following and of clinging or holding on to someone. She cites several case histories which suggest that the children did not show these proximity seeking behaviours until they had established some rapport with a familiar person. This sort of account supports the idea of the main problem facing the thalidomide damaged child in developing an understanding of people being the lack of opportunity to form such relationships, perhaps as a result of being institutionalized.

Another way of examining a child's understanding of people is to look at how she represents people. Gouin Décarie and O'Neill (1973/4) looked at this ability in several ways with the original sample of 22 thalidomide damaged children and eight others, when they were 6 years old. In one task the children were given cut-out parts of the body and face, piece by piece, and asked to position each part correctly in turn. Although detailed results are not given, it is clear that some of the thalidomide children were very good at this. Gouin Décarie and O'Neill explain this by pointing to the fact that although a thalidomide damaged child may be missing parts of her own body, a lot of interest may have been paid to her body and this may have drawn her attention to her body and how her body is different from other people's. Surprisingly, the children were not good at constructing a body when they were given all the pieces together. However, the scoring method for this task requires that the body is constructed within a certain space, and because of their physical handicaps some of the children failed to keep it within this area. Thus, although the construction itself was quite good, they were given a low score because of where they had positioned the figure.

Gouin Décarie and O'Neill also examined how the children drew themselves and other people. They found that the children's ability to draw a person on the Goodenough-Harris Human Figure Drawing Test (Harris, 1963) was below average. The mean quotient of the children on this test was 88. Out of the 30 children, 19 scored below average, and only five above.

Pringle and Fiddes also gave this test to their group of thalidomide damaged and similarly handicapped children. They found that the children damaged by thalidomide who were not profoundly deaf had a quotient on this test of 87.5, whereas the mean quotients for the deaf thalidomide damaged children and the non-thalidomide damaged children were 79.4 and 95.5 respectively. This suggests that thalidomide damage may contribute to the child's poor representation of people. Certainly, of Pringle and Fiddes's authentic cases, those with moderate and severe physical handicaps had much lower quotients of 83 and 82 respectively than those with a mild handicap who had a quotient of 98 on the Goodenough. However, what is unclear from these scores is the nature of the differences: how are the figures represented? Are parts omitted, are they drawn in the wrong place or are the parts drawn inaccurately? From Pringle and Fiddes's six case studies it looks as though the figures correspond to those drawn by younger non-handicapped children.

Gouin Décarie and O'Neill add some information to account for the low scores of the thalidomide damaged children's drawings. They found two main differences between the drawings by the thalidomide damaged children and those by normal children. First, the thalidomide damaged children were worse at drawing fingers and feet. Second, the thalidomide damaged children were worse at drawing the body parts in the correct proportions, so that certain parts might be disproportionately large, others too small. In all other respects the drawings by the thalidomide damaged children are just as good as, if not better than, those of normal children.

Why should the thalidomide damaged children show these differences in their drawings? Gouin Décarie and O'Neill point to two factors. The first factor arises from the restrictions imposed on the children by their handicap. Of the 19 children who had scores below average, 13 had upper limbs which were severely malformed. For these children their handicap prevented them from reaching easily over the whole sheet of paper on which they were drawing. If you cannot move your arm and hand freely over the sheet of paper it is much more difficult to keep the parts of the body in proportion, and to draw hands and feet accurately since these are at the extremes of the figure. Obviously these problems can be overcome by keeping the drawing small. This was how three children with malformed arms managed to achieve scores which were above average.

The second factor that Gouin Décarie and O'Neill point to is that the test itself is in some sense like a projective test, and the drawings probably reflect aspects of how the thalidomide damaged child feels about people, as well as indicating her perception and understanding of people.

There is some evidence that both spina bifida and cerebral palsied children have difficulties in correctly relating the different parts of the human body in their drawings, and this difficulty has also been seen when cerebral palsied children are asked to assemble the cut-out parts of a human figure or face (Abercrombie, 1964). There are also reports of these children representing aspects of their own handicap in their drawings. An 18 year old boy with mild athetosis drew a man with his hands in his pockets saying, 'I can't draw hands. Anyway, his probably aren't any better than mine, and mine certainly are a hurdle to me' (Cruickshank, 1976). However, we should not conclude from these sorts of observation that physically handicapped children have a different understanding of people from non-handicapped children. Both cerebral palsied and spina bifida children also have difficulties in correctly relating the parts of non-human figures in their drawings, so it is not a problem which is specific to their drawings of people.

In conclusion, there is relatively little evidence to suggest that the physically handicapped child's understanding of people is any different from that of a non-handicapped child's. There are many gaps in the literature which would make fascinating study: for example, what does the physically handicapped child understand about the ability of people to act on objects; how is this understanding reflected in early language, and does the child's understanding of objects parallel her understanding of people?

### *Does the physically handicapped child have difficulties learning to read, write and do arithmetic?*

Many spina bifida children, especially those with hydrocephalus severe enough to need a shunt, are of below average intelligence, as are severely spastic cerebral palsied children. Not surprisingly, these children are slow to learn to read, and some will never acquire this skill. Spina bifida children do not appear to be any slower than non-physically handicapped children of the same intelligence, but almost half of all cerebral palsied children over 8 years who took part in a survey between 1957 and 1966 were found to be backward in reading by two years or more for their mental age (Wilson, 1970). This particular area of difficulty for the cerebral palsied child probably reflects a number of factors, including their speech and language learning difficulties, their interrupted schooling and the perceptual problems they have with letter reversals and mirror images (see p. 85). For thalidomide damaged children, Pringle and Fiddes (1970) found no particular difficulties in reading amongst their young children, provided that the profoundly deaf children were omitted. According to teachers' ratings, the hearing thalidomide damaged children's reading abilities were comparable to those of non-handicapped children.

Writing difficulties also seem to be associated with low intelligence amongst spina bifida and cerebral palsied children with the exception of those with athetosis. The latter children, who are often of normal intelligence, may be unable to control their movements sufficiently to write, and this may be particularly frustrating for them. A television documentary of Joey Deacon, a cerebral palsied athetoid, portrayed the laborious writing of his book *Tongue Tied* (Deacon, 1974): Joey spoke a sentence; Ernie, who could understand him, repeated the sentence; someone else wrote the sentence down since Ernie could not write; a nurse corrected the spelling; Joey spelled out each corrected word and gave the punctuation; Ernie repeated each letter and punctuation, and yet another person typed out each letter. Writing in the conventional way may be difficult or impossible because of a physical handicap as in some thalidomide damaged and cerebral palsied cases, and other means may be sought. This has obvious practical implications.

Arithmetic seems to present a greater problem for these physically handicapped children than either reading or writing. This is most likely related to the fact that the schooling of a physically handicapped child is frequently interrupted for hospital treatment. In contrast to reading and writing which, once begun, can improve just with use, arithmetic is much more dependent on the child being taught the various stages and procedures. Absence from school will interfere with this learning (Pringle and Fiddes, 1970).

## The development of communication

Physically handicapped children are different from normal children in a variety of ways. Do these differences influence the way in which these children communicate with their parents before they acquire any language? Unfortunately no studies have specifically examined the early communication between physically handicapped children and their parents. Such studies would provide a way of examining the contribution of certain factors to the communication between children and their parents: for example, the physical characteristics of the child; the parents' attitude to the child; the child's understanding of her world; and her mobility and dexterity. This information would provide a means of answering questions such as: how important is it that the parent and the child can take the initiative in beginning and directing the course of communication and how important is it that the child shows an interest in and can direct her parents' attention to things in the environment?

These sorts of study could contribute a great deal to our understanding of the processes involved in early communication and the relationship between this and language. A few studies have examined the language of physically handicapped children and these point to some of the factors which may be important for normal language development. For example, as we saw earlier, Gouin Décarie found that the performance of the thalidomide damaged children on the Griffiths subscale assessing speech and hearing was inferior to their performance on any of the other subscales. Pringle and Fiddes's observation of the incidence of deafness suggests that this factor is likely to play a major part in these depressed scores, although Gouin Décarie reports that only two of the children had hearing difficulties. The argument put forward by Gouin Décarie concerns the environmental opportunities available to the children. The scores were depressed regardless of whether the child lived mainly at home or mainly in an institution. Gouin Décarie proposes that interaction with adults was limited in both environments: in the institution because of the lack of a stimulating environment and the opportunity to form a one-to-one relationship, and in the home because of the effect that the child's handicap had on the parents.

Thus these thalidomide damaged children's difficulties do not seem to be due to the actual handicap but rather due to consequences of it. Other reports also suggest that children who are just physically handicapped can acquire language, and use it in very similar ways to non-handicapped children. For example, Pringle and Fiddes report that Fiona, the thalidomide damaged child born without arms and with dislocated hips who spent her first 18 months in plaster from her knees to her shoulders, began to speak at 8 months. Unfortuantely, what she said and how her language developed are not reported. A more detailed account is provided by Kopp and Shaperman (1973) in their case history of a non-thalidomide damaged boy born without limbs. From the age of 2¾ his language seems very similiar to that of non-handicapped children of the same age: he refers to action, makes distinctions between himself and others, and uses prepositions and plurals. The following extract give a feel of his language at the age of 2¾. His foster mother is changing his nappy (diaper) and putting on his artificial limb:

> No change diaper, my not wet
> no take my shirt off, my get shirt on
> wash my arm, dirty, it stinks
> Mom look no got more arm there.

By this age this child had reached the end of the sensorimotor period, and it is clear from this quote that his understanding of the environment is comparable to that of a non-handicapped child. Neither his cognitive development nor his language seem to have been adversely affected by the fact that he has no limbs and is limited in how he can interact with his environment. He talks about things which are going on around him and things he knows. His language reflects what he knows.

Children with spina bifida, especially those with hydrocephalus, present a somewhat contrasting picture. Their verbal skills seem to stand out as rather good, especially in comparison to other areas of their development. This suggests that language may not be dependent upon other areas of development. However, closer inspection, or listening, shows that much of what they say may be inappropriate and irrelevant, albeit said using complex syntax. They seem to be particularly adept at remembering things they have heard: commercials, nursery rhymes and phrases they have heard adults use. Tew and Laurence (1972) found this to be true of 28 per cent of the population they studied, whilst Anderson and Spain's study (1977) in London, England, found that around 40 per cent of 6 year olds showed this hyperverbal behaviour. In general this phenomenon was more typical of girls who had shunts and who were more physically handicapped than of the other children.

It is quite clear that many children with cerebral palsy have problems speaking, and some of them fail to communicate at all orally. The survey carried out between 1957 and 1966 (Wilson, 1970) reported that in 1957 just over half (52 per cent) of the children who were 9 or under had some form of speech defect. Nine years later, in 1966, 7 per cent still could not speak, the speech of 9 per cent was hard to understand and a further 16 per cent still required speech therapy. The difficulty is knowing whether these children have anything to say and are prevented from doing so by some motor difficulty or other problem, or whether they do not speak because they are severely impaired cognitively. In some cases, particularly those with athetoid cerebral palsy, it seems likely that the motor difficulty explanation is correct. For these children the difficulty is one of production: they are unable to coordinate the motor movements involved in making an utterance, and their efforts come out as noises which are hard to comprehend. If they are given some other way of communicating they can often demonstrate that they have plenty to say.

Some cerebral palsied children seem to be too handicapped intellectually to communicate, and here any communication may be very one sided, as the following extract from one of Hewett's parents shows. The mother is talking about her 2 year old daughter.

Some days she'll want me to nurse her and other days she'll sit hours, and I just keep going up to her and talk to her, and she'll smile and that's it. She wants you to talk to her - 'cos I think they've got a terrible life - they're terribly lonely. I mean, they're left out a lot, I should say. When you talk to her, you know, you don't know how much she understands or what she's thinking.

However, even in this case it is difficult to be certain how intellectually impaired the child is. Nevertheless, it is clear that this child is contributing very little to this interaction, and this must have a marked effect on what the parent says to her.

Denhoff and Holden (1951) found that delays in saying the first words were not correlated with intelligence amongst cerebral palsied children, but that intelligence scores did correlate with the onset of two and three word utterances. Those children who did not produce such utterances until they were more than 30 months old tended to be backward intellectually. However, there is a problem here in that intelligence tests often rely on verbal skills and it may be that the sort of problems which prevented language production also prevented the children from demonstrating their real intellectual level.

A great deal more needs to be found out about the way physically handicapped children and their parents communicate, both about the parent's contribution and the child's. The existing evidence suggests that physically handicapped children do manage to communicate about things they know: thus if what they know or can experience is limited, then what they talk about will be limited also. What is not known is how these limitations might affect the process of communication.

## Social development

### *How is interaction with others affected by a motor handicap?*

There are many factors which have the potential to affect the interaction between a physically handicapped child and her parents: for example, the parents' own reaction to the handicap; whether or not they are separated from their baby early on; and the actual nature and extent of their child's problems. It seems very likely that these factors will influence the nature of the interaction between a physically handicapped child and her parents. Unfortunately little relevant work has been carried out.

Gouin Décarie examined the ability of her thalidomide damaged children to keep close to and in contact with other people. She found that even some of the most severely handicapped children were able to cling. One of the children, who had no arms, used her chin and shoulder to grip around her parent's neck whilst her legs supported her weight. Another child, who had no arms or legs, managed to follow people by moving on her head and her hips. It would be fascinating to know what effect this ability had on the way other people interacted with these children. Certainly Gouin Décarie's data seem to suggest that thalidomide damaged children may be delayed in how they respond to people, but this seemed to be more a function of how long they had spent in an institution than of how handicapped they were.

Spina bifida children, especially those with hydrocephalus, are often described as friendly and socially responsive, presumably because they often have lots to say even though much of what they say may be inappropriate. However, many of these children are of below average intelligence. It would be interesting to know whether having plenty to say is more or less important than what is said in determining the nature of any social encounter. Unfortunately, there is no relevant research in this area.

We are all sensitive to the way other people look and behave, and we treat people differently depending on how we perceive them. In view of this it would be surprising if we were to interact with physically handicapped people in the same way as non-physically handicapped people. Although we have very little data about the interaction between physically handicapped children and other people, we do know something about how physically handicapped people react to their own handicap. This is important since how a person feels about herself is likely to affect how she interacts with other people, and her behaviour will influence how others interact with her.

### *Do children with motor handicaps adjust successfully to their handicap?*

Some physically handicapped children adjust well, whilst others flounder. Some even feel positive about being handicapped: 'Now I am going to tell you how CPs feel. They feel like you, but they can't walk like you. If they aren't CPs, they grow up like nothing, but if they are CPs they have to work like mad. I am a CP and I like being a CP.' This was said by a 13 year old with cerebral palsy (Cruickshank, 1976).

A physical handicap alone is not a prescription for mental handicap, and it seems likely that physical limitations will be particularly frustrating for an otherwise able child who is aware of her problems. The child who is physically handicapped is in a very different position from the child who is blind or deaf. It is hard to imagine how a blind child or a deaf child would conceive of these senses in an intact person. They can never really understand the sense that they are missing unless their loss is partial or occurred after a period of useful vision or hearing. The paraplegic cannot know how it feels to walk or run unless a period of normal development preceded the handicap, and yet she has access to this experience by watching others and by observing her own inability or limited attempts. The blind child cannot experience another person's sight, nor a deaf child another person's hearing, except in a very indirect way.

Further comments from cerebral palsied adolescents illustrate the frustrating effect that a physical handicap can have: 'Sometimes I have to repeat myself and I get embarrassed.' 'When I can't succeed in something and when I know I could succeed if I weren't a CP, I get more than discouraged because I'm so helpless. You're stuck and you hate yourself for being stuck' (Cruickshank, 1976).

This second comment is from a 16 year old quadriplegic athetoid who cannot walk and needs help with eating, and who wonders, 'why [did] the doctors let me live when I was born. I am no use to anyone the way I am.'

This illustrates the extent of the despair which may occur in severely physically handicapped people. Physically handicapped children are reported to experience more depression and anxiety than non-handicapped children, and it is those children with neurological problems who are especially at risk.

Seidel et al. (1975) found the incidence of psychiatric disorder in 5-15 year old cerebral palsied children and children with hydrocephalus to be as high as 24 per cent, compared with 12 per cent in children who had a physical handicap which did not involve the brain. In agreement with this, Pringle and Fiddes report that approximately 12 per cent of thalidomide damaged children show symptoms of maladjustment and that the only difference between this figure and the figure for the non-handicapped population was in the relative proportions of boys and girls. More thalidomide damaged girls than boys had problems, whereas the reverse is the case for the non-handicapped.

A depressed child cannot be said to be adjusting normally. The very young physically handicapped child is unlikely to show any symptoms of depression, although if her caretakers are finding it difficult to accept her she may begin to show some of the characteristics. As she gets older she will become increasingly aware of her limitations, her dependence on others and how she is different from other children. The child who is severely handicapped physically may be competely dependent on the services of other people for the whole of her life. As she gets older this may become increasingly hard for her to accept. There may be aspects of her handicap which are particularly distressing, such as incontinence. Whilst many aspects of physical handicap are visible, incontinence is not and it may raise social and emotional problems. Anderson and Spain (1977) report that spina bifida boys who had to use a penile bag often had problems, as did girls who were incontinent. However, Gulliford (1971) points out that children who are severely physically handicapped have less severe adjustment problems than children who are not so handicapped. He suggests that this may be the result of the parents of severely physically handicapped children being more realistic and accepting than the parents of less severely handicapped children. Parents of less severely handicapped children may have unrealistic expectations.

Pringle and Fiddes reported that, although the thalidomide damaged children showed great social confidence for their age, they tended to be concerned that they should be accepted by the adults around them. They were often uncertain about how adults felt about them, and this could cause them anxiety. In agreement with Gulliford (1971), Pringle and Fiddes found that the most disturbed were not necessarily the most handicapped. What seemed to be of greater importance was how favourable their environment was. This was based on their home background, the attitude of their parents and the availability of education. The more favourable the environmental circumstances of the child, the more satisfactory her emotional adjustment. There was also a relationship between adjustment and handicap but it was less consistent and less marked than the relationship between adjustment and environmental circumstances. This is interesting since it illustrates the importance of the environment for the emotional development of such children. Even in the face of a severe physical handicap a child can be emotionally well adjusted if her environment is favourable.

Pringle and Fiddes suggest that more girls have problems than boys because girls are more concerned at a younger age with how they look than are boys. A concern with how they look is likely to become an increasing problem for all physically handicapped children as they get older, especially as they approach adolescence.

Because they are often relatively immobile compared to their peers, the physically handicapped are particularly likely to be socially isolated. Social isolation may become even greater after the physically handicapped adolescent leaves school, as opportunities for employment are likely to be particularly bleak for those who are severely disabled. This can contribute to problems of adjustment.

In view of all this perhaps it is surprising that less than a quarter of all physically handicapped children show some disturbance. What does seem clear is that a supportive environment contributes a great deal to the extent to which a physically handicapped child adjusts to her disability and comes to accept it.

# 5

# How do children with Down's syndrome develop?

## Introduction

One of the main reasons for examining the development of children with Down's syndrome is to ask whether their development is quantitatively or qualitatively different from the development of normal children? Does the Down's syndrome child follow the same pattern of development as the normal child but just go through each stage more slowly, or do different processes underlie her development? This idea of delay as opposed to difference in the development of mentally handicapped people was first articulated by Zigler in 1967, and more recently it has been applied to Down's syndrome in particular.

Many aspects of the development of Down's children have been studied and although most of these studies have not been with the intention of exploring the developmental delay/difference question, this is one way of interpreting their results. The answer to this question is obviously very important both for determining how these children may be assisted in their development and also for our theoretical understanding of the processes of development.

Down's children form the largest group of mentally handicapped people and are usually identified at birth. For these two reasons they have been the subject of much research. Currently, there are three main groups of researchers, one in England, a second based in Australia and a third in the USA. Interestingly these groups do not share the same view when it comes to the question of delay versus difference. The group in the USA (e.g. Cicchetti and Serafica, 1981) have argued that the Down's person's development is delayed. They consider that although these children do develop more slowly than normal children they face similar problems and pass through the various stages at developmentally appropriate ages. They also support the delay model because of their evidence that Down's children maintain their individuality over time. Those children who are more able than others in a particular area of development will be more able at a later date too. These workers suggest that Down's children may provide a way of examining, in slow motion, how various aspects of development unfold. The two other groups, although less explicit, seem to favour a difference explanation (e.g. Berger and Cunningham, 1981, in England; Berry et al., 1981, in Australia).

## Motor development

Studies of Down's children's motor development tend to report either the ages at which the children attain particular motor landmarks, or indicate the degree to which their motor development deviates from that of normal children. These data are not relevant to the delay/difference question. However, they are important because if the motor development of Down's children is behind that of other children, there may be implications for other areas of development. For example, Cicchetti and Stroufe (1976) found that of their sample of 14, the four most floppy or hypotonic Down's children were the slowest to laugh or smile, the last to show any fear and had the lowest mental scores in their second year of life.

One study reports that aspects of the Down's syndrome child's motor development, such as holding up her head and rolling over, are within normal limits up to the age of 6 months (Fishler et al., 1964). These findings have not been substantiated by other research. Cowie (1970) examined a mixed group of home and institution reared Down's children at 2 weeks of term-related age, that is the child's chronological age after adjustment has been made for gestation lengths other than 40 weeks. She reported poor muscle tone and the absence of normal traction (pulling to a sitting position) and placing (when held upright, stepping up on to a surface when the top of the foot brushes the edge of the surface) responses. They all had poor posture when suspended horizontally in space face downwards (ventral suspension) and, although they showed a normal response when held on their backs and the head and upper part of the body was dropped a couple of inches (Moro reflex) and a normal palmar (hand) grasp, these took longer to disappear than reported for normal babies. Other studies have reported delays in being able to hold their heads steady and rolling over, although in all these studies some of the children performed well within the normal range (e.g. Carr, 1975).

This evidence, particularly Cowie's, points to some young Down's children being backward in motor development from as near birth as has been tested. This continues, and the gap between the age at which Down's children and normal children reach various motor milestones widens as the children get older. Sitting unsupported and crawling are reported to occur on average at about 12 months, compared to 7 or 8 months in the normal child. A similar picture emerges with the landmarks of standing alone and walking with and without help. These occur at around the end of the first year in the normal child, but are delayed on average until the end of the second year in the Down's child. However, for all these developments there is enormous variation. For example, a range of 6-36 months has been reported for sitting unsupported (Erbs and Smith, 1962), and a range of 11-48 months for walking with help (Fishler et al., 1964).

Interestingly, a study by Kučera (1969) found that the age of walking of a group of Down's children was related to the year in which the child was born. Children born before 1954 walked by an average age of 30 months, whereas for those born between 1955 and 1966, the corresponding age was 22 months. Kučera argues that this reflects an increasing number of later born Down's children being reared in a more stimulating environment, their own home, than the earlier born Down's children, which implies that the delays observed are not an inevitable consequence of Down's syndrome. Indeed the range of ability reported in most studies supports the view that the motor developments of Down's children who are reared at home are on average in advance of children who are brought up in some form of institutional care (e.g. Centerwall and Centerwall, 1960). Of course, this observation is not just restricted to children with Down's syndrome, but is found amongst children generally.

A number of studies report motor quotients rather than the ages at which particular motor landmarks are attained. These quotients indicate the degree to which the child's motor development is in line with that of the average normal child. A quotient of 100 means that the development is average, and a quotient below 100 means that development is below average. One study suggests that the Down's child's motor development is within normal limits up to 3 months (Dameron, 1963), but falls outside the normal range from 6 months although the actual motor quotients are not reported. In contrast to Dameron's study there are two others which report below average motor quotients for Down's babies of 6 weeks (Carr, 1970, 1975) and 4 months (Dicks-Mireaux, 1966, 1972).

In support of the findings reported for motor landmarks, motor quotients also suggest a detrimental effect of institutionalization. Stedman and Eichorn (1964) compared the performances on the Bayley Scale (Bayley, 1969) of home and institution reared Down's children. The children in the two groups were matched for age which ranged from 17 to 37 months. The home reared children obtained a higher average motor quotient than the institution reared children and, although the difference was not significant, it is in the same direction as Centerwall and Centerwall's (1960) finding. Carr (1970) also found an adverse effect of institutions, although not until the children were 10 months old or more.

Poor motor skills have been reported in much older Down's children. A study by Zekulin et al. (1974) examined performance on placing pegs in holes on a pegboard. They found that Down's children aged from almost 6 to 10 years were slower than either normal children or other non-Down's mentally handicapped children of similar mental age. The children had two minutes in which to place 25 pegs in holes, and it was in the first minute that the Down's children were slower. The authors point out that the difference may have reflected the Down's children being more uncertain about the task than the others. This problem could also be true of how the Down's child performs on developmental tests generally.

It is quite clear that Down's children attain the various motor milestones later than normal children. However, it is not clear from the available literature whether their development is following the same pattern as that seen in normal children or whether the pattern itself is actually different.

## Perceptual development

Much of the research on perception has examined the Down's adult rather than the Down's child. The Down's adult is often reported to be functioning intellectually at the level of a 4–6 year old normal child. If the Down's adult behaves in a different way from normal children then this has implications for the processes underlying the development of individuals with Down's syndrome. However, there is a problem. Down's adults and normal children, even if of the same developmental level, are of very different chronological ages and with very different experiences. The normal child may process the environment differently because of the level of development she has reached; the Down's adult may process the environment differently because of the additional years of experience she has had.

### Are the visual abilities of the Down's person different?

O'Connor and Berkson (1963) found that Down's adults made many more eye movements than normal adults and non-Down's mentally handicapped adults, both in darkness and when looking at various light presentations. This suggests, particularly if the findings could be confirmed under more natural conditions, that the Down's adult may look at her environment in a different way from that of other people, whether they are mentally handicapped or not.

A number of studies, comparing the abilities of Down's adults, non-Down's mentally handicapped adults and normal children to discriminate patterns and shapes visually, fail to find any differences provided that the people are matched for developmental age (e.g. Gordon, 1944; O'Connor and Hermelin,

1961). On the other hand, when the comparison is between Down's children and normal children of the same chronological age, differences in visual ability have been found (e.g. Miranda and Fantz, 1973, 1974; Fantz et al., 1975).

The differences which have been reported between normal and Down's children of similar chronological age are interesting. Miranda and Fantz (1973), using a visual preference technique, found that 8 month old Down's babies looked at the patterns for longer and showed fewer preferences between the patterns than the normal babies. However, a further study by the same group of workers found evidence that Down's babies develop the same preferences as normal babies when the patterns differ in form (e.g. straight versus curved lines) but at a later age (Fantz and Miranda, 1975). Few differences in the ages at which the normal and Down's children developed preferences were found when the form of the pattern (squares) was kept constant but the number and size of the elements varied. Fantz et al. (1975) interpret these findings as indicating that the emergence of preferences for patterns with more, smaller elements is probably related to the development of elementary visual and neural mechanisms involved in pattern perception, and these they consider to be developing as normal in the young Down's baby. However, the fact that Down's children's visual preferences lag behind those of normal children when the patterns differ in form is taken by the authors as evidence that these involve higher processes, which they argue are retarded in the Down's child.

Further support for this comes from studies examining recognition memory. The most interesting study is a longitudinal one by Miranda and Fantz (1974). Down's and normal children were seen between 8 and 16 weeks, between 17 and 29 weeks and between 30 and 40 weeks. The normal children showed recognition memory of abstract patterns at all ages, the Down's children only at the two older ages. Recognition of one of two photographs, and of a circular or chequerboard arrangement of squares, was demonstrated in the two older normal groups, but only the oldest Down's group showed recognition of a photograph, and no Down's group showed recognition for the arrangement of squares. Finally, the oldest normal children, but none of the Down's groups, showed recognition memory for colours. These results suggest that the Down's children lag behind the normal children for recognition memory of these four stimulus variations by at least two months. This lag was confirmed in a longitudinal study in which significant recognition memory was shown first by the normal children at 9 weeks and by the Down's children at 17 weeks.

The particular problem facing the Down's baby seems to be one of remembering what she has seen rather than an inability to make the discrimination in the first place. This was shown by Miranda (1976) who found that, although pairs of abstract patterns could be discriminated by Down's babies of 7 weeks of age using the preference method, they failed to show any sign of remembering these same patterns until they were about 17 weeks old. In comparison the normal children remembered the patterns at 9 weeks of age.

Thus, despite the fact that people with Down's syndrome appear to move their eyes differently, there seems to be no great difference in how they perceive the environment visually, provided that they are compared with normal people who are functioning at a similar developmental level. If they are of the same chronological age then differences do occur, but these data seem to favour a quantitative rather than a qualitative difference, although their ability to recognize something they have seen before seems to be limited, at least in the first few months. However, two things should be noted: first, the tasks on which this conclusion is based are only examining a minute portion of the visual abilities of individuals with Down's syndrome; second, similar end points can be reached by different routes. It is still possible that the Down's child is processing her environment visually in a way that is different from that of the normal child.

### Are the tactual abilities of the Down's person different?

The majority of the studies in this area have examined the tactual abilities of the Down's adult and adolescent and, despite the fact that different studies have employed different tasks, there seems to be general agreement that, on tactual discriminations, the Down's person is inferior to normal people of the same developmental level and non-Down's mentally handicapped persons (e.g. Gordon, 1944; O'Connor and Hermelin, 1961).

However, these and other studies say nothing about such abilities in young Down's children. A study by Lewis and Bryant (1982) provides some evidence that young Down's children do have some sort of difficulty with touch. The ability of Down's children aged 12-46 months to recognize objects visually that they had previously either seen (visual-visual tasks) or touched (tactual-visual tasks) was compared to the ability on the same tasks of normal children of similar developmental level. None of the Down's children performed above chance level on any of the tasks involving touch, whereas the normal children were successful on at least one task involving touch. For the normal children, but not the Down's children, their performance on that tactual-visual tasks improved with increasing age. The performance of the Down's children on the visual-visual tasks was also inferior to that of the normal children. This study suggests that Down's children have a difficulty either in discriminating objects tactually, or in remembering the tactual information, or in relating tactual and visual information.

This paper reported a second experiment which examined the consequences of the tactual deficit on how Down's children look at patterns and objects. Here it was found that if Down's children are allowed to touch patterns or objects whilst looking at them, this has much the same effect on how they look at them as touching patterns and objects has on the looking behaviour of normal children. In particular, when touching was allowed, the children looked at the patterns and objects less often, but each look was longer, on average, than when touching was not allowed. This suggests that touching may serve the purpose for both groups of focusing their attention on the pattern. Interestingly, Krakow and Kopp (1982) found that Down's toddlers were as likely as normal toddlers to touch and handle objects.

Taken together, the results discussed in this section on perceptual development indicate that certain processes in the individual with Down's syndrome, particularly those involved in tactual discrimination, may be different rather than just slower to develop. Nevertheless, despite these signs, much of the Down's child's development appears to be very similar to that of the normal child's.

## Are Down's syndrome children musical?

It has been suggested that people with Down's syndrome are particularly musical. Probably the earliest reference to this ability was that of Fraser and Mitchell in 1876, only ten years after Down's original paper. Since then frequent reference has been made to this. Shuttleworth (1900) said of the mongols 'their love of music great; their idea of time as well as tune remarkable'. A few years later, in 1908, Tredgold described them as being very fond of music and as having a 'marked sense of rhythm'. Similar descriptions abound. But is there any evidence to support these claims? Is this particular ability superior to that found in the normal person? Are people with Down's syndrome more musical than either non-Down's mentally handicapped people of similar mental age, or normal children of similar mental age?

The evidence is sparse, and that which there is either can be criticized on methodological grounds or shows that although their sense of rhythm may be superior to that of other mentally handicapped persons, when compared to non-mentally handicapped people they are not especially musical.

One of the earliest studies was performed by Rollin (1946), and illustrates how limited some of the studies in this area have been. Rollin examined the musical abilities of a large group of people with Down's syndrome aged 8-48 years. The majority had been institutionalized for most of their lives and over half of them had recorded IQs of below 20. The wide age range, low IQ and the extent of the institutionalization are limiting enough factors, but the method itself leaves even more to be desired. They were all seated in a semi-circle in a hall whilst dance music was played. Their facial expressions were observed to see how much they were enjoying the music. This experiment provided no support for a marked sense of rhythm and fondness of music by the person with Down's syndrome. In addition, it was reported that none of them danced spontaneously, and only two danced when they were invited to.

More rigorously designed research has been reported since 1946. In 1959, Cantor and Girardeau reported that normal pre-schoolers were better than Down's children of similar mental age at saying at which of two possible rates a metronome was beating and tapping in time with the beat.

There are a number of problems with this study. As Stratford and Ching (1983) point out, one of the tasks required a verbal response which may have been more difficult for the Down's children than for the normal children. Stratford and Ching also ask whether a response to a metronome beat can be taken as an indication of musical ability. In their own study, they found that Down's children were as good as normal children, all with mental ages between 3½ and 4 years, at tapping in time to three rhythms varying in complexity. A group of non-Down's mentally handicapped children did not do so well. Both the Down's children and the normal children anticipated the rhythms once they had heard them.

Two further studies have used more realistic stimuli. The first by Glenn et al. (1981) found that normal and Down's babies aged between 5 and 14 months showed a preference for listening to a sung nursery rhyme over listening to a repeated tone. In addition, over half the normal babies and the Down's babies more often selected the rhyme sung by a woman than the same rhyme played on an instrument. Although very different in design from the previous study, this study again suggests that the individual with Down's syndrome may not be especially musical, in terms of comparisons with normal people. However, Glenn et al. did report that there were some differences in the nature of the two groups of babies' responses. In particular, the Down's babies had a significantly longer response duration: when they were listening to either of the two alternative patterns they listened to them on average for longer than did the normal babies. This raises the possibility that the way in which the two groups are processing the material may be different.

An extension of this research was reported in 1982 by Glenn and Cunningham. In this study Down's babies were matched with normal babies for mental age, which ranged from 7½ months to 13 months. All the babies had mothers who regularly sang them particular nursery rhymes. The choice for the baby was between a familiar rhyme and a nonsense rhyme in which the words in the familiar rhyme were replaced by nonsense words containing the same number of syllables. The authors took various measures of the babies' preferences: how long they listened to each; how often they listened; and the average duration of each period of listening. On the first two measures, but not on the third, both groups showed a preference for the familiar rhyme. As in the earlier study, the Down's babies listened for longer, both in total and on average, than the normal babies. As the babies got older in terms of mental age they showed an increasing preference for the familiar rhyme.

This study is interesting because it reiterates the similarity between Down's babies and normal babies in what they like to listen to (out of the choices supplied) and it also says something about the nature of what the babies are responding to. It is not just intonation and stress patterns, although these are important and will be used if there is nothing else. Glenn and Cunningham's study shows that they appear to listen to the characteristics of single words which are familiar. The words probably do not have any meaning for the babies at this stage, but nevertheless they are recognized at some level.

Thus, despite the often reported observations that people with Down's syndrome are musical, there is really no evidence to suggest that they are any more musical than normal people, although they do seem to have a better sense of rhythm than other mentally handicapped people. There is some evidence that they may take longer to process musical information, which may link with the memory limitations noted earlier.

## Cognitive development

Cognitive development is an area which is particularly pertinent to the question of delay versus difference. Does the Down's child pass through the same cognitive developments in the same way as the normal child but take longer, or is her cognitive development different? Does she have a different understanding of her environment from the normal child? In the next section I shall examine some studies of the intelligence of Down's children and some of the factors which seem to affect this. In the two subsequent sections I shall examine the Down's child's understanding of particular aspects of her environment. It is these latter sections which are most relevant to the question of delay or difference.

### How intelligent is the child with Down's syndrome?

Individuals with Down's syndrome do not usually reach the same levels of intelligence as normal people. What level can they attain? Does their intellectual ability remain the same throughout their lives? Do particular circumstances affect their intelligence? These are some of the questions on which the literature in this field has focused.

There seems to be general agreement that although the Down's child has an IQ of around 70 in her first year, this declines as she gets older. However, there is some disagreement as to whether she begins life with average intelligence or is handicapped from birth. There are a couple of studies which report that the 3 month old Down's baby's IQ is within the range for the normal baby (Dameron, 1963; Cunningham and Sloper, 1976). Cunningham and Sloper report average mental quotients of between 80 and 90 at 6, 12 and 18 weeks of age for their group of Down's children. Although the mean quotient fell below that for the normal child it was within the normal range, and in fact some of the babies had quotients between 90 and 110. However, after this age the mean quotient fell, falling to between 50 and 60 for the second half of the first year. Two other researchers have reported below normal ability from 16 weeks (Dicks-Mireaux, 1966, 1972) and 6 weeks (Carr, 1970).

On the basis of these studies, although the development of some Down's babies may fall within the age range of normal development, the development of many Down's babies is slower than that of non-handicapped babies, from as early as 6 weeks. For many Down's babies, their rate of development seems to slow down considerably from the age of 6 months, compared with the rate of development of non-handicapped children. At about this age the normal child is learning rapidly.

Reports of Down's babies of under a year who have IQs of 70 or more are not uncommon (e.g. Øster, 1953; Loeffler and Smith, 1964). The authors of the last paper also report that of a group of children with Down's syndrome of 3 years and under, 30 per cent had IQs between 20 and 50, 47 per cent had IQs between 50 and 70, and the remaining 23 per cent had quotients over 70. These proportions are similar to those of other reports.

As Down's children get older, reports show that the gap between their level of development and that of non-handicapped children widens (e.g. Loeffler and Smith, 1964; Cornwell and Birch, 1969). Interestingly, Down's females seem to be more able than Down's males (e.g. Connolly, 1978), although this female superiority may only be significant at the younger ages (e.g. Clements et al., 1976).

The picture which is emerging from the literature is one of great variability in the intelligence of Down's syndrome children. Their ability ranges from severe retardation to near normal, although it is fairly clear that there is an increasing gap between their developmental level and that of normal children with increasing age. One of the factors which seems to influence the developmental outcome is the nature of the environment in which the child is reared. For example, the evidence is quite clear that Down's children reared in an institutional environment are cognitively behind those brought up at  home (e.g. Carr, 1970). Interestingly, children who live at home for the first couple of years and who are then institutionalized maintain their superior cognitive development for at least three or four years over those Down's children institutionalized from birth (e.g. Shipe and Shotwell, 1965).

Additional evidence for the importance of the environment comes from studies reporting an increased rate of development in institutionalized children when they are given additional stimulation (e.g. Lyle, 1960; Tizard, 1960; Bayley et al., 1966), and from studies of Down's children living at home who have been involved in various intervention programmes, and whose development is exceeding that which has been characteristically expected of the Down's child (e.g. Brinkworth, 1975; Cunningham and Sloper, 1976; Rynders et al., 1978; Buckley, 1985). These latter studies are the most interesting, because they indicate that Down's children may require a different environment from normal children if they are to develop maximally. For example, some of the children who took part in Cunningham and Sloper's study were visited every six weeks from birth, and when they were 1 year old they were ahead of children who were referred to the study when they were between 6 and 12 months old and who therefore received fewer visits. The early referrals were also ahead, at 1 year, compared with the children in Carr's (1975) study who were only visited three times in the first year. Carr's children and the late referrals in Cunningham and Sloper's study were of similar mental ability at 1 year of age. The late referrals gradually caught up with the early referrals as they received more visits. Cunningham and Sloper suggest that these children may have benefited from the frequent visits through their parents getting ideas about how to play with them as a result of watching the assessments that were being carried out. Obviously these parents were also getting a lot of support and often this is not readily available.

Further support for the idea that the development of the Down's baby, who is living at home, can benefit from early intervention comes from Brinkworth's (1975) work. He reports that Down's children whose parents had followed his early stimulation programmes from the time of the child's birth had an average quotient on the Griffiths Developmental Scale (Griffiths, 1954) of 66 by the time they were in their second year, compared with an average quotient of 56 for children who were involved in his programmes from 1 year of age.

All of the studies discussed in this section show that the child with Down's syndrome is not as intelligent as the normal child, although in the first year or two of life some of these children may show near normal ability. The gap between their intelligence and that of normal children seems to widen as they get older, and this is especially true if they live in an impoverished environment. Like all children, they thrive on stimulation, and indeed some of the recent studies indicate that their actual potential may not have been fully tapped. However, even though the gap between their intellectual ability, as measured by an intelligence quotient, and the intellectual ability of normal children may widen as they get older, the Down's child's intellectual ability is developing. It is not that they are able to do less and less as they get older; the

decline in IQ reflects the fact that their cognitive development is not keeping
pace with their age. Development is occurring, but whether it is normal
development slowed down, or different development, cannot be answered by
this sort of study.

### *What does the Down's syndrome child understand about objects?*

Over the first two years babies are learning a great deal about objects. Given
that the development of most Down's children fails to maintain a normal rate
over this period, it seems likely that the Down's baby will take longer to reach
each stage of object understanding compared with the normal baby. But will
there be any qualitative differences in what they understand about objects?

One of the most detailed studies on object understanding is reported by
Morss (1983, 1985). He followed eight Down's babies and a group of normal
babies longitudinally. At the beginning of the study they were aged between 8
and 22 months. Morss assessed their developing understanding of objects on a
variety of Piagetian object permanence tasks (Piaget, 1953). These tasks
involve hiding toys in a variety of different ways and observing the child's
searching behaviour. Not surprisingly, Morss found that the Down's children
were delayed compared to normal children in succeeding at each of the tasks.
In addition, the pattern of results was different. Once the normal children had
succeeded on a particular type of task, they would continue to be successful
on this task on later occasions. The Down's children were more varied. They
showed fewer examples of the sorts of error which are thought of as
characteristic of these tasks, and Morss argues, from these findings, that the
Down's syndrome baby is developing in a different way from the normal
baby. Whilst the normal baby seems to follow the sequence of developments
predicted by Piagetian theory, the Down's baby does not. In particular, she
does not show the same sort of pattern of errors, and an understanding at one
level does not seem to be consolidated and built on to the same extent as is
observed in a normal baby.

A further study on older Down's children by Moore et al. (1977) reported
that the order of difficulty of object permanence tasks was identical to that for
the normal child, albeit delayed. Interestingly, they found that whereas the
children's language ability was correlated with their understanding of object
permanence even when mental age was partialled out, there was no significant
relationship between mental age and the mean length of their utterances. We
shall come back to this later when we consider communication.

One of the developments which can be observed to start somewhere in the
second year of the normal child's life is that of symbolic or pretend play. This
indicates that the child understands that one object can stand for another. Hill
and McCune-Nicolich (1981) looked at pretend play in a group of Down's

children aged 20–53 months, with mental ages from 12 months. The level of symbolic play was much better correlated with mental age than with chronological age, and the development of symbolic play followed the same sequence as found in normal children, thus supporting a delay account of this development.

A more detailed study of symbolic play in 3, 4 and 5 year old Down's children was carried out by Motti et al. (1983). Also, since the children were part of a longitudinal project investigating a range of developments, the authors had access to information about their earlier progress. It was found that various aspects of the children's play intercorrelated strongly, indicating consistent individual differences in the play of the Down's children. In addition, the children's developmental age at 2 years on the Bayley Scale (Bayley, 1969) was predictive of their level of symbolic play one, two and three years later: the higher the developmental quotient, the more advanced their symbolic play, the more symbolic play they engaged in, the more actively they explored, the more enthusiastic they were and the more positive affect they showed. There were also some predictions from even earlier behaviours. For example, more sophisticated play was found in children who, at 16 months, had been observed to cry when an object loomed towards them, and in children who had begun to laugh before the age of 10 months. Although some of these correlations may be due to chance, they do suggest that what the Down's child understands of objects at one age is related to her understanding at a different age. This supports the idea of a delay in their development rather than a difference. However, Morss's contrary evidence should not be forgotten since this is the only study which really attempts to say anything about the process by which the Down's child comes to an understanding of object permanence, and here a difference in processing was implicated. More work is needed to settle the question of delay versus difference.

### What does the Down's syndrome child understand about herself and other people?

The literature supports the view that the Down's child is qualitatively similar to the normal child in her understanding of herself and others. However, most of the studies have been limited to the reactions of Down's children to strangers and to separation from, and later reunion with, their mothers.

One study by Mans et al. (1978) stands apart in that they examined the reaction of Down's children, aged between 1¼ and 4 years, when they saw their reflection in a mirror and when, without them realizing, a smudge of rouge was put on their noses. The most obvious indication that the child realizes that what she sees in the mirror is a reflection of herself is if she touches the rouge on her nose. Normal children begin to respond in this situation by around 15 months and the response is well established by 22 months (e.g. Bertenthal and Fischer, 1978). Only a quarter of the Down's children of 22 months or younger touched their noses, and these were the most developmentally able. Amongst the older children, a greater proportion responded in this way. The authors argue that this development follows the same process as in normal children, since its emergence is dependent more on the child's mental age than on her chronological age. Other behaviours were also recorded, and about three-quarters of the children showed some sort of change in their behaviour when their noses had been coloured. The most common reaction amongst the youngest children was a change from a positive response to one of puzzlement or sobriety, whilst the other children were more likely to show some sign of surprise or an increased positive response.

I now want to discuss the results of three studies which have focused on the responses of Down's children to being separated from a parent, in all cases their mother. All of these studies used some version of the classic Ainsworth and Wittig (1969) paradigm, in which the child is initially in a strange room with her mother, followed by a number of brief episodes, in various orders, in which the child is left in the room, either alone, with a stranger, or with the stranger and her mother. Only one of the studies included normal children. This was a study reported by Serafica and Cicchetti in 1976. They observed the behaviours of Down's and normal children of around 3 years. Overall the Down's children reacted less than the normal children. For example, when the parent left, most of the normal children cried, but only one Down's child cried. When their mothers returned, the Down's children spent less time in physical contact with them than the normal children. This all suggests that the Down's children were less perturbed by the separation, and less concerned about getting close to their mother upon her return. This sort of explanation is backed up by what happened when they were alone: the normal children looked more towards the door and tended to move around the room, whilst the Down's children looked more around the room generally and kept fairly still. There was, however, no difference in the amount of smiling and movement towards the mother when she returned. Cicchetti and Stroufe. (1976) interpret these results as indicating a delay or lag in the development of fear reactions in the Down's child.

A similar conclusion is drawn by Berry et al. (1980) from a study of Down's children of around 2 years old. They argue that Down's children and normal children show qualitatively similar sensitivities to strange situations in which they find themselves separated from their parent and in the presence of a stranger. However, in contrast to the previous study, most of the Down's children cried when they were separated from their mother, especially when they were left completely on their own. In this study, the mother was absent for longer and this difference in methodology, plus the fact that the Down's children were a year younger, may account for the different findings. This illustrates the difficulties of reaching any firm conclusions as to the nature of the Down's child's development. For example, if the crucial factor is the length of time that the parent is absent, rather than the child's age, this would be consistent with the idea of the Down's child taking longer to process information than the normal child. This would imply a qualitative difference.

In Berry et al.'s study the Down's children seemed to be more aware of the strangeness of the situation and, in particular, of the exits and entrances of their mother and the stranger, than were the children in Serafica and Cicchetti's study. For example, the Down's children tended to watch the door most when they were alone, and least when they were first in the room with their mother. They kept in closer contact with their mother, and looked at her more after her return than before her departure. Unfortunately, as Berry et al. did not include any normal children, it is difficult to compare the two studies.

The third study is a further one by Cicchetti and Serafica (1981) with Down's children of around 3 years old. Again they argue that, although there may be quantitative differences between how normal and Down's children react in strange settings, the patterns of responding are similar. However, they do point out that such conclusions are tentative. The Down's children showed a slight wariness towards the stranger, but generally responded quite positively, looking, smiling, approaching and even touching the stranger if the mother was there as well, although they did vocalize less in the stranger's presence. This suggests that Down's syndrome children are less distressed than normal children on being left alone with a stranger. When the stranger became increasingly intrusive, the children's reactions became more negative, and their reaction on being reunited with their mother was much more positive than their reunion with the stranger.

These studies show that young Down's children have a similar repertoire of behaviours towards people as do normal children, although they seem to be rather less intense in their responses. Cicchetti and Serafica suggest that they may show less fear because they are less easily aroused. However, none of the studies discussed has really examined the mechanism involved and so the possibility remains that the processes underlying the behaviours are different in Down's and normal children.

## The development of communication

*How does Down's syndrome influence the early communications between these children and their parents?*

Down's syndrome has obvious physical signs which mean that a diagnosis is often made within a few days of the baby's birth. Therefore the parents are usually aware, from the earliest days, that their new baby is different, and they will probably hear things about the characteristic abilities and disabilities of individuals with Down's syndrome from a variety of sources. They may also have their own expectations, correct or incorrect, of the implications of Down's syndrome. All these factors are likely to influence how they approach their baby and interact with her. In addition, Down's syndrome babies develop more slowly than normal babies, and there may be ways in which development is actually different from that of a normal baby. How will all this influence the way in which these babies and their parents communicate with each other? In this section I shall first examine the behaviours of the Down's baby, and then I shall consider some of the evidence concerning the way in which adults characteristically react to these children. Finally, I shall examine the nature of the interaction between the Down's child and her parent.

Do Down's children provide their parents with different signals? Crying is one of the earliest signals from a baby and several studies have found that the cry of the Down's baby in the first year is different, both in quality and quantity. For example, they cry less frequently when in pain, their cries show more variation in intensity and are lower in pitch than the cries of normal babies (Fisichelli and Karelitz, 1966). They take longer to cry, make more whimpers and fewer gasps, fewer bursts of vocalizations and fewer sounds than normal babies (Fisichelli et al., 1966). Their pain cries are longer with a monotonous flat melody form and the pitch is lower (Lind et al., 1970). Thus the cries of Down's babies are less intense than those of normal babies. It is interesting to speculate whether or not this less intense response to pain is related in any way to the less intense response shown towards strangers by 2 and 3 year old Down's children (see pp. 117–18).

How are these differences perceived by adults? Freudenberg et al. (1978) asked adults with varying experiences of children to listen to tapes of Down's babies and normal babies crying. The cries were matched for the age of the baby, and the intensity and length of the cry. The normal babies' cries were more likely to be interpreted as the baby needing immediate attention, and were rated as much more unpleasant than the cries of the Down's babies. It did not matter how experienced with children the adults were. The cry of a normal baby is perceived as a much stronger signal than the cry of a Down's baby.

These findings accord with the common description of Down's babies as 'good' babies. They are often perceived as not particularly demanding, seldom crying for attention. This will influence the amount of time that the baby and adult come into contact. However, this view that Down's babies are 'good' babies is not supported by the literature on Down's children aged over 6 months. In 1972 Baron asked the parents of 6–18 month Down's babies to fill in a questionnaire about how their babies behaved in everyday situations.

On the basis of their responses, Baron concluded that Down's babies did not differ temperamentally from normal babies. Some of them were easy, others were difficult. Baron suggests that the general impression of them as easy may originate from parents having low expectations of Down's children.

This suggestion of Baron's was followed up by Gunn et al. (1981) who compared the temperamental characteristics of a group of Down's children, as rated on a questionnaire about their everyday behaviour, with the mothers' own perceptions of their children based on interviews with the mothers. The children were aged from 6 months to 3 years. The questionnaire data failed to support the notion of Down's children as being particularly easy. Also the mothers felt that their children were easier than the analysis of the questionnaire data warranted. This supports Baron's suggestion, but Gunn et al. raise a further possibility. This is that the mothers have acquired successful coping skills, which result in them perceiving their children as easier than they actually are. Interestingly, the older Down's children in this study seemed to be easier than the younger Down's children. Gunn et al. (1983) provide some support for this, finding a tendency for difficult 1 year old Down's to become easier by the age of 3. However, in addition to crying behaviour, there are differences in how Down's babies and normal babies behave in the earliest months which are likely to influence interactions with adults.

Berger and Cunningham (1981) observed normal and Down's babies once a fortnight until they were 6 months old. The Down's babies made eye contact with their mothers at an average age of almost 7 weeks, about 2½ weeks after the normal babies did. There was also a difference in how much the two groups looked at their mothers over the six months. The normal children increased the duration of eye contact with their mothers up to 6 or 7 weeks, and kept at this level until the fourteenth to sixteenth week, after which the time they spent in eye contact diminished rapidly. The Down's babies made very little eye contact up to about 3 months, when the duration gradually began to increase, and continued increasing throughout the study, so that by 6 months they spent more time in eye contact with their mothers than the normal babies.

More eye contact with their mothers at 6 months and at 9 months by Down's babies compared to normal babies was also reported by Gunn et al. (1982). These findings of greater eye contact by the Down's babies may be related, in some way, to the longer looking times reported by Miranda and Fantz (1973) in their visual preference studies (see p. 108). The study by Gunn et al. (1982) also reported that the Down's babies spent much less time than the normal babies looking around the room. There also seems to be a difference in the extent to which Down's babies and normal babies involve others. Jones (1977) found that 1-2 year old Down's children were much less likely than normal babies of similar mental age to look from a toy towards their mother's face, and then back to the toy or activity. The bringing together of people and objects or activities is part of what communication is all about, and so already we are seeing differences between the normal child and the Down's child.

Returning to the very early behaviours of the Down's child, the study by Berger and Cunningham (1981) found that the Down's babies smiled first on average by 7 weeks, three weeks after the normal babies. For the normal children, the amount of smiling increased and peaked during the fourth month, after which it declined. The Down's babies, as well as starting to smile later, never attained the same levels as the normal babies. The amount they smiled increased more slowly, reaching a peak at around the beginning of the fifth month, after which it declined. It was also more difficult to elicit smiles from the Down's babies than from the normal babies.

There were also differences in their vocalization patterns. The number of vocalizations made by the normal babies increased over the first three or four months, and then declined. The Down's babies began much more slowly and made fewer vocalizations than the normal babies up to the fourth month. However, the Down's babies showed no decline, and by the twentieth week they were making significantly more vocalizations than the normal babies. Berger and Cunningham (1983) suggest that the decline in the normal babies' vocalizations after the fourth month is because they are taking more notice of what other people are saying, and are spending an increasing amount of time listening. The Down's babies do not show this decline, although they may later, and so are not listening or taking so much notice of the fact that the other person is speaking. These differences may be due to, or exacerbated by, the hearing difficulties often associated with Down's syndrome (see p. 22).

There are several reports that from the end of the first year Down's children make fewer noises (e.g. Buckhalt et al., 1978; Greenwald and Leonard, 1979). Greenwald and Leonard observed that the normal children, who were matched with the Down's children for mental age, were more likely to use words. None of the Down's children used words, rather they tended to rely more heavily on gestures. It may be that the Down's baby, after initially vocalizing less than the normal baby up to about the fourth month, then vocalizes more, whilst the normal baby is concentrating on listening and attending to what is going on around her. This may give the normal baby an entry into increasingly sophisticated means of communicating, including using words, and so she vocalizes more. At the same time, the Down's child is vocalizing less and less, perhaps because she is not taking enough notice of what others are communicating. This may partly explain the delay in, and sometimes complete absence of, the development of meaningful vocalizations by some Down's children. Certainly young Down's children seem to have particular difficulties imitating gestures, sounds and words (e.g. Dunst and Rheingrover, 1983), although this may possibly be related to the poor memory which was noted for visual patterns on p. 108.

One further study supports the idea that Down's children pay less attention to what others are saying than normal children do. Glenn and Cunningham (1983) gave normal and Down's children the opportunity of listening to recordings of their mother talking to either another adult or a baby. The children were seen twice: the Down's babies at about 12 and 24 months and the normal babies at about 9 and 17 months. All the children preferred to listen to baby talk on both occasions. However, by the second visit the normal children were listening for significantly longer, both in total and on average per response, than they were during the first visit. For the Down's children there was a significant decline in response durations to the baby talk by the second visit, although they still preferred listening to the baby talk. Also, whereas on the first testing the normal and the Down's children both listened less to an adult talking than to a rhyme, by the second testing the normal children spent much longer listening to the adult talking. There was no such change for the Down's children. Thus, somewhere between the end of the first year and the end of the second year, the Down's child has become less interested in listening to adults talking to her, whereas the normal child has become more interested.

Therefore there are many ways in which the Down's child reacts differently from a normal child when she is with an adult. How do adults behave? Do they behave in a different way because the child they are interacting with has Down's syndrome? If there are differences, are they due to the adult responding to the differences in the child's behaviour, or to the adult behaving differently because she knows the child has Down's syndrome?

A number of studies have reported that the mothers of Down's babies talk more and more as the babies get older (e.g. Berger and Cunningham, 1983), especially when the mothers are teaching their child how to play with something new (Buckhalt et al., 1978), whereas mothers of normal babies vocalize less and less as the babies get older. The parents of a Down's child may talk more to her because they are trying to help her. Certainly mothers of 1-2 year old Down's children give more verbal directions than mothers of normal children of similar mental age (Jones, 1977). The lengths of the mothers' utterances to Down's and normal babies are similar up to the age of about 17 months (Buckhalt et al., 1978), but at later ages the utterances of the mothers of Down's children are shorter (Buium et al., 1974) than those of the mothers of normal children. This is probably due to the mothers of the normal children increasing the length of their utterances in line with their own children's rapidly expanding language skills. Not only do the mothers of Down's children make shorter utterances, but more of their utterances are incomplete and consist of only single words. Both of these are characteristics of how adults talk to young children. When 1 and 2 year old Down's children are matched with normal children for mental age there are no differences in the speed or length of the utterances made by their mothers when speaking to them (Glenn and Cunningham, 1983).

Thus the behaviours of the Down's child and of her parent are different in a number of ways from the behaviours of the normal child and her parent. How smoothly does the interaction itself proceed? Several studies have demonstrated that when a child has Down's syndrome many more clashes or overlaps occur between the child's vocalizations and the parent's vocalizations (e.g. Jones, 1977; Buckhalt et al., 1978). This lack of synchrony seems to be there from the earliest months in the Down's baby, and the frequency of overlaps greater than one second increases over the first six months (Berger and Cunningham, 1981, 1983). A number of factors may contribute to this. For example, the Down's child, as she gets older, seems to pay less and less attention to what other people are saying, and at the same time her parents are talking to her more than they would if she were normal.

It is clear that the early communication which occurs between Down's syndrome children and their mothers is different from that which occurs between normal children and their mothers. But does this matter? Is it important for the Down's baby's subsequent development? If our present understanding of the relevance of early interaction for the development of the normal baby is correct, then it seems that these delays and differences must have effects. It may be impossible to disentangle these likely effects from effects directly to do with the fact that the child is a Down's syndrome baby. Nevertheless, such possibilities should be considered, particularly since they may have implications for how these children's development could be aided.

An interesting study by Berger and Cunningham (1981) suggests that it may be possible to change certain aspects of the interaction between Down's babies and their parents. Berger and Cunningham (1981) noted that the increase in eye contact, which the Down's babies made with their mothers from 3 months onwards, seemed to be associated with the mothers becoming much more positive and involved with their baby. They additionally found that if the mothers of Down's children of around 23 weeks are asked to imitate their babies' facial and vocal behaviours and not to initiate anything themselves, their babies smiled more than when their mothers interacted with them normally. The Down's babies also made more noises when their mothers imitated them than when they interacted normally. This suggests that the behaviour of the mothers may be inhibiting the Down's babies' behaviour and that if the parents of Down's babies fit their behaviour to the babies' then the babies respond more.

There are therefore many ways in which the early interactions which occur between the Down's syndrome baby and her parents may be slower to develop and in certain ways different from the sort of interactions which occur between the normal baby and her parents.

## What are the characteristics of the Down's child's language?

Down's children are delayed in beginning to speak, although their babbling sounds seem to be quite similar and to follow the same developmental sequence and times of appearance as is found in normal babies (Rondal, 1981). However, there is considerable variability in the age at which children with Down's syndrome begin to use words. Some of this variability may be due in part to variations in hearing loss (see p. 22). In 1955 Levinson et al. reported that although some Down's babies began to use words at around the age of 12 months, others did not start until they were 6 years old. A more recent study (Melyn and White, 1973) found that amongst a group of non-institutionalized Down's children, most spoke their first word between the ages of 6 months and 7 years, although some never spoke at all. Phrases began to occur between the ages of 1 and 8 years, and sentences between 1½ and 11 years. Rondal (1981) commented that the onset of meaningful speech was usually delayed by at least eight to nine months, and it seldom occurred before 2 years of age. Even at this age it was reported as constituting less than 5 per cent of the child's verbalizations. This percentage increased slowly up to the age of about 4 when the earliest two and three word combinations were heard.

The pitch, or fundamental frequency, of the speech of the Down's child is higher than that of the normal child (e.g. Weinberg and Zlatin, 1970). However, as the child gets older the difference may diminish (e.g. Montague et al., 1974), until by adolescence it is actually lower (e.g. Goueffic et al., 1967). Another characteristic is poor articulation which often makes it difficult for others to understand what the Down's person is saying (e.g. Lenneberg et al., 1962).

Rondal's study supports the idea that the Down's child's language development follows a similar path to that of the normal child. The Down's children were found to use the same range of relational meanings as normal children: they commented when objects or people disappeared or reappeared; they remarked on attributes, possession and location; and they referred to situations in which actions occurred. In support of this idea is a study by Moore et al. (1977). They found that the mean length of utterance produced by 3½-5½ year old Down's children was related to their understanding of objects, and of the ways in which objects relate to one another and to people, rather than to their chronological or mental age.

However, for any given level of understanding of people and objects, the Down's child's language is inferior to that of a normal child (e.g. Dunst and Rheingrover, 1983). The Down's child's utterances tend to be shorter, less complete and less complex than those of normal children of similar mental age (e.g. Ryan, unpublished a, b), although their noun vocabularies may be more extensive (Ryan, 1975). Ryan suggests that this last finding is due to their being chronologically older than the normal children and having therefore been exposed to language for longer. However, the finding of more extensive noun vocabularies may also relate to the differences in how parents of normal children and parents of Down's children talk to their children (see p. 122).

## Social development

### *Are Down's children particularly sociable?*

In his account of Down's syndrome, Down wrote: 'they have considerable power of imitation, even bordering on being mimics. They are humorous, and a lively sense of the ridiculous often colours their mimicry' (1866). This view of the Down's person as a sociable, friendly, outgoing and amusing person has almost become as accepted a part of the syndrome as mental handicap. Just as there is variation in the extent of the mental handicap, it is presumed that there is variation in their sociability. Nevertheless, the over-riding view is that the Down's child is especially affectionate and easy to get on with.

One explanation of this view of individuals with Down's syndrome being particularly sociable could be that other people have low expectations of the person with Down's syndrome and, as a result, any sociable behaviour is overemphasized simply because it is not expected. A study by Gibbs and Thorpe (1983) attempted to overcome this difficulty. They asked non-professional aides in schools for mentally handicapped children to say which of over a 100 adjectives characterized individual Down's and non-Down's mentally handicapped children of about 11 years old. Although the raters were very familiar with each child they rated, some of the raters, even with repeated questioning, failed to show any awareness of the child's diagnosis. These latter raters were called the naive group. A number of adjectives were found to be consistently associated with Down's syndrome and distinguished them from the other children. These fitted in quite well with the stereotype of the Down's child as being outgoing and sociable. When the naive and non-naive raters were compared, it was found that the non-naive raters perceived the Down's children as fitting the stereotype more closely than the naive raters, although the stereotype still emerged from the naive raters. This supports the idea that adults' interpretation of a child's behaviour depends to some extent on what they expect to see. However, there was a marked difference between the naive raters' ratings of the Down's and the non-Down's children, which suggests that Down's children of about 11 are perceived as more sociable than other mentally handicapped children.

Thus Down's children may be more sociable than other mentally handicapped children, although this view of them is influenced by the commonly held idea that they are happy and cheerful people. As Gibbs and Thorpe (1983) point out, the stereotype may not reflect the genetic basis of Down's syndrome, rather it may say more about how they have been treated as children.

### In what ways is interaction with others affected by Down's syndrome?

There have been a number of reports suggesting that the social abilities of individuals with Down's syndrome are in advance of their mental abilities (e.g. Benda, 1949; Cornwell and Birch, 1969). Also, like their mental quotients, the social quotients of Down's people seem to decline as they get older.

Several studies have examined the development of particular social behaviours in young Down's children, some of which were discussed in the section on early communication. Cicchetti and Stroufe (1976) looked at the development of smiling and laughing over the first two years of life. The children were observed in their own homes and their mothers played with them in a variety of ways designed to elicit smiles and laughter. The median age for the children first laughing was 10 months compared with 3-4 months for normal children. One child in the study never laughed. Just like normal children, the Down's children were more likely to laugh earlier at auditory and tactual events than at visual or social events. However, the Down's children were more likely to smile when the normal child would laugh, and they took longer to respond. This again supports the idea that they may take longer to process information. Even by early on in the second year, the Down's children still did not laugh at sights such as their mother pretending to suck on a bottle.

This study found a clear relationship between the children's cognitive ability and their responses to their mothers. When the group was divided into those who first laughed before the age of 10 months and those who laughed later, there was no overlap between the developmental scores on the Bayley Scales (Bayley, 1969) for the two groups. The four most floppy children did not laugh until they were more than 13 months old. Cicchetti and Stroufe argue that these data support a delay in the development of smiling and laughing in the Down's child and that the sequence is similar to that in normal children.

Several studies have focused on the ways in which Down's children interact with adults. Jones (1977) found the mothers of 1-2 year old Down's children to be more directive when playing with their child than were the mothers of normal children of similar developmental level. A similar finding was reported by Stoneman et al. (1983) for 5 year old Down's children compared with normal children of the same chronological age. Whereas the parents of the normal children interacted with them more as playmates, the parents of the Down's children managed the playing more, often assuming the role of teacher. Although the Down's children were less responsive than the normal children, the responses of the parents of the Down's children were determined much more by what the children were doing than was the behaviour of the parents of the normal children. It would be interesting to see what would happen if Down's children were compared to normal children of similar developmental age.

One of the problems with these studies is that most of them are concerned with group differences. Crawley and Spiker (1983) argue that by examining groups and ignoring individual differences the studies fail to provide data by which to interpret any differences that are seen. From a practical point of view an understanding of individual differences and of how different factors interrelate is very important.

In their own study, Crawley and Spiker looked at relationships between various aspects of the child's behaviour, and the mother's behaviour, whilst 2 year old Down's children played with their mothers at home. They found significant relationships between how sensitive the mother was, the elaborateness of her play, how much stimulation she provided and how much positive affect she showed to the child. They found no correlation between how sensitive she was and how much she directed what went on. For the child, social initiative, play maturity and social responsibility were all positively intercorrelated, and correlated with the child's developmental level as assessed by the Bayley Scales (Bayley, 1969). They found no relationship between how much the mother directed the situation and any of the measures to do with the child's competence. If the mother was directive in her behaviour, then the child was likely to be less interested and seldom to initiate play with objects. The more competent children were more likely to play in harmony with their mothers. These mothers combined sensitivity and directness in ways that provided their children with appropriate stimulation. This study demonstrates clearly the individuality of both the Down's children and the adults with whom they are interacting.

One factor which may influence parents' attitudes to their child and their interaction with her is the impact her birth has on the family. Much has been written about the effects of the knowledge that a child is handicapped on those around her, but we will discuss just a few studies. Gath (e.g. 1972, 1973, 1974, 1978) has examined, in some detail, the consequences of the birth of a child with Down's syndrome for the rest of the family. The initial response of the parents is, not surprisingly, one of shock and grief at the knowledge that they have a child with a lasting handicap. The parents can often be seen to go through characteristic stages (e.g. Drotar et al., 1975), although Gath points out that the effect will be different for each family. About a third of the mothers were clinically depressed during the child's first two years of life. The relationship between the parents may be jeopardized, although if there was a good relationship before the birth, the parents may be drawn closer together afterwards. Gath also found that problems may arise for the other children in the family, especially sisters.

Any handicap in a child is going to have effects on the family, but there are likely to be particular effects of Down's syndrome because it is one of the few mental handicaps which is diagnosed when the baby is only a few days old. From the beginning, the parents will have been told that their child will probably be unable to do certain things when she is older, and yet the parents may be unable to see any difference between their baby and other babies. Cunningham and Sloper (1976) point out that parents may not really notice any difference until their baby is about 7 or 8 months old when she fails to start to do things that other babies of this age are doing, like sitting up on their own, crawling and standing with help.

Another study examined the way in which parents are told of their child's handicap. Cunningham et al. (1984) carried out a survey of parents to discover how satisfied they had been with how they had been told. Many of the parents had complaints. For many there was, for no good reason, a delay in when they were told. Others found the way they were told abrupt and unsympathetic. Some felt that they were not given all the information they needed, or that they were fobbed off. Sometimes the parents were not together when they were told. More than half of the parents expressed some form of dissatisfaction.

As a result of their survey Cunningham et al. (1984) designed a 'model' service which incorporated the points raised by the survey. The parents were to be told together, as soon as possible, and in private. Ideally, the baby was to be present. They were to be told by a consultant paediatrician in a direct way concentrating on the positive aspects, together with a health visitor who worked with handicapped children and who would see the parents again whenever they wanted. It would be arranged for the parents to see the paediatrician and the health visitor again the next day. All the parents who received this 'model' service expressed satisfaction with how they were told of their child's handicap.

Many of the parents who were satisfied with the way in which they had heard that their baby had Down's syndrome were positive and confident about the support services which were available. It seems very likely that such an attitude will make it easier for the parents to accept the child. This is bound to contribute to how the parents interact with their child.

# 6

# How do autistic children develop?

## Introduction

Following Kanner's 1943 article the main disability facing the autistic child was thought to be a difficulty in forming, or even a failure to form, any kind of social relations with other people. The autistic child seems withdrawn from the world of people. A difficulty with this view is that it cannot account for the other behaviours which characterize autism. More recently the view of autism which has become increasingly accepted is that it is the result of a basic cognitive deficit (e.g. Rutter, 1983). The exact nature of this deficit is not yet clear, although the evidence strongly suggests that it is associated with communication functions.

Autistic children seem to have difficulties in extracting meaning from situations and events, especially social situations and events, and in representing this information in a useful way for reference in the future.

This lack of certainty as to the exact nature of the problem underlying autism makes this chapter rather different from the previous chapters. A further difference is that much of the literature on autism has been concerned with describing and explaining the behaviours of these children. It has been less concerned with their development. Indeed, the main comment which is made about their development is that the symptoms often become less severe as the child gets older.

Like other handicaps discussed in this book there is tremendous variability in the sorts of behaviours and abilities exhibited by children labelled autistic. In this chapter I shall focus on extreme forms of the behaviours, although the behaviours will not be present to the same degree, nor manifested in the same way, in all children given the label of autism.

## Motor development

The autistic child reaches the main motor milestones at much the same age as the normal child, although there may be a slight delay. However, certain aspects of motor behaviour are abnormal. For example, autistic children have a characteristic way of standing. They can very often be seen standing with their heads bowed as though they were gazing at the floor in front of them, and their arms flexed at the elbow with their hands flopping down from their wrists as if they were extremely heavy. When they walk, many of them go along on tip-toe without swinging their arms at all. Very often autistic children can be seen to repeat a particular movement over and over again. For example, they may rock backwards and forwards from one foot to the other; they may wave their arms and legs about and they may pull the same face again and again. These repetitive behaviours seem to be associated with times when they are excited or are absorbed in some sensory experience like watching a light flash on and off. At other times autistic children seem to provide stimulation for themselves. For example, they may twist their hands around in front of their eyes, or they may spin round and round for long periods without apparently becoming dizzy. Some severely handicapped autistic children may even injure themselves: the ultimate in self-stimulation.

Similar sorts of behaviour can often be seen in handicapped children who are institutionalized. One explanation of these behaviours in institutionalized children is that the repetitive rocking and spinning behaviours provide the children with stimulation not available from the environment. This cannot explain the behaviour in autistic children because they often behave in this way when the environment is quite stimulating. However, they seem to take little or no notice of external stimulation, appearing to prefer the repetitive stimulation they provide themselves. This could result from an inability to make sense of the environment and to represent it in any meaningful way. Simple repetitive activities may provide autistic children with sensations they can experience. Normal children, because of their understanding of their environment, can interact with it, and can use their imagination to devise games and ways of involving themselves in their surroundings. In order to be able to interact with the environment meaningfully children need to be able to make some sense of it. Without this understanding they may turn in on themselves, seeking simple repetitive sensations.

## Perceptual development

*How does the autistic child respond to sensory stimuli?*

The autistic child's reaction to her sensory experience is often bizarre. At times she may act as though she does not experience the noises, sights and smells around her, or feel things that touch her. She may show no response to a loud noise. She may show no recognition of a person she knows well. She may be indifferent to pain or cold. At other times she will show that her senses are intact. She will turn to the rustle of a piece of paper. She will gaze intently at a lighted lamp, a spinning top or a portion of a patterned wallpaper. She will scratch or tap a surface for hours. Even more bizarre is the observation that some autistic children have an intense fear of certain everyday objects, a fear that can only be quelled by removing the object. On the other hand, they may seem oblivious to events that would be quite frightening to a normal child. This selectivity in the attention that the autistic child pays to her environment has been confirmed experimentally. For example, Koegel and Wilhelm (1973) trained profoundly retarded autistic children and normal children to select one of two cards. On each card were drawings of two everyday objects. When the children had learned this discrimination the extent to which their selection was based on both drawings was examined by presenting cards with drawings of single objects. The autistic children tended to respond to only one of the trained drawings, whilst the normal children responded to both trained drawings.

There is also some evidence that the senses of the autistic child are not as distinct as the normal child's. For example, she may cover her eyes when she hears a sound which she finds distressing.

How can these behaviours be explained? Many of the experiences which seem to be attractive to the autistic child are repetitive: gazing at a patterned wallpaper or at her fingers flickering in front of her face; listening to bells chiming; tapping or scratching on a surface. Many of the things she seems to ignore require that meaning is extracted from past experiences and used in the present situation. The autistic child often behaves as though she cannot interpret her separate experiences. At times she seems to have no way of giving meaning to things, of going beyond the sensory impressions.

Despite these observations, on many other occasions autistic children, including those of low ability, recognize everyday objects as meaningful. For example, they respond appropriately to cups, spoons, chairs and doors. They can also learn about places, for example, where the biscuits are kept, where to hang up their coats or how to get from one place to another. It is also quite evident that they come to recognize people they know well. Extracting meaning from sounds does seem more difficult for the autistic child, although obviously those who acquire some useful speech are making sense of the sounds. However, as will be discussed later, those autistic children who do acquire some spoken language show little evidence of using their language in creative and flexible ways.

Thus in some circumstances the autistic child appears to make sense of her perceptual experiences, although in many other situations she seems to behave in a way which suggests she is just responding to the sensations.

## *Does the autistic child possess special visual-spatial skills?*

When Kanner (1943) made his original observations he noticed that very often there is something at which these children are particularly good, at least in comparison to the rest of their behaviour. A number of these areas of ability involve visual-spatial skills. For example, in his original paper Kanner reports that all of the children did well on the Séguin form board. Certainly their performance on items in intelligence tests which require such skills is superior to their performance on items requiring other sorts of skill (e.g. Lockyer and Rutter, 1969). An experiment by Shah and Frith (1983) supports this. Autistic children and adolescents were matched with mentally handicapped and normal children for mental age, and their ability to locate a shape embedded in a drawing was examined. The autistic children were more accurate and quicker than either of the other two groups. Their accuracy was commensurate with that expected of normal children of the same average chronological age. Shah and Frith (1983) suggest that the autistic children may have been relatively good at finding embedded figures for the simple reason that the pictures in which the shapes were hidden did not have as much meaning for them as they did for the other children. As the authors point out, the pictures did have some meaning for the autistic children since they were able to name them, but the suggestion is that the meaning of the pictures may not be as dominating as it is for normal children and children with other forms of mental handicap. Similarly, the performance of autistic children on form boards is good because they are able to focus on the details of each shape.

Some autistic children seem to be particularly adept at doing jigsaw puzzles. They may put a puzzle together over and over again, but in a mechanical and un-creative sort of way. They may pay no attention to the picture, even doing the jigsaw with the picture side facing the table. They seem disinterested in doing the puzzle in order to create a picture; it is just the act of putting all the pieces together with which they are concerned. They may also be good at the sort of toys that are constructed from a number of parts but, once again, it is not the end product that they are interested in, just the process of repeatedly assembling and dismantling something.

These findings can also be explained by autistic children having difficulties making meaningful sense of the environment. Autistic children may not perceive the toy they construct as a representation of something in the real world. The jigsaw picture may mean little to them; they are not interested in its meaning and what it represents. In addition to their visual-spatial skills, autistic children are good at remembering the positions of objects and their ability to do jigsaws and constructional toys may reflect some of this ability. If you can remember where each piece of a jigsaw goes, the act of completing a jigsaw can be quite repetitive. Similar pieces of wood are fitted into other pieces, and this process is repeated until the last piece is put in. Much the same is true of constructional toys. But why should they do these sorts of task? Another of their behaviours suggests a possible answer. They enjoy collecting and arranging objects tidily, and it may be that the pieces of a jigsaw attract them and they put the pieces together to create order out of all the pieces. Similarly, they may want to put in order all the parts of some constructional toy.

Other observations of superior visual-spatial skill can also be explained by autistic children making less sense of the environment than non-autistic children. For example, an autistic child will often notice a tiny object on the carpet, which an adult would miss, and pick it up. This may be because she is not dominated by the overall pattern of the carpet. These children often spend long periods of time arranging objects in a precise way, and notice the slightest change in how familiar things are arranged. They seem to be especially sensitive to the spatial arrangement of objects. It is as though they collect and arrange objects purely for the sensations that they gain from the objects. Neither the objects nor the arrangements seem to have any particular meaning for them. A normal child might collect stones and use them as pretend food for her teddy. For the autistic child the emphasis is on the perceptual value of the collected objects, and it is to changes in this respect that she responds.

An outstanding example of the autistic child's sensitivity to the spatial arrangement of objects is the exceptional drawing ability of a small number of autistic children (Selfe, 1977, 1983). The children studied by Selfe produced pictures far superior in terms of their photographic likeness to reality than those of normal children of a similar age, in some cases equivalent to those of trained artists. These drawings reflect the fact that the autistic children are not basing their drawings on what they know, rather they are copying the lines and details which they see in front of them or which they remember. In this way they produce a far more accurate representation than the average normal child who is hampered by her understanding of what she is trying to represent. For example, a normal child may draw the four legs of a cat because she knows that cats have four legs; the autistic child may draw only one leg if that is all that can be seen of a cat who is lying in its basket and three of its legs are out of view. The autistic child draws what she can see and is not hindered by a need to represent her knowledge, since the object has less meaning for her than for the normal child. If this is correct, then all autistic children should draw exceptional pictures, whereas only a minority do. However, this small group of autistic children do differ in one important respect from the majority of autistic children: they have exceptionally good visual memories. This, together with the lack of interpretation of what is seen, may be the reason for their exceptional drawings.

## Cognitive development

### *How intelligent are autistic children?*

Despite Kanner's original statement that the cognitive potential of these children is normal, it is now clear that the majority of autistic children are intellectually retarded. The findings vary, but there seems to be agreement that over half of all autistic children have IQs below 50 (e.g. Lotter, 1967a; Rutter and Lockyer, 1967; DeMyer et al., 1974). Wing (1976) calculated from Lotter's Middlesex data that only 19 per cent of the children in the nuclear and non-nuclear groups (see p. 26) had non-verbal IQs over 70. DeMyer et al. (1974) reported that 94 per cent of 155 autistic children with a mean age of just under 5½ had IQs below 68, and that three-quarters of the children had quotients below 51. The verbal IQs of autistic children are usually lower than their performance IQs: DeMyer et al. (1974) give means of 35 and 54 respectively for the 5½ year olds.

In his 1983 article Rutter cites a number of studies which together support the suggestion that many autistic children have a cognitive deficit which cannot be explained by the social aloofness which Kanner saw as primary. If the social problems were the cause, all autistic children should be mentally handicapped, but this is not the case, as is clear from the evidence cited above. Rutter argues that the IQs of autistic children are fairly stable and correlate reasonably well with school achievement, although this is less true for autistic children with IQs in the normal range. He points out that even when autistic children become more sociable, whether as a result of some intervention or not, their IQs do not change appreciably. He quotes work with Clark which ruled out two possible explanations of their poor performance on IQ tests. The first explanation was that autistic children might know the answers but deliberately avoid giving them (Clark and Rutter, 1977). The second explanation which was eliminated was that autistic children's performance is determined by the nature of the test situation, rather than by the task difficulty (Clark and Rutter, 1979). In this experiment it was found that as test items became harder, the autistic children failed more and vice versa, although the test situation remained the same. Finally, he includes the evidence that many autistic children start having epileptic fits when they reach adolescence. This is much more common amongst autistic children of low IQ than amongst those who are of normal intelligence. In contrast, other mentally handicapped children are more likely to begin to have fits in childhood.

In the same article Rutter argues that this cognitive deficit is in fact the basic handicap in the sense that it is responsible for all the other problems which characterize the autistic syndrome. He uses two findings to suggest this. First, the likelihood of autism increases as the IQ declines, although it is fairly infrequent amongst children with IQs below 20. Second, the intelligence of the autistic child is a better predictor of her psychological and social development than are her other behaviours.

Rutter goes on to show that although a cognitive deficit is at the root of autism it must be very specific. Autism is not the result of just any cognitive deficit. He points out that a general deficit cannot account for those few autistic children who are of normal intelligence, since they obviously do not have a general cognitive deficit. Also, although autism is more common amongst children of low intellectual level, it is very unlikely if the child has some other handicap such as Down's syndrome. Finally, the intellectual profile of autistic children is quite distinct. They do much better on non-verbal items than on verbal items, their visual-spatial skills stand out as being particularly good, and their rote memories are often exceptional. It seems to be in the area of language and language related skills that the autistic child performs so badly.

One of the main difficulties for autistic children seems to be in going beyond their current experience, and of using previous experience to help them understand the present situation and to look ahead to future experiences. They seem unable to plan and organize what they are doing. However, they will classify and order objects which they find in their immediate environment in an extremely systematic and repetitive way. They seem fixed in the present.

They seem to lack an imagination which could take them beyond the here and now. They seem unable to imagine how it would be if . . . . In order to illustrate this and other phenomena we will examine the autistic child's understanding of people and objects.

### *Do autistic children have the same understanding of objects and people as other children?*

Since the majority of autistic children are not diagnosed until they are 2 or 3 years old, relatively little is known about their development before this age. This is the time when the normal child's understanding of people and objects is developing rapidly. However, Rosenthal et al. (1980) have managed to examine some aspects of this period by studying home movies of 14 children, nine of whom had been diagnosed as autistic, and comparing them with films of normal children.

Films were available for six of the nine autistic children until they were at least 2 and, of these, three had been filmed up until they were 3. The films were examined using Piaget's sensorimotor period as a framework (Piaget, 1953). One of the main achievements of this period is the realization by the child that objects exist independently of and separate from herself. According to Piaget, this understanding is reached in the normal child between 18 and 24 months. Only one child in Rosenthal et al.'s study showed behaviours characteristic of the end of the sensorimotor period, and this was seen when the child was 29 months old. The behaviours of the majority were characteristic of developments reached earlier in the sensorimotor period, for example, finding an object which the child has watched being hidden, and which has not been hidden anywhere else immediately before.

One interpretation of these data is that autistic children are delayed and reach various stages of development later than normal children although, from this study, it is unclear whether or not autistic children reach these stages of object understanding at a similar mental age as non-handicapped children. It may be that the development of autistic children over the first few years is delayed, rather than different from that of normal children. However, there are numerous accounts of older autistic children behaving in a bizarre way towards objects.

They often seem to be fascinated with regular patterns of objects. They will collect and arrange objects which they find in an extremely systematic and repetitive way. They will make collections of things like stones and leaves, and get very upset if their arrangements are disturbed. They do not seem to collect objects for any apparent reason. They are likely to handle objects carefully, looking closely at them, turning them around, sniffing them and licking them, as though what are crucial are the sensations they get from the objects, rather than either what the objects are or what they could be used for. They may appear only to be interested in part of a toy or object. An autistic child may hold a toy car and just watch the wheels as she spins them around endlessly. Again, this would be consistent with an apparent interest in the sensations rather than in what the toy is. She focuses on only a part of the toy, seemingly oblivious to how it can be used. She is not interested in the car wheels as that part of the car which enables it to be pushed across the floor. She is only interested in the effect of spinning the wheels around and around.

Another aspect of their behaviour towards toys and objects is that very few attempt to use them spontaneously in pretend play, although Gould (1986) has demonstrated that 5–12 year old autistic children can produce pretend play using miniature versions of everyday objects under structured test conditions. However, Baron-Cohen (in press) has shown that, compared to normal 3–5 year olds and 2–13 year old Down's syndrome children, 4–13 year old autistic children seldom use non-realistic objects in spontaneous pretend play, that is, autistic children do not use objects to stand for something else. In their spontaneous play some autistic children may appear to produce pretend play. For example, they may line up all their teddies and dolls and, from what they say, appear to be playing at schools. But, more often than not on these occasions, the child will just be repeating verbatim things which have been said to her. She will not go beyond her own actual experience, even using the same wording as has been used to her. Of course, non-handicapped children also recreate in play situations they have experienced. However, the non-handicapped child's play reflects an amalgam of different experiences, combined in a creative way. The autistic child does not invent new games or talk about things which have not actually happened to her. The autistic child will not even talk about things which have happened to her, in any normal sense. She may make isolated statements about things she has done in the past, or repeat phrases she has heard in the past, but she will not converse about past experiences.

Thus, from her behaviour, the autistic child does not seem to understand objects in the same way as a normal child. What sense does she make of other people? One of the main characteristics of autism is a lack of relationships with other people. However, not all autistic children withdraw from social situations. In particular, more able autistic children will approach familiar people, and like games involving physical contact. They may sit on a familiar adult's lap and enjoy being hugged and tickled and stroked. More able autistic children may be extremely upset if a familiar caretaker is absent. Thus a lack of relationship with other people is not absolute amongst the autistic population. However, an experiment by Langdell (1978) demonstrates that the way in which autistic children recognize familiar people may be different from the way in which normal children recognize familiar people.

Langdell compared the ability of autistic children and adolescents with that of normal children of the same mental age, normal children of the same chronological age and mentally handicapped children of similar chronological and mental ages to recognize photographs of their peers. The autistic subjects were relatively able, both groups having mean IQs above 60, with sufficient language to understand and respond to the task. There were a variety of ways in which the photographs were shown: upside down; nose only; eyes only; mouth and chin; nose, mouth and chin; eyes, nose, mouth and chin; eyebrows and above; eyes and above; and finally the full photograph was shown in the correct orientation. In line with previous research the normal children were more accurate when they were shown features in the upper part of the face than when they were shown the lower part of the face. The non-autistic mentally handicapped children were similar, but the younger autistic children were better when shown the lower features than the upper features. The older autistic children were as good as the younger ones on the lower features, but as good as the normal children of the same chronological age with the upper features. Another bizarre result was that the older autistic children were more accurate than their controls at identifying the photographs when they were presented upside down. The younger autistic children were no different from their controls with this presentation.

This study shows that more able autistic children are able to recognize familiar people from photographs. However, the findings suggest that autistic children go about this process of identification in a rather different way from non-autistic children. The non-autistic children seem to be particularly responsive to features which can be thought of as especially social, the eyes and the orientation of the face. In contrast, the autistic children do not give these characteristics any particular priority in their recognition of faces.

On some occasions autistic children will show an awareness of other people, although even then they behave very differently from normal children. For example, if an autistic child wants her parent to do something for her, perhaps spin a top, she will get hold of her parent's hand and put it on the top. She will not look at her parent, but simply place her parent's hand on the handle of the top. This demonstrates that she knows that her parent, or rather her parent's hand, can operate the top. This is very different from how a normal child would get her parent to spin a top. A normal child, who could not yet use words to ask her parent to spin the top, might take the top to her parent, and, as she pushes it into her parent's hand, look back and forth between her parent's face and the toy. She might try and make the top spin herself, and accompany her glances toward her parent with demand-like noises. Both the autistic child and the normal child 'know' that their parent can make the top spin, but there the similarity seems to end. The autistic child just reacts to what it is that does the spinning: her parent's hand. There is nothing in her behaviour to suggest that she understands anything other than that this hand can make the top spin. The normal child, on the other hand, knows that it is her parent who will carry out the action of spinning, albeit using her hand, and therefore any request should be directed to her face, not to her hand. The autistic child does not seem to understand the relationship between her parent's hand and the rest of her parent's body. The hand carries out the action, and therefore the request is made to the hand.

Although the autistic child may get her parents to carry out actions in this way, she is unlikely to mimic an action carried out by another person. Often the only way to get an autistic child to learn a new action is to move her body through the appropriate action. Once she has experienced the action herself she can repeat it. This difficulty in copying other people's actions could reflect an inability to view the world from a perspective other than her own. However, some research by Hobson (1984) suggests that autistic children are no worse than Down's children or normal children of a comparable mental age at recognizing another person's visual point of view. The autistic children were 9–16 year olds and their language abilities were superior to those of many autistic children. One of the tasks involved a cube being placed diagonally between the child and the experimenter who were sitting opposite one another. There was a different colour or picture on each of the four vertical sides of the cube. The child was only able to see two sides of the cube. After some practice the child was able to say what was on each side. The test consisted of a doll being placed at different points around the cube and the child having to say what the doll could see. At a later point a second doll and an identical cube were introduced and the child had to place the cube so that the second doll could see the same as the first doll. The autistic children were just as good as the normal 3–7 year olds at this task. They also found a hide and seek task quite easy in which they had to hide a doll from one or two seeker dolls behind different arrangements of screens. All this requires that the child take account of what the doll or dolls can see. This shows that at least by the time more able autistic children are approaching early adolescence and beyond, they are able to take account of other perceptual perspectives. However, as Hobson himself points out, these tasks are not particularly social and the skills which the autistic child has demonstrated in these tasks may have no relevance for how they would react in social situations.

The behaviour of autistic children in a more social situation was studied by Baron-Cohen et al. (1985). A scene was acted out between two dolls who were introduced to the children as Sally and Anne. First, Sally put a marble in a basket, and then she left, leaving the basket behind. Anne then transferred the marble to a box. Sally returned and the children were asked where Sally would look for the marble. Over 85 per cent of 3–6 year old normal children and a similar proportion of 6–17 year old children with Down's syndrome answered this question correctly. In contrast, 80 per cent of 6–17 year old autistic children gave the wrong answer, although they could remember where Sally had put the marble originally and knew where it actually was. The authors interpret this finding as an inability by the autistic children to impute beliefs to others. It would be interesting to repeat this experiment using people rather than dolls.

Related to this last study is evidence that the autistic child has problems imagining how she would feel if she were another person. An example of this is her inability to respond appropriately when something happens to someone else. If she sees someone fall over she may laugh. The fact that she responds in some way suggests that she realizes that some reaction is expected of her, but she cannot put herself in the other person's place and imagine how she would feel. The ability to take another person's point of view is not essential for responding appropriately in such a situation. The child could respond appropriately just by interpreting the behaviour of the other person. Young normal children can be seen to comfort another child who is crying. The normal child abstracts an understanding from the crying behaviour and responds on this basis. Thus, as well as having difficulty putting herself in the place of another person, the autistic child seems unable to make sense of the behaviour of other people. She cannot interpret their behaviour. This observation is supported by more of Hobson's research (1982, 1986). In one study autistic, normal and non-autistic mentally handicapped children were shown short videos. On these videotapes a variety of emotions, people and things were portrayed. The children had to match the videotapes to drawings representing emotions, people and things. There was no difference between the autistic children and either the normal or the mentally handicapped children when the subject was things. However, the autistic children were much worse than either of the other two groups when people or emotions were involved. This is a much more realistic task than Hobson's perspective-taking one, and it strongly supports the idea that the autistic child has great difficulty in appreciating how others are feeling, and also that the autistic child has problems with tasks which require that she takes notice of people.

There is evidence to suggest that the autistic child does have some of the same sort of understanding of herself as a person as normal children do, albeit at a later age. Ferrari and Matthews (1983) examined the behaviour of 15 mentally handicapped autistic children between the ages of 3½ and 10½ when the children viewed their reflection in a mirror after some rouge had been put on their noses. If the child touches the rouge on her nose, this indicates that she must realize that she is looking at a reflection of herself. In this situation normal children of 21–4 months will touch their nose, although from the age of about a year they show some sort of response (e.g. Bertenthal and Fischer, 1978). Eight of the autistic children touched their noses and, although there was no difference in the mean chronological ages of this group and the children who did not touch their noses, the nose-touchers were further ahead developmentally. The eight who touched had a mean mental age of 38 months whereas the other seven had an average mental age of 22 months. Of the non-touchers, three touched the mirror whilst four either avoided looking or appeared indifferent.

The authors argue that these results do not support the view of the autistic child as having an undeveloped sense of self, assuming that this is what the test assesses which is in itself questionable. Rather, any difference in their understanding of themselves can be explained by their delayed development.

A more detailed study of exactly the same phenomenon was reported by Spiker and Ricks in 1984. Thirty-six out of a group of 52 autistic children aged between 3 and 13 touched the green makeup when they saw themselves in a mirror. When the authors compared the children who showed recognition with those who did not, a number of differences emerged. Those failing to show any recognition were more likely to be mute or to lack any communicative speech; to be on medication of some sort; to have been untestable in other situations; or to be functioning at a lower level. Almost all of the children who had some communicative language, even if it was very limited, showed visual self-recognition. However, the authors point out that self-recognition cannot be solely dependent on communicative ability since a few mute children showed recognition and a few non-mute children did not. As these authors point out, further work is required in which these sorts of relationship are examined in much greater detail.

Spiker and Ricks also analysed the expressions on the faces of the children throughout the experiment. Only three children showed any surprise when they saw themselves with green makeup on. Forty-one of the children remained completely expressionless. This is in marked contrast to the way in which normal children behave in such a situation, and these qualitative differences need to be explored further.

### *How good are autistic children at remembering things?*

Kanner noticed that autistic children are often exceptionally good at remembering certain things; indeed this was one of the observations which led him to argue that these children were potentially clever. Although this view is no longer supported, Kanner's original observation is accepted. Some autistic children remember entire passages of conversations they have heard; others can recite nursery rhymes and poems without making an error. Many are particularly good at recognizing a piece of music on the basis of a few bars. They may also notice when the slightest change is made in a room, such as the order of books on a shelf or the position of an ashtray on a table. Their memories are very exact, with experiences appearing to be stored precisely as they occurred. Another feature is that the things that they do remember do not appear to be of any great importance; they do not seem to have selected particularly useful things to remember.

What seems to distinguish the memories of autistic children from those of normal children is that autistic children commit things to memory without changing them in any way. The things the autistic child hears and the things she sees are remembered exactly as they happened. She does not select things to be remembered. Many of the things she does remember seem irrelevant and of no use to her. She seems to have just learned something for its own sake, rather than because of what it means. By contrast, a normal child may also be able to recite a nursery rhyme, but she is unlikely to be word perfect. She is much more likely to understand what the rhyme is about. She is likely to be able to tell you what is happening in her own words. The autistic child cannot do this. She remembers the order of the words, but often seems to be unaware of what the chain of words mean. This is supported by the work of Hermelin (Hermelin and Frith, 1971; Hermelin, 1976) who found that although normal and non-autistic mentally handicapped children are better at remembering things if the things to be remembered make some sort of sense or follow some sort of rule, this sort of aid does not help autistic children.

This view has been questioned by Prior and colleagues (e.g. Fyffe and Prior, 1978; Prior, 1979). Fyffe and Prior found that autistic children may be able to use meaning to help their recall, albeit less effectively than normal children. Additionally these workers found that more able autistic children are quite good at recalling sentences and on the basis of this they argue that rather than supporting the idea that autistic children have problems in coding things to be remembered, any differences they may encounter can be explained by recourse to their developmental level.

Another characteristic of the autistic child's memory is that what she remembers is not modified by subsequent events. Each memory seems to be kept quite separate from her other memories. One of the characteristics of a normal child's memory is that it gets updated. She too will remember particular events, but her memory of them may become associated with other memories. One memory may lead to many others. Similarly, something which happens to her may set her off remembering a whole series of past experiences. Memories are not linked in this way for the autistic child. They are far more rigid and are triggered by very particular associations. Autistic children's limited pretend play could be related to their memory peculiarities. A real cup may trigger off the action of drinking, but when her parent pretends to hold a cup and to drink from it, the autistic child does not see the similarity between this and her memory of the real object. Indeed, her memory may be so inflexible that she will only drink out of one particular cup.

Thus the autistic child's memory skills are extremely limited even though they may give the initial impression of being rather good. It is possible that she remembers things exactly as they happen because she has difficulties making sense of situations and abstracting meaning from them.

## The development of communication

The absence of any intention to communicate meaningfully with other people was one of the characteristics of autism which Kanner identified. About half of all autistic children never acquire any useful speech (e.g. Lockyer and Rutter, 1969) and, in those children who do learn to speak, what they say and how they say it is very different from the language of normal children and even from the language of children with other severe language problems (e.g. Rutter, 1978). One view of autism is of a basic cognitive deficit associated with particular difficulties in the area of language and language related skills. Certainly the language achievements of an autistic child are good predictors of their subsequent development. The more limited their language at the age of 5 or 6 years, the poorer the prognosis for their future development (Rutter et al., 1967; Lotter, 1974).

*How do autistic children and their parents communicate?*

This section in the other chapters has been mainly about the sorts of communication which occur between adults and young handicapped children in the period before the children begin to speak. Since many autistic children do not acquire any language, this section will not be restricted to observations of particularly young autistic children. In fact, because of the usual age of diagnosis, we know little about the very early communications of the autistic child, although Ricks (1975) does report that the babbling patterns of many autistic children are abnormal. This suggests that there may be difficulties from fairly early on. However, since even those autistic children who do have some language are unlikely to use it for communication purposes it would be surprising if their non-verbal communication in their earliest years was completely normal.

Observations of older autistic children support this. They tend not to communicate with other people non-verbally (e.g. Bartak et al., 1975; Ricks and Wing, 1975). They do not use gestures in the same way as normal children. A study by McHale et al. (1980) found that about three-quarters of the behaviours of groups of 4–9 year old autistic children were asocial when four of them were left alone without a teacher. However, the authors report that these children, especially those who were more able, did exhibit some communicative behaviours. When the teachers were present more social communication and less self-directed or asocial communication occurred. Also in the presence of the teachers more gestures and symbolic communications were observed, although it was noteworthy that these interactions were more likely to involve the teachers than the other children.

A further observation is that an autistic child tends not to point to things she wants, although she may lead her parent to whatever it is that she desires. This shows that she knows that other people can get things for her but, as we saw earlier on p. 139, she goes about this in a very different way from a normal child. Autistic children do not seem to communicate with their parents.

Much of the early communication between parents and normal children arises out of a shared interest in things that are going on around them. Unlike the normal child, the autistic child does not invite her parent to share her interests. She will not glance up to her parent as she plays with a toy. She will not offer objects to her parents. She is interested in objects and events for the immediate sensations they provide her with. She is not interested in sharing any of this with other people.

She may pay little or no attention to what other people are doing. However, a study by Tiegerman and Primavera (1984) shows that it is possible to change this behaviour. Six autistic children aged between 4 and 6 took part in the study. The child sat opposite the adult and they each had an identical set of toys. There were three conditions: either the adult imitated everything the child did with the toys immediately, or the adult simultaneously did something different with the same toy as the child was handling, or the adult's behaviour with the toys bore no resemblance to the child's. At the outset the children hardly looked at what the adult was doing, but over the course of a number of sessions the first two conditions, and especially the first, produced quite marked increases in how much the child attended to the adult's behaviour. This study is encouraging since it shows that the looking behaviour of young autistic children can be altered. It remains to be seen if such a change would generalize to other situations and conditions.

### What are the characteristics of the autistic child's spoken language?

Most autistic children have severe language learning difficulties. Lotter (1966, 1967a, b) found that six out of 32 autistic children aged between 8 and 10 years were mute, and all these children had IQs below 55. A further 10 of the children had very limited language, just a few words, which they used neither for communication or conversation. Thus about half of all autistic children acquire little or no language. But what of the language of the rest?

The language of the autistic child who talks is very different from that of a normal child, both in the sort of things she says and in the ways she uses her language. The beginning of speech is almost always delayed and, when the autistic child does begin to talk, she shows none of the delight and enthusiasm seen in many normal children. There is no rapid expansion of her vocabulary and much of what she says consists of meaningless echoing of things she has heard. This is called echolalia. She may just repeat odd words that she has heard, or she may repeat whole sentences, or even entire conversations. As well as reproducing verbatim what someone else has said, she may also copy the way they talk, imitating their accent and intonation. This echolalia does not necessarily occur immediately. It may be delayed for days, or weeks or even years. It may occur repeatedly or just once. Often the echoed utterances are irrelevant to what the child is currently doing, although this is not always the case.

For a number of autistic children this echoing of heard words or phrases is as far as their language goes, but some do move on and speak spontaneously. This spontaneous speech often shows the sort of immaturities seen in young normal children, but, unlike the normal child, these characteristics usually persist (Wing, 1969). One of the most common mistakes is their misuse of the personal pronoun. For example, rather than saying, 'I would like a drink', the autistic child is much more likely to say, 'Do you want a drink?' This may be a direct result of their tendency to echo. They have lifted a phrase they have heard another person use to them, and have used it without changing it as is appropriate. They are 'you' to themselves, rather than 'I' because that is how other people refer to them. Alternatively, it may reflect a more general difficulty with deictic words. These are words such as this/that, here/there and I/you, whose meaning depends on an understanding of the circumstances in which they are used. Very often the understanding of the word is derived from the person being an active participant in the conversation.

Both their echoed phrases and their spontaneous speech tend to be of words which are emphasized in sentences. They will often mimic being ticked off by their parent when their parent is likely to be talking more loudly than usual. They often omit underemphasized words like prepositions and conjunctions. However, the lack of emphasis may not be the only reason why they leave out these sorts of word. A more likely explanation is that they do not understand the meaning which is conveyed by these words in the sentence. Much of autistic children's vocabulary consists of nouns, the names of objects and things around them. They talk about things which are concrete and real in their environment. Like their perception and understanding of the world, their language concentrates on discrete aspects of this environment, rather than on making statements about how various aspects of it may relate to one another. We use prepositions and conjunctions to talk about relationships between different things, for example: 'The kettle is on the stove'; 'I would go for a walk but it is raining'. The autistic child has difficulty understanding these relationships, and so is less likely to use these words herself, and if she does they are often used incorrectly.

When they speak spontaneously they sometimes get the words in a sentence in the wrong order. For example an autistic child might say: 'Put table drink on' instead of 'Put the drink on the table'. In this sentence the autistic child is failing to order the words meaningfully. This may be because she cannot make sense of the situation, or, more likely, because she fails to understand how this sense is conveyed in language. She just says the relevant words, ignoring their order. They may also confuse words which sound similar or which have similar meanings. If the latter is correct it implies that such autistic children do have some awareness of meanings. Interestingly, Wing (1969) also noted that some autistic children describe certain objects by referring to their use. For example, one child said 'sweep-the-floor' for 'broom'. This is interesting because, by describing objects in this way, these children are showing some understanding of the objects. Their use of the object's function as a way of describing it shows that they have some understanding of it. These children, certainly for those objects they label in this way, do not appear to be focusing on separate parts of the objects; rather they seem to have related the parts to the whole and have interpreted its use. Alternatively, it is possible that all they are doing is echoing what others say when they pick up a broom: 'Let's sweep the floor'. To sort out these possibilities the way in which the child comes to use such phrases needs to be examined. Unfortunately, such developmental data are not available for autistic children.

A few autistic children eventually manage to speak grammatically, but even these children still rely a great deal on repeating phrases they have already heard. Their language is literal, and the absence of idiom, metaphor and allusion is noticeable. They tend to speak with a flat monotonous voice. They still tend to talk about concrete things, rather than about anything abstract or things in the future, and what really seems to set their language apart from that of normal children is an absence of any sort of discussion. They may be able to talk non-stop, and apparently quite knowledgeably, about something which interests them, but as soon as anything new is introduced they seem unable to include it. For example, an autistic child may be able to talk at length about a particular piece of music, but be unable to make any sort of comparison with another piece, or to say why she prefers a recording by one orchestra to another's. She may say she enjoys one and not the other, but be quite incapable of saying why. In addition, even if their language skills are adequate, their conversational skills are extremely limited. Very few autistic children can manage to hold a proper conversation. The majority fail to take turns appropriately and do not adjust what they are saying to take account of what the other person is saying (e.g. Bartak et al., 1975).

The difficulties that the autistic child has with language are not just confined to her use of language, but also to her understanding of what other people say. Some autistic children appear to have no understanding of what is said to them, whilst others seem to understand quite a lot. However, their understanding is limited to concrete things and events, and breaks down if the conversation becomes abstract. They interpret things that are said to them literally. One of Kanner's original cases, Alfred, was asked, 'What is this picture about?', to which he replied, 'People are about.' Another boy, when asked to put something down, put it on the floor. Often the understanding that an autistic child has of a word is the meaning it had when she first learned the word. Once again we see that the autistic child is rigid in her behaviour and cannot modify something she has already learned. Because of this inflexibility she cannot understand (except in a literal sense) idiomatic expressions such as: 'Have you lost your tongue?' This inflexibility of meaning is not just confined to their understanding of what other people say, but also to what they say themselves. Another of Kanner's original cases learned to say 'yes' when his father told him he would put him on his shoulders if he said 'yes'. For a long time afterwards 'yes' was used by the boy to mean 'I want to go on your shoulders.'

Before concluding that these problems have their origins in autism, it is important to rule out the possibility that they are due to, or aggravated by, the parents of autistic children talking to their children in an abnormal way. A number of studies have reported that the language learning environments of normal and autistic children are very similar (e.g. Frank et al., 1976; Cantwell et al., 1978; Wolchik, 1983). In her study, Wolchik compared the way in which the mothers and fathers of 10 autistic children interacted with the way parents and normal children interacted. The autistic and normal children were of similar language ability and their average ages were almost 4 and almost 1 respectively. There were some differences: for example, the parents of the autistic children used less language which was related to the child's own verbal behaviour and tended to ask more questions and provide more labels. This difference may account for the over-representation of nouns and names in the vocabularies of those autistic children who acquire some spoken language. There were no differences in terms of the parents giving the children directions about what they should or could say or in how much praise they gave their children's attempts. The similarities far outweighed the differences, and it would be impossible to account for the idiosyncratic language of autistic children by any of the differences which have been observed. Most of the differences can be accounted for by the fact that the autistic children were much older when they began to speak.

A further study demonstrates that although the more able autistic child may learn to speak, the way in which she interacts when she is talking seems to be very different from a normal child. This is a pilot study by Mirenda et al. (1983) of four autistic children aged between 6 and 15 who had good language skills. They were compared with four normal children aged between 6 and 12. The looking behaviour of the children was examined in two situations. In one the children did all the talking. They were asked to tell the experimenter a story, or to describe something that had happened to them. The other condition was more of a dialogue, in that the experimenter chatted to the child, generally eliciting information from her. There was no overall difference in how much the normal and the autistic children looked at the adult. The mean lengths of their gazes were similar, although there was more variability in the lengths of the autistic children's looks. However, there was a tendency for the children to behave differently in the two conditions. When the children were doing all the talking, the monologue condition, the autistic children tended to look more often and for longer at the adult than did the normal children. The reverse was seen in the dialogue condition, when the normal children tended to look more than the autistic children. These results are very interesting because they suggest that there may be qualitative differences in the looking behaviour of normal and autistic children during interaction with others, albeit in a somewhat artificial set-up. Normal people look at another person more when they are listening to what the other person is saying than when they themselves are talking. Mirenda et al.'s study suggests that the autistic child may fail to behave like this. This may well be related to their poor conversational skills as discussed earlier in this section.

Although some autistic children do acquire some useful language, the majority do not. However, words are not the only way in which we refer to the world. We also use many non-verbal means of communication. In the next section we consider whether or not autistic children can learn to communicate non-verbally. If the autistic child really has problems in extracting the meaning of situations and in representing them in some abstract way we should not expect her to succeed with non-verbal ways of communicating.

### Can autistic children understand and use non-verbal means of communication?

Autistic children tend not to communicate non-verbally. Their faces show little expression and they do not use their hands and bodies in the way that a normal child does. The autistic child does not use gestures spontaneously to compensate for any of the difficulties she has with speech. Compare this with the deaf child who, even though she may have no spoken language, shows a desire to communicate and may invent gestures to get others to understand her.

However, the autistic child does use some form of non-verbal behaviour. As babies and toddlers these children are often reported as crying and screaming to indicate that they want something. Apart from this screaming they may not give any clues as to what they want, and it is up to their parent to guess. This is rather like the way in which a very young normal baby behaves, but there is an important difference here. Ricks (1975) has demonstrated that parents of 3–5 year old non-verbal autistic children can recognize the message of their own child's cries and those of non-autistic non-verbal handicapped children of the same age, but that they cannot identify the cries of other non-verbal autistic children.

As the autistic child gets older she will show her parent what she wants rather than just screaming but, as we have seen, she does it in a very different way from a normal child. Very few autistic children point or use their direction of gaze to indicate what they want. They very rarely nod or shake their heads to show agreement or disagreement.

As well as not communicating non-verbally themselves, autistic children seem to have little understanding of other people's gestures and expressions (see pp. 140-1). Autistic children seem unable to interpret correctly the feelings of other people and, as a result, may respond inappropriately.

Despite all this, there have been many attempts to teach autistic children non-vocal ways of communicating. In an extensive review of the literature in this area, Kiernan (1983) concludes that although there are many methodological problems with most of the studies, there is some evidence that even some of the most handicapped autistic children can learn to communicate basic needs using signs and symbols, and that this may actually aid the development of their spoken language. Kiernan's review is useful because not only does it summarize a great deal of research, but ideally it will encourage more thorough and better executed studies in an area which is obviously vital for practical as well as theoretical reasons.

## Social development

### *How does autism affect interaction with others?*

Autistic children are particularly handicapped when it comes to interacting with other people. Indeed it was their social aloofness which Kanner proposed as their primary problem although, as we have seen, a cognitive account offers a more parsimonious explanation of the other characteristics of autism.

There are few data on the early social behaviours of autistic children. However, Wing (1971) asked a group of parents about the early behaviour of their 6–15 year old autistic children. Fourteen of the 27 children were thought to have been handicapped from birth. According to their parents, a number of these children failed to show various social behaviours at the appropriate age, or even when they were older: 10 failed to lift their arms up when their parent came to pick them up; 7 showed very little response to their mother's voice and 11 did not draw their parent's attention to things by pointing. All of these behaviours are part of normal social interaction. Other reports of autistic children (e.g. Rutter, 1978) also note the absence of the sorts of attachment behaviour which are characteristic of normal children. Autistic children tend not to keep close by their parent, and may not even show any acknowledgement of their parent's return after an absence, let alone any sign of greeting. They do not seem to use their parents for comfort, although they will enjoy a game of rough and tumble. Indeed Rutter (1983) suggests that one of the characteristics of the autistic child's social behaviour is their failure to seek bodily contact to gain comfort or security.

Yet, under certain circumstances, autistic children will interact with other people. Clark and Rutter (1981) found that, as the demands for a social response from autistic children were increased, the children were more likely to produce a social response. This ties in with the findings of McHale et al. (1980) who found almost no social behaviour between autistic children when the group was left alone, but when a teacher was with the children the level of social behaviour increased. However, this social behaviour occurred towards the teacher rather than towards the other children and most of it was initiated by the adult. Encouragingly, this study also reported that over an eight month period the amount of social behaviour exhibited by the children increased, whilst there was a decrease in their asocial behaviour. Nevertheless, their social behaviour with other people was still very different from that of normal children.

It is often commented that autistic children avoid making eye contact. However, we saw earlier in this chapter that, in certain situations and with more able autistic children, there may be no quantitative difference in the amount of eye contact made when talking to or with another person but that there may be marked qualitative differences (Mirenda et al., 1983). In this study the autistic children looked at the other person more when they were talking themselves than when the other person was talking. It was the reverse for the normal children. It is as though the autistic child does not have the same understanding as the normal child about interacting. From early in the first year normal babies show a reciprocity in their behaviour with other people; they do something then the adult does something, and so on. The interaction is balanced, although initially it is likely that this is achieved by the adults fitting their behaviour around that of the baby's. It is this absence of a reciprocity of social interchange that Rutter (1983) suggests is another of the main features of the autistic child's social abnormalities. Autistic children seem to be unable to predict what other people will do, and they seem unable to adjust their behaviour to that of others.

Some of the autistic child's behaviour could be explained by her inability to imitate what other people do. She tends not to smile back when someone smiles at her; she may not wave goodbye when others wave, and she may not clap her hands when everyone else is clapping. But, given some of her other behaviours, it seems much more likely that her failure to reciprocate in these social situations, especially the first two, is due to an inability to understand the reciprocal nature of social interaction.

In particular, autistic children and adults are poor at interpreting other people's feelings from their non-verbal behaviour. An autistic person may not realize that the person she is talking to about one of her interests is bored, despite the fact that the person is gazing out of the window and yawning. She shows little or no ability to adjust her behaviour to the needs of other people.

This is a persisting problem. Bemporad (1979) reports a follow-up of one of Kanner's original cases. At the age of 31 this man, although of normal intelligence, was unable to comprehend other people's feelings and could not predict how they might behave. Rutter (1983) also describes a young man who sought help because he was forever offending and upsetting people. He seemed unable to react appropriately towards others. However, the fact that this man sought help suggests that he had some understanding of other people's feelings, and realized that the difficulties were likely to recur.

The explanation of the autistic child's social behaviour is not obvious. Her behaviour sometimes gives the appearance of a failure to differentiate between people and objects, and yet at other times she does show an awareness of some of the things which differentiate people from objects. For example, many autistic children show an awareness that their reflection is a reflection of themselves (e.g. Spiker and Ricks, 1984), and Hobson (1984) has shown that they can recognize the perspective of a doll in a visual-spatial task, although Baron-Cohen et al.'s (1985) study showed that autistic children do not appreciate the knowledge of others when this differs from their own. They can recognize photographs of friends (Langdell, 1978) although they seem to go about this in a rather different way from normal children. Rutter, in his 1983 article, suggests that the problem for the autistic child is in processing information which has social or emotional meaning. It is clear that this is an area where more research is needed.

### Do autistic children adjust to their handicap?

Unlike children with many other sorts of handicap, the autistic child shows little sign that she realizes that she is handicapped. However, the two adults mentioned in the previous section do indicate that more able autistic adults may be very aware of some of the problems that their handicap causes them in social encounters (Bemporad, 1979; Rutter, 1983). Yet autistic children often seem unaware of how odd some of their behaviour may be. An autistic child may exhibit quite extreme behaviours, such as taking off all her clothes in the street or making rather loud embarrassing remarks about other people. Unlike a normal child, who might behave like this on the odd occasion, the autistic child does not seem to do such things as a way of attracting the attention of people around her. The purpose seems not to be the effect of her behaviour on others and, given her problems in appreciating how other people feel, it seems unlikely that this could explain this aspect of her behaviour.

However, her inability to make the same sort of sense as a normal child of her environment, and her ability to remember certain things as they first happened in great detail, can lead her to show distress in certain situations. One of the characteristics of autism is a dislike of changes, changes in things like routines and the arrangement of objects in a room. An autistic child may get extremely agitated at a slight change, such as the order of the books on a shelf, and yet ignore other changes. What seems to be happening is that the autistic child remembers certain things she perceives in great detail. Because she seems to focus on the sensations she gets from the environment rather than interpreting it, any alteration to the things which provide her with particular sensations is noticed. This causes disturbances because things are not as they are remembered. Often the autistic child's distress persists until the original order or routine is re-established. In this sense the nature of the autistic child's handicap can cause her extreme distress.

Autistic children often appear to be unhappy children. They may cry and be very miserable for no apparent reason. On other occasions, the source of their distress can be identified, for example, a change in their environment as described above. They also become distressed through frustration and failure. This suggests that they may have greater awareness of how they differ from other people than is indicated by many of their other behaviours.

# 7

# Some practical implications of the studies

## Introduction

The previous five chapters have examined the ways in which certain handicaps can affect development. In this chapter I want to consider some of the practical implications of the studies discussed in these chapters. I shall restrict myself to implications which arise from the studies discussed in this book and will use illustrations from the handicaps I have described. Although a particular point may be illustrated with reference to one handicap only, many of the implications will be relevant to all the handicaps included, and also to children who are handicapped in ways other than those described in this book. Some of the suggestions I shall be making are already in operation, although even when this is the case, they are often not available everywhere, and even when they are available they are not always as effective as they could be. Because of this, I have not attempted to indicate which suggestions are in practice and which are not.

## The individuality of handicapped children

Although the overall incidence of handicap is surprisingly high, the incidence of individual conditions is often very low. As a result, many people have no personal experience of particular handicaps. However, stereotypes abound. These stereotypes are often misleading and incorrect, and may be particularly distressing for parents who have just discovered that their child has a handicap. Many people have a stereotyped picture of individuals with Down's syndrome which is not very appealing, yet this is not realistic. The literature shows how variable people with Down's syndrome are in ability and how they have been underestimated in the past. As Rynders et al. (1978) point out, the limits of the Down's child's educability are virtually unknown.

Stereotypes may not just paint a depressing picture, they may also be damaging in terms of what is expected of the child. This is particularly true of children with motor handicaps, and is supported by case studies of physically handicapped people who have surprised everyone by their achievements once an appropriate channel for communication has been found. Often these people are quite old by the time that their abilities are realized and given an outlet. It is probably true that some physically handicapped children, because of additional brain damage, are unable to achieve a great deal, but the danger is in assuming this to be the case in a child who appears to show the same lack of interest and inability to communicate. These children must be given every opportunity to demonstrate their capabilities.

This has particular relevance for assessment. Assessors need to be sensitive to the child and her circumstances, and to be creative in attempts to find a way through to each child. Assessors should also be aware of their own influence on the testing situation. They need to watch for the child developing along different routes from the non-handicapped child, and demonstrating similar developments in different ways. Testing procedures must be modified to take account of each child's problems, and efforts should be made to distinguish between behaviours which result from the handicapping condition itself and behaviours which result from some additional problem. Only if this is achieved will the clinician be in a position to advise parents and teachers how they can best help each child.

Although it is very important that the abilities of handicapped children should not be underestimated, the opposite is also true. The spina bifida child whose language gives the impression that she is quite capable may, as a result of this, not be given help from which she could readily benefit. The autistic child who can recite nursery rhymes or remember shopping lists may have very little or no understanding of what she is saying. If an estimate of her ability, based on these isolated skills, results in her being treated inappropriately, she could be at a disadvantage. However, this is a delicate area since the parents of such children may feel that these apparent abilities show that their child is more capable than otherwise might be thought. Understandably, their child's ability may be very important to them, and they may find it hard to accept that an isolated skill does not reflect a general ability.

The studies have shown the need for us to be aware of the problems which may arise indirectly from the handicap. Children with motor problems may have fewer opportunities to experience their environment and may have restricted surroundings, particularly those who spend a large proportion of their lives in institutions. Again, the source of the problem needs to be identified: in the case of motor handicap, is the child unresponsive because of her physical handicap or because she has never been given the opportunity to respond?

Children who superficially have the same handicap will be quite different from one another, and the environments in which they grow up will also differ. In order to be able to help each child, it is essential that her particular needs are considered. This is clearly illustrated by Fraiberg's two cases of Toni and Peter. Although they are described at very different ages, it seems likely that the ways in which these two children and their families could have been helped early on, given our understanding of the problems facing the developing blind child in her earliest years, would have been very different. Toni's mother seemed to have adjusted to Toni's means of experience, whereas Peter and his mother seemed to have failed to achieve any way of sharing their experiences. The literature may describe problems that a blind child is likely to have but, to be of use to an individual child, this needs to be considered alongside the particular circumstances and characteristics of each blind child and her family.

Children with different handicaps have different educational needs and each individual child will be different and have her own particular needs. This means that the educational system must be flexible, so that each child's educational attainments can be maximized. It is especially important that the educational placement of children is not guided by stereotyped views of particular handicaps and that teachers, whether in specialist or mainstream schools, are as fully informed as possible as to each child's particular strengths and weaknesses. Each child should be placed according to her ability, and her placement reviewed regularly.

In England, the Warnock Report (1978) made many recommendations about the education of handicapped children, including proposing that they should be referred to as children with special educational needs, rather than by their particular handicap. Many of the Warnock recommendations were incorporated in the 1981 Education Act which came into operation on 1 April 1983. This Act refers to children with special educational needs and introduces a number of important changes in educational procedure. One is a requirement to integrate children with special needs into ordinary schools wherever possible and practical. Another change is in parental involvement. Under this Act parents have a right to request and to be involved in assessments of their child and decisions about school placement. Following an assessment, a statement of special educational need is provided for each child between 2 and 19 for whom it is decided, on the basis of the assessment, that special educational provision is required. This statement sets out the educational provision for the child. Parents also have the right to appeal against this statement if they disagree with it. One of the recommendations of the Warnock Report that was not adopted in the Act was for the appointment of a 'named person' for each child who would coordinate all the information and decisions concerning that child. However, if a child is in need of special educational provision the local Education Authority must provide the parents with the name of someone to whom they can apply for information and advice.

This legislation is important because it makes a change in the approach to educational provision for young handicapped people in England.

## How can parents and teachers aid the development of handicapped children?

### *The blind child*

Probably the most important factor to emerge from studies of blind children is an understanding of the way in which blind babies and children, who are not otherwise handicapped, experience their surroundings. Parents expect babies to look around, to smile at familiar faces, to turn towards sounds, to babble in response to conversation and so on. The parents of a blind baby can be helped to understand that their baby's behaviour does not indicate disinterest and passivity. It is just that she shows her interest in what is going on around her in different ways from a sighted child. Parents can be directed towards reading the signals in their baby's hands, and towards understanding the reasons why a blind baby may drop her head and go quiet. The parents can be guided towards thinking about the experiences that their child has, the noises she hears, the things she feels and smells, and helped to adjust their behaviour so that it is appropriate to their child's experience, rather than focusing on the visual nature of their own experience. In other words, parents can be helped to get inside their child, to think about how she experiences the world, and the sense she is likely to make of this experience.

In the first few months, parents can be helped to think about how their blind baby comes to recognize them, and encouraged to provide opportunities for recognition: for example, talking to the baby, using varied intonation, holding her and encouraging her to explore with her hands. They can be alerted to signs of recognition in their baby's hands. Blind babies often really enjoy boisterous games, and smile readily during familiar tickling and physical games. The majority are just as robust as sighted children and their movement should be encouraged, perhaps devising actions to accompany nursery rhymes or elaborating their own. A blind baby studied by Urwin (1978) developed a game with his father: Jerry would stand on a table and when his dad said, 'Ready, steady, go' Jerry hurled himself towards his father. This delighted them both and probably helped Jerry come to realize that sounds have sources and that there were objects and people beyond his reach. After all, the safe outcome of his leap depended on this. This game is likely to have helped him to achieve mobility.

Once parents become sensitive to how their baby may interpret her experiences, and the possible misinterpretations she may make, they will be in a far better position to help their child develop a realistic understanding of the environment. It is very easy for us to take our knowledge for granted and to fail to consider other alternatives. For example, we know that cups must be put down on a flat surface for safety, but a blind child, who always gets handed a cup, may drop the cup when she has finished, thinking that she is putting it on to an invisible shelf, or because she thinks that cups only exist when they are in her hand and cease to exist when she lets go. If her parents have an awareness of these possibilities, they can adjust their behaviour appropriately: for example, rather than handing their child a cup and taking it when she has finished, they can encourage her to pick up the cup and put it down herself, even if initially they need to guide her hand to the table top and help her feel for the cup. All of this can be accompanied by appropriate conversation, talking to her about what she experiences. For example, when juice is poured into her cup and the cup put on the table, her parent might say, 'Hear that, I'm pouring your juice into your cup and now I'm putting it on the table in front of you', rather than just saying, 'Here's your juice'. Of course, many parents will pick up on their baby's signals and show sensitivity to her experiences without any help. But for some parents this will be difficult, and they may be much encouraged to learn that their baby is interested in the people and objects around her and to appreciate how she shows this.

For all parents, an awareness of the potential problem areas can be useful since this may help them to spot the problems at an early stage and think about ways of overcoming them. For example, we saw how Toni lay passively on the floor before she became mobile, and how this behaviour disappeared once she started to move. Parents can be made aware of the problems of mobility for their blind child and of the other sorts of stimulation that the child may discover. Parents can be encouraged and helped to think how their child's mobility can be developed. Parents may not realize that their child's lack of mobility is related to the fact that she does not yet understand that there are objects and people beyond her reach and, without direction, may not see how encouraging her to reach out, and to discover the control she can have of her environment, will aid her mobility. From a very early age parents can draw their child's attention to her hands and feet, perhaps putting little bells on her ankles and wrists, or by encouraging her to use both hands to hold a bottle or cup. Toys which make a noise when touched and which do not roll away are useful, such as rattles which can be stuck to the side of the cot or wobbly toys which sit on the floor or table. These sorts of experience will provide opportunities for the blind child to discover that there is an environment beyond, and that she can act on it.

As she gets older one way of encouraging mobility is by providing auditory incentives for movement. For example, the parent can crouch in front of the child who can stand, and talk to her, and as soon as she makes a movement forward she can give her a big hug. Gradually, greater movement can be demanded of her. It is interesting that Toni's mobility first came by her use of a baby walker. Fraiberg makes it clear that she would not recommend this sort of equipment as she feels that it prevents independence. For the same reason, she does not favour playpens. In some cases it may even be necessary to go to extreme lengths to combat particularly limiting behaviours in the blind child. For example, Scott et al. (1977) suggest that if a blind child spends a great deal of time just lying on her back, a hard object should be tied on to prevent her from lying on it. The blind child needs to be helped to discover that there is an environment around her, and once she begins to realize this, her experiences will widen as she moves around, finding new things to play with and places to explore. It is in these ways that our understanding of development makes us increasingly aware of how apparently different behaviours relate to one another.

One of the most important developments for the blind child and her parents, as for any child, is the beginning of language. This can present problems for the blind child. I have already commented on the value of parents talking about aspects of the environment which their child can experience: for example, 'Hear that, I'm pouring the juice into your cup'. Names should be provided for things the child hears, smells and feels. It is essential that the parents talk about things which are relevant to their child and encourage their child to make noises, perhaps by imitating noises that she makes. When she begins to talk, she should be encouraged to talk about things she knows, rather than just parroting things that her parents say, although obviously imitation does play a large part.

One of the difficulties facing the blind child and her parents in the area of language is that they have less to talk about than the sighted child and her parents. The blind child is also less likely to initiate conversations. She will not point towards something she wants and grunt appealingly at her parent. Although this obvious requesting behaviour is absent, the blind baby may make requests. She may make a slight movement of her hands towards the noise of an object, and parents must be alerted to the significance of this sort of behaviour which may otherwise go unnoticed and disappear.

As soon as the blind child has some language she should be encouraged to use it. Many parents feel a need to protect their blind child, and they may try to compensate for her handicap by not demanding too much of her. For example, they may interpret what it is that their child wants, rather than insisting that she asks for it. The child should be given the opportunity to make decisions. This could be done by asking the child which of two things she wants. This may also reduce the echolalia often heard in blind children. After all, if you are asked, 'Would you like a sandwich or a biscuit?' it makes no sense to reply, 'You would like a sandwich or a biscuit.' Language can be used to promote the child's exploration of her environment. For example, rather than passing the child a biscuit when she asks for it, the parent could say, 'Fetch one yourself, they are on a plate in the middle of the table by the window.' At times this may seem hard. I remember vividly as a teenager thinking how unhelpful the mother of a blind friend of mine was when she said, 'For goodness sake, Christopher, don't just stand there holding your empty glass, find a table and put it down.' And that was in a house he did not know particularly well. But now that I know more about the problems facing the blind child I can see that this parent's attitude probably played a major role in Christopher's realistic understanding of his environment and in his independence.

Blind children may not develop a full understanding of people and objects until sometime after they have begun to talk. Because of this, and since they have no visual reminder of their parent, they may have problems reconciling the cross parent with the loving parent. One way of minimizing this difficulty is for parents, when they are cross with their blind child, to keep in contact with her, holding her, rather than isolating her. In this way she will be helped to realize through touch that this is one and the same person who can be cross and be kind.

Many of the implications discussed so far in this section are relevant for teachers working with blind children, as well as for parents. Pre-school provision should be available to all families with a blind child. As soon as blindness is diagnosed a peripatetic teacher, who will visit regularly, should be assigned to the family. As has been seen, there are many ways in which the parents can help their blind child develop, and help from trained and experienced people should be made easily available to all families. For the blind child to derive the maximum from her intact senses, and to be able to achieve independence and satisfaction as she gets older, there must be support and advice available to her parents from the beginning. Such provision should help to minimize the numbers of blind children who run into developmental difficulties later.

The transition to school may be traumatic for the young blind child and she must be introduced gradually to the idea of being away from her family. Small nursery schools can be especially valuable. Ideally every blind child should have the opportunity to attend a school or unit for the blind which is situated locally. The main reason for this is not because it will foster integration, although this may be an important and valuable spin-off, but because the blind child will be able to live at home surrounded by familiar objects and people. This means that more units for visually handicapped children are needed, both for those with additional problems and for those whose only handicap is blindness, so that every blind child can live at home for as long as possible.

Unfortunately, in many cases the decision to send a blind child to a residential school arises because she has reached the age of 5 and there is no available alternative. Wills (1981b) has pointed out quite clearly that, for many blind 5 year olds, boarding will be very disturbing. She argues that the decision to send a blind child to a residential school should be based on factors other than her age. A child who is still very dependent on her parents, and who finds it hard to cope in new surroundings and with new people, is going to flounder if she is sent to a boarding school with no sight to help her make sense of the experience. Wills suggests that the age of 8 or 9 years will be plenty early enough, although the most suitable age will vary with each child. This means that earlier education must be provided either in the form of peripatetic teachers or small units, at least until the age of 8 or 9 years.

Within the educational system itself, there are implications for how and what blind children should be taught. Learning, as in the pre-school period, must be made relevant to the child's own experience, and the experience that the child has must be maximized. Each child should be encouraged to make as much use as possible of any residual vision. Since it is more difficult for a blind child to learn to read braille than for a sighted child to learn to read print, there is a need for more research into how braille can best be taught. It may be appropriate to delay the teaching of braille until the child is 8 or 9. In other areas of education as well, the blind child needs to be considered more from her perspective rather than from the perspective of what a sighted child of the same age is learning. Parallels should be drawn with sighted children only with great caution. Blind children need to be taught in different ways and educators need to be aware that they may not be ready to learn certain things at the same age as sighted children. Their lack of vision makes it harder for them to integrate their experiences, and this may be an argument for extending their education beyond the usual school leaving age.

One of the positive benefits of much of the recent work with blind children is that it has questioned a number of earlier views that blind children are intellectually inferior to sighted children. It is no longer believed that they should just be taught basket weaving and that education for them is out of the question. Blind children can achieve just as much as sighted children, and education is gradually becoming increasingly sensitive to the different ways in which they can learn to do things. Sighted people are often hampered by their own view of the world and their own ways of doing things, and the main implication for education is the need for a greater awareness of other ways of achieving the educational goals set for sighted children. Educators must think differently, rather than expect blind pupils to think like sighted pupils. It is encouraging that many teachers of the blind are themselves blind.

### The deaf child

The majority of the profoundly deaf population fail to acquire adequate spoken language and, for this reason, I believe that signing should be encouraged. This view is not shared by everyone and because of this it is important to examine the arguments against as well as the arguments for signing.

It has been argued that sign languages are inherently concrete and so are inferior to spoken language. However, this sort of position has been refuted by recent linguistic work. Let me illustrate this by considering American Sign Language (ASL). The signs in ASL consist of symbolic gestures, many of which stand for whole concepts. The meaning of each gesture is dependent on the shape, the location, the movement, and to a lesser extent the orientation of one or both hands. These components which occur simultaneously are called cheremes and correspond to the phonemes or sounds which occur successively in the production of a word in spoken language. Many of the signs are iconic, that is, they are not arbitrary like words, but are based on pantomime type gestures. However, signs in ASL, as in British Sign Language (BSL), differ in several crucial ways from pantomime gestures, and this is one of the factors that makes linguists consider such languages to be proper languages. A pantomime gesture involves the action of the hands 'as if' representing an action or object, whereas a sign requires a particular shape, location, movement and orientation of the hand or hands, and no other. Variations in any of these changes the meaning of the sign. Signs are much more sophisticated than pantomime gestures. Also, there are rules for combining cheremes, which would not be evident if it were just pantomime. For example, if the hands move independently they must be of the same shape and move in the same way, whereas if the hands are of different shapes one hand must be stationary. Finally, if ASL and other natural sign languages were based on pure pantomime they would be readily understood by 'foreigners', but in fact a BSL signer is incomprehensible to an ASL signer and vice versa.

There are several other features of ASL which contribute to its language status. It is unique in that it is not derived from written or spoken American. It has its own lexicon which does not correspond to American and it also has its own grammar. For example, the signs for 'I see you' and 'you see me' are only differentiated by the direction of hand movement. This shows how the visual-spatial nature of the system has been utilized, rather than attempting to copy the sequential nature of grammar in the spoken language.

Other arguments used against signing are based on the consequences of signing for the deaf child's use of a spoken form of language. It has been suggested that if a child learns a sign language this may interfere with, or detract from, her learning spoken language. ASL, for example, has its own syntax. However, there is no supportive evidence for interference. Again, it has been argued that once a child has an effective means of communication, she will not bother to learn a spoken language which is admittedly more difficult. Here, it is important to consider the purpose of having a language. Obviously one important function is to communicate with others, and a second function is as a medium through which we can learn more about the environment. Since the majority of deaf people actually fail to acquire much intelligible spoken language, they are unlikely to be able to communicate with other people very easily using spoken language. In reality, although deaf people may work alongside hearing people there is little social mixing.

It seems essential that deaf children, from an early age, are given a system through which they can communicate effectively and can find out about things from others. Admittedly, if they learn a sign language, their communication will be limited to those who can also sign, but the number of people with whom they can communicate orally will be limited anyway. Conrad (1981) reported that teachers of the deaf found it extremely hard to understand three-quarters of their deaf pupils who had losses greater than 90 dB. It seems hardly likely that the person in the street will fare any better, and more likely that they will understand even less.

However, it is important to acknowledge that there are some members of the profoundly deaf population who do manage to communicate effectively within a hearing world and have excellent oral skills. Many parents and practitioners seem to cling to this hope, and hope is all it is. We have no idea why it is that some people, even when profoundly deaf from birth, manage to acquire good oral skills. We should be asking why. If we could be sure that we could put every deaf child on the road to good spoken language then I would not be arguing for signing. In the meantime, the deaf child must be put first and given the maximum opportunity to develop skills which enable as rich communication as possible.

Signing also has its positive side. Parents of hearing children delight in their child's acquisition of spoken language, but Gregory and Mogford (1981) make it quite clear that for the parents of the deaf child this process is hard work. The parents talk of working on a particular word. The joy seems to have gone out of it. It is not just for the parents that it is hard work, it is hard work for the child as well. Imagine saying to a child 'Give the doll a bath', and the child offering the bath to the doll. The deaf child has a much harder task before her if she is to crack the code of spoken language sufficiently for her to be able to comprehend it, let alone speak it. Imagine trying to explain the meaning of the expression 'to catch the waiter's eye' to a deaf adolescent. If sign language were used these sorts of difficulties would be reduced, and accompanying this would be a decrease in the frustration and confusion which exists for the deaf child and her parents. Deaf children themselves prefer to shift to a sign mode if they have a loss of 70 dB or more.

Therefore a very obvious implication is that the deaf child should be given the opportunity to sign from an early age. This is reliant upon early diagnosis and qualitative assessment, to the extent that this is possible. The child may have some residual hearing which would benefit from auditory training. The earlier the diagnosis can be made the sooner the parents can be alerted to the importance of them learning a sign language, and becoming tuned into their baby's early gestural communications. Provisions for teaching parents and other members of the family to sign should, ideally, be a priority. Families should be supported emotionally and financially throughout. The processes underlying the deaf child's understanding of objects and people is probably different from a hearing child's, and the parents of a deaf child need to be made aware of the different routes that their deaf child's development may take and how to facilitate this: for example, using toys which change visually when the child acts on them.

Apart from communication problems, the greatest handicap for deaf children is educational. Their reading and writing skills rarely get beyond an elementary level, and many may never be able to read in a way that can be useful to them. Yet many schools for the deaf seem to place a great deal of emphasis on these skills, and much of the deaf child's time is spent trying to achieve them, and often failing. All this time is time during which the hearing child can be learning more and getting even further ahead. Are there ways in which the deaf child can be assisted more effectively?

Many deaf children would benefit enormously if they were given the opportunity to communicate through signing. Some evidence suggests that signers may be advantaged in reading although, as Conrad (1981) points out, most of these studies have been poorly controlled. In his own study he found no advantage for the signers, but although these were signing children, signing was not common in the schools. These were children who signed at home with their parents, and went to a school where signing was frowned upon. Conrad is cautiously optimistic that acceptable levels of reading can be taught provided that signs are used. He argues that for reading, the correspondence rules between phonemes and graphemes, that is between letter sounds and letter shapes, are not a prerequisite. The child does not need to know the sound of each letter in order to match it up to its shape. Knowing these rules obviously helps us to read out loud an unfamiliar word and recognize it, but reading at the word level would enable the deaf child to translate straight into signs. And for her there would be no confusion between words that sound alike, for example, 'I see the sea'!

As with blind children, one of the difficulties for deaf children is that they are always being compared to normal children. Here is a child who cannot hear and yet in all other respects is like a normal child. The tendency is to have similar expectations, to expect the deaf child to do similar things at similar ages to the hearing child. This comparison should not be made and teachers should use the deaf child's own readiness to guide her education. It may well be that the deaf child would be better off if the teaching of reading and writing were delayed.

The implication is that many deaf children, if not the majority, should be given the opportunity to learn and to use a sign system at home and at school. However, some caution is necessary. All the evidence suggests that signing will benefit the deaf child's acquisition of these skills, but this still needs to be proved. What is certain is that the adoption of signing will not impede the child's development. Given the current state of deaf children's educational achievements they must be given this opportunity for improvement.

If schools adopt signing this should make signing more acceptable to parents as an effective means of communication, and ideally more parents will learn how to sign. This should bring real benefits for parent-child communication. If signing is to be used in schools, it follows that all trainee teachers of the deaf must learn to sign fluently.

I have been emphasizing signing as a means of communication for the deaf. However, some deaf children, especially those who are partially hearing, do become fluent speakers and read and write well. For this reason deaf children should be talked to as well as signed to, since the deaf child who can use spoken language is at an advantage. This means that in schools there needs to be one teacher or assistant per child, so that help for the child is maximized. In addition Wood et al. (1986) propose that teachers should examine how they communicate with deaf children and, in particular, they suggest that more attention should be paid to what deaf children are trying to communicate than to correcting their language. Spoken language as well as signing should be used at home as well. If the child's parents are also deaf then the child should be provided with spoken language experience outside the home.

### The child with a motor handicap

Many physically handicapped children are not just handicapped physically, but they have other disabilities as well. These additional problems vary between children and, even within the main types of physical handicap, the children will differ in the nature and extent of their individual problems. For this reason it is only possible to examine very general practical implications since the relevance of them for any particular child will depend on her particular circumstances.

Children who are severely handicapped physically can develop cognitively, and can have an understanding of objects and of people, provided that they have some means of acting on the environment. These children may not be able to interact with objects and people in a conventional way, but they may still reach a level of understanding similar to a non-handicapped child, albeit by an alternative route. If the child has no way of interacting, or opportunities are not provided, then these developments may be delayed or even absent. It seems clear that ways and means must be found to provide these sorts of experience for the physically handicapped child who, if left alone, would have no way of interacting. The child who cannot sit up unsupported needs to be provided with a special chair so that her head and body are supported and her hands are free to manipulate toys. If she cannot use her hands in this way, or has no hands, then some other way must be found of providing her with such experiences. For example, if she can only move her head from side to side then a way should be devised so that this action can alter something in her environment: perhaps some arrangement so that she can move her head against a board which triggers the carousel on a projector to advance a slide. She would then be able to have a direct effect on her environment by changing what is projected on a screen in front of her. Obviously, the more meaningful and useful to her that her interaction with the environment can be made to be, the better. Recent developments in applications of microchip technology for the handicapped are exciting and need to be made readily accessible (e.g. Behrmann, 1984; BBC series, *With a little help from the chip*, 1985).

Many of these children will be dependent on others to provide all their experiences. Other people will have control over what and how they experience the environment. Parents of non-handicapped children, who are sensitive to their development, get ideas from their children about appropriate ways of interacting with them. These parents do not need to be taught about the different developments which follow one another. But the situation may be very different for a parent of a physically handicapped child. These parents may unwittingly restrict the experiences of their child, for example, by underestimating her abilities, by not being aware of subsequent stages of development, by being embarrassed to take her out to public places or by being overprotective and fearful of her coming to harm if they let her explore potentially dangerous situations like climbing the stairs. These parents may need help in choosing appropriate things to do with their child, and advice about ways of compensating for their child's particular problems. Parents must be encouraged to widen the experiences of their child, and given the necessary support, whether financial or emotional, to do this.

Parents of children who are physically handicapped but who are not handicapped mentally may see education as particularly important. Some of the parents in Pringle and Fiddes's study of thalidomide damaged children felt that their children's physical problems would preclude certain sorts of work later, and that the sorts of work they could do would require educational achievements. There is certainly a feeling that parents are often unhappy with their child's educational placement or lack of it. Hewett's parents felt very dissatisfied with the way in which their children were assessed and thought that their children were much more responsive in their own homes.

There is an urgent need for the provision of more nursery opportunities for physically handicapped children. In her study of 180 cerebral palsied children, Hewett reports that, out of the 55 children who were under 5, 34 had no nursery day care, 16 went for one or two days to a voluntary centre and five attended some form of local authority care. These children may lead very restricted lives at home. Hewett also reported that 17 of the total sample, (almost 10 per cent) were very severely handicapped and spent most of the day in a special chair or pram, 11 of them rarely moving out of one room. At a nursery, even if they cannot join in many of the activities, they will have the opportunity to observe other children and to interact with people outside their immediate family. There will also be benefits for their parents in addition to having a break from their child. The parents will have the opportunity to talk to parents of other handicapped children (if the nursery group caters for several handicapped children) and the opportunity to observe what other children are doing; these opportunities may give them ideas about how to play with their own child. It is not only the provision of more nursery facilities that is needed, but also help for the parents if it is difficult for them to get their child to nursery or school.

Many of these children spend a great deal of time in hospital, and this may be especially disrupting to their education. A study by Woodburn (1973) of spina bifida children aged between 1 and 17 found that a quarter of them had gone into hospital 8-15 times. Almost 7 per cent had been in hospital 16 times or more. One way to deal with this would be to provide better facilities in hospital so that the child's education could be continued. Another way might be to involve parents in their child's education to a greater extent so that they could provide some of the continuity. Some of the things which are taught at school can be improved just by practice: for example, reading and writing. But others, like arithmetic, require a more directed input. It is in these sorts of area that the hospitalized child may miss out and where help is needed.

Schools need to be responsive to the particular problems that individual children may have in coping with school subjects. A child's motor control may be so poor that her writing is unintelligible, but she might be able to learn to use a typewriter or adapted computer keyboard. A child who has little control over her hands may, nevertheless, be able to operate a computer with some part of her body over which she does have control. Teachers need to be sensitive to the reduced experiences of many physically handicapped children and attempt to build on those experiences that they do have.

Most parents of a handicapped child would hope that their child could attend an ordinary school. They may feel that a special school is too geared to handicap, has too low expectations of its children, is overprotective and unchallenging. This has implications for ways in which special schools should change and for integration as an alternative. In their book, Pringle and Fiddes make a number of suggestions for change through: 'special individual tuition and assignments; by remedial teaching; by a heightened awareness among teachers concerning the positive value of adopting higher expectations; and, perhaps above all, by acceptance of the fact that challenging, enriching and stretching a child's mind is not synonymous with educational pressure or intensive coaching.' They suggest that if special schools were to change along these lines, some of the thalidomide children in their study who were in special schools might develop sufficiently to transfer to mainstream schools. In fact, Pringle and Fiddes found that 17 out of 79 children were incorrectly placed: some were in special schools and should have been in a mainstream school, whilst others were in a mainstream school but were more suited to a special school, either a school for the mentally handicapped or a school for the hearing impaired. An alternative, for these latter children, would be that provision in mainstream schools should be changed to meet their needs, rather than the children being moved out of mainstream education. Hodgson (1984) makes a number of practical suggestions as to how the needs of physically handicapped children can be met in the mainstream school. These range from collecting as much information about the child before entry to the school to providing the necessary support in the classroom, both in terms of equipment and additional adult help.

One of the additional problems about their child attending a special school which may concern parents is that she will be more isolated from her peers when not at school than if she could attend the local mainstream school. Isolation may be a problem for those children for whom mobility is very difficult. It seems clear therefore that, if it is necessary for a child to attend a special school, a great deal of effort must be made to establish and maintain links with non-handicapped children. This has implications not just for special education but also for mainstream education, and society generally.

### The child with Down's syndrome

There may appear to be no difference in the development of a Down's baby and a normal baby in the first few months, but later on in the first year the

Down's child usually begins to fall noticeably behind. They often give the appearance of following the same pattern of development as the normal child, but at a slower rate. However, there may be differences in how they develop and support services need to be alert to this possibility. It is clear that help early on can be beneficial. Cunningham and Sloper (1976) found that Down's babies who were visited by the research team from before they were 6 months old were doing more at a year than babies who were visited first when they were over 6 months. Cunningham and Sloper recommend visits every four weeks, since there was no difference at a year between babies who were visited once every two weeks and babies who were visited once every six weeks, and those families who were visited every six weeks would have liked more visits. Early intervention could be provided either through specialist advisers visiting the Down's baby and her family or by involving the parents and child in some form of specialist pre-school care. What is important is that this help is provided early, preferably before the baby is 6 months old.

Initially the Down's baby may give the appearance of being undemanding and easy. But to leave the baby alone at this time is to miss opportunities which could be spent giving the baby attention and stimulation. This time will coincide with the parents trying to come to terms with the handicap and careful, sensitive support is crucial. The parents need to be shown that their baby is developing. It is useful if they can observe developmental tests being given, so that they can become increasingly aware of just what their baby is doing, and what things are just beyond her. This will give them ideas of how to play with her. They need someone who can answer their questions honestly and sensitively.

There are several schemes available providing help and support for parents of handicapped children, and many of these are well suited to the needs of Down's syndrome children and their parents. For example, the Education of the Developmentally Young (EDY) project started by the Hester Adrian Research Centre at Manchester University was designed to teach those working with young handicapped children the skills for modifying the behaviours of these children (e.g. McBrien, 1981; Farrell, 1982). Home-based support is widely available through the Portage project which began in Wisconsin in 1969. This involves a trained person visiting the family at frequent intervals and working with the parents and child. During these visits, the parents and the Portage visitor agree on what skills the child needs to acquire next and how the parents can achieve this by working with the child each day (e.g. Daly et al., 1985).

A number of the studies discussed in chapter 5 suggest that the Down's baby and young child take longer to process information than the normal child. Compared with normal babies and children, Down's babies and children need to look at objects for longer in order to recognize them; they spend longer listening to one thing before listening to something else; and they are slower to smile and laugh. This has implications for how adults should interact with them. The Down's baby and child need to be given time in which to respond. Others must wait and fit in with her behaviour to a greater extent than is necessary with the normal child. Parents should be helped to make their behaviour contingent on the baby's behaviour, so that the baby is the one who is directing the speed with which things happen. This is particularly important for communication. Unlike the normal child, the Down's child in her second year is not so attracted to the sound of her mother's voice. Parents need to be helped to talk clearly, slowly and simply to their Down's child, repeating phrases and leaving longer gaps between utterances than they might otherwise do (Glenn and Cunningham, 1983). These same authors also suggest that, because Down's children seem to be especially attracted to nursery rhymes, the possibility of using rhymes to teach words should be explored.

A further problem for the Down's child seems to be in relating separate pieces of information together. For example, there is some suggestion from Morss's (1983, 1985) studies that the Down's child does not build on her previous experience, in that on one occasion she may understand particular things about objects and yet, on a later occasion, she may appear to have forgotten this. Just because normal children seem to build on what they have previously learned, it cannot be assumed that this will be the case with the Down's child. Tasks need to be repeated and, when a new skill is about to develop which relies on several earlier skills, the Down's child may need to be reminded of these earlier skills. All this requires that parents are given clear information about how developments at one age are related to or are pre-requisite for developments at a later age. This also has implications for people who are carrying out assessments. The Down's child should be assessed over a period of time, since her performance at any one time may be unreliable. Another example is that she seems to have difficulty in combining what she knows about people with what she knows about objects. If the people working with the Down's child are aware of these problems they can be sensitive to ways of helping her.

Nursery or playgroup opportunities are important for Down's children. There should be the choice of attending groups organized for non-handicapped children as well as specialist groups. In the past, there has been a tendency to put all Down's children with other children who are thought to be mentally handicapped. However, the range of ability amongst children with Down's syndrome is large and, because of this, it is crucial that each child's pre-school or school placement is decided on the basis of her particular capabilities. Educational placement must not be based on the stereotyped view of Down's syndrome. Recent research has demonstrated that the abilities of the Down's child have been underestimated in the past, and their ultimate potential is not yet known. With more opportunities for early intervention it can no longer be assumed that these children are necessarily best placed in special schools for the mentally handicapped. Many Down's children will benefit from attending schools for the non-handicapped and this should be encouraged. Only when it is felt that the needs of the Down's child and the mainstream children would be better met if the Down's child attended a special school should such a transfer be arranged. Before implementing such a transfer, the possibility of modifying the mainstream school should be explored fully.

Teachers who are working with Down's children must be aware that these children may take longer to make sense of particular tasks. Also, they must be aware of the possibility that Down's children do not incorporate old skills into new skills in the same way as non-handicapped children. Down's children must be given more opportunities to rehearse skills which are prerequisite for later ones, and to experience the relationship between different pieces of information. All this requires that teachers design teaching programmes for individual children, taking particular account of each child's educational needs and abilities. The increasing use of curricula which specify detailed objectives for each child (e.g. Ainscow and Tweddle, 1979) should meet this need.

Above all, it must not be assumed that these children are as incapable as has been believed in the past. Such expectations can be self-fulfilling and detrimental to the child and her family.

## *The autistic child*

The implications of the studies for parents and teachers of autistic children are less clear than for the other handicaps. This is mainly because of the complexity of the condition, our lack of understanding as to the actual nature of the handicap and the enormous range of ability of individuals with autism, from those with a severe mental handicap to those who can succeed in higher education.

Many children will not be diagnosed as autistic until the age of 2 or 3 years. Before this diagnosis is made, parents and specialists may feel that something is wrong with the child but be uncertain as to the actual diagnosis. Because of this, any pre-school facilities must be especially sensitive to the particular needs of the individual child.

One of the main problems facing anyone wanting to help the autistic child is knowing what to work on. Should the emphasis be on modifying behaviours which seem to get in the way of the child developing behaviours which might be of greater use to her, or should the strategy be to take these restricting behaviours into account when trying to develop a new skill? For example, should the aim be to make her more accepting of change in the first instance, or should the aim be to adjust situations to take account of her dislike of change? It is quite clear that it is possible to change at least some aspects of the autistic child's behaviour. For example, Tiegerman and Primavera (1984) showed that the autistic child's apparent lack of interest in what other people are doing could be modified. This is encouraging, although it is not reported whether the changes which occurred generalized to other situations. Generalization of behaviour is often limited in autistic children, and parents and teachers need to take this into account.

Rather than deciding in favour of either modifying the autistic child's behaviour or modifying the situation, an alternative approach is to make use of both, as appropriate. Some of the autistic child's behaviours may be particularly resistant to modification and, where possible, the teaching situation should be adjusted accordingly. For example, the autistic child's environment and teaching routine should be well structured (e.g. Bartak and Rutter, 1976) to minimize the number of changes to which the autistic child is exposed. If changes are necessary, they should be introduced gradually, rather than attempting to alter the autistic child's dislike of change. Other behaviours may seem to be particularly handicapping and restricting and the feasibility of modifying them should be explored. For example, wherever possible autistic children should be taught some form of communication, whether oral or manual. Behavioural methods, using immediate and relevant rewards, such as food, and applied by people familiar to the child can be successful. Each task needs to be broken down into tiny steps, and the autistic child taken through step by step, with the adult ensuring at each point that the autistic child is paying attention.

Autistic children seem to have little understanding of the reciprocal nature of social interchanges. They do not seem to have picked up the unspoken rules of social interaction. The Mirenda et al. study (1983) demonstrates that even able autistic children do not seem to adjust their non-verbal behaviour to the situation in the same way as normal children. A study to explore the possibility of modifying the autistic child's non-verbal behaviour during social interactions would be valuable.

It has also been shown that autistic children tend to look at different parts of the human face when recognizing people compared with non-autistic children. It seems important for people who are working with autistic children to be aware of such differences.

It is quite clear from the studies that autistic children generally take very little notice of people and social situations, although many show recognition of familiar people. It seems unlikely that this can be changed substantially, and so any teaching which is attempted needs to take account of this. Ideally, each autistic child should have the opportunity to form long term relationships with one or two teachers. In certain situations an autistic child's inability to imitate what others are doing can be overcome by taking the child through the action herself, rather than expecting her to copy what the adult is doing. In situations where it is possible, it makes sense to try to teach the autistic child in as impersonal a way as possible. Autistic children often show great interest in and competence at computer-type games. Their ability to interact with machines should be exploited, since this is a medium through which they can be taught more effectively than by traditional classroom methods. Other islets of ability should be made use of in the teaching situation wherever appropriate.

The choice of school will be between a mainstream school, a special school catering for a range of handicaps and a special school for autistic children. There are advantages and disadvantages to each of these. Mainstream education will provide the more able autistic child with valuable social opportunities. However, it is crucial that non-specialist teachers, whether in mainstream education, or in special schools catering for children with a variety of handicaps, are alerted to the characteristics of autistic children. For example, that autistic children's actual ability on key school subjects, such as computation and reading, may appear to be much better than it actually is because they utilize good memory for mechanical arithmetic and recall of written words. Similarly, non-specialist teachers must recognize and accept autistic children's need to have collections of objects, such as stones, with which to fiddle. There may also be difficulties for the autistic child coping with the frequently changing classroom displays and reorganizing of furniture, which are a particular characteristic of mainstream primary classrooms.

The main advantage of special schools catering solely for autistic children is that the teachers will be aware of the characteristics of autism and can adjust the system accordingly. However, because of the relatively low incidence of autism, many of these schools are residential, ranging from full-time residential to weekly boarding. Residential schools provide needed relief for families who cannot cope with the child at home. They will help accustom those autistic young people, particularly in adolescence, who will be unable to live in the community, to living away from home. However, the transition between home and school is likely to be difficult and far more disruptive when the child is residential than when the child attends school on a daily basis and lives at home. If the child does need to board, and is not fully residential, then a great effort must be made for the parents and the teachers to keep in close contact. The autistic child's preference for routines and the environment staying constant means that she is very likely to fail to generalize what she has learned in one setting to another setting, unless the conditions in the two settings are fairly similar. It is therefore vital that the parents and the teachers communicate closely with one another about the child's development and the ways in which they are working with the child, such as ways of dealing with particular behaviour. Weekly boarding may be a useful way of keeping the child in contact with her home environment, provided that the family can manage at weekends and during the holidays.

## Support for the parents of handicapped children

All parents need support at one time or another, and some families will need more help than others. Parents who have a handicapped child are no exception, but there may be times when they are particularly vulnerable, and there may be certain sorts of help which will be especially useful to them.

Support is especially important when the parents are first told that their child has a handicap. Help at this time can be beneficial to both the parents and the child. Parents who receive sensitive support are more likely to be able to accept the child and as a result are more likely to be less distressed and more attentive and positive towards their baby than parents who are not helped through the early days. The opportunity to talk with parents of a similarly handicapped child at this time may be especially helpful.

No two familes are likely to react in exactly the same way to the news that their child is handicapped. However, the study by Cunningham et al. (1984), on how parents are told that their baby has Down's syndrome, suggests that some ways may cause less distress to the parents than others. Although this paper is specifically concerned with Down's syndrome, its recommendations are relevant to other handicaps. It is clear that, ideally, the model service described in this paper, or something similar, should be available. Sadly, the paper demonstrates that even though such a policy may be introduced it may be difficult to maintain. Changes in the junior medical staff during the course of this study led to a lapse in the model service, and dissatisfaction on the part of those parents who did not receive the model service. How parents are first told is very important, and the adoption of such procedures really should be given priority.

In the model service described in the Cunningham et al. paper, the parents were told in a direct way and were given a balanced viewpoint. However, as well as pointing out to parents how variable handicapped children are, parents need to be given a realistic description. They also need to be told about possible problems which may arise, such as feeding difficulties in Down's babies (e.g. Berry et al., 1981).

An implication of giving parents a description which is well informed and realistic is that the person who tells the parents needs to know about the handicap and have personal experience of how such children develop. They need to have had some specialist training. All of this requires that a procedure is set up for telling parents, and that it is followd. As personnel change, the new members of the team need to have the procedure explained to them and any necessary training should be provided.

One of the features of the model service outlined by Cunningham et al. was that it provided support for the parents after they were first told. A specialist health visitor was available to see them at any time and visited them regularly at home. Support for families is essential. After the model service was introduced, 11 Down's babies were born. The parents of seven were told in accordance with the procedure and all were satisfied. For the other four the procedure was not followed, and of these, two families abandoned the baby in the hospital. Since one of the clearest practical implications to come out of the studies on Down's syndrome is that the Down's child who lives at home, even if only for the first few years, develops much further than the child who is institutionalized from the beginning, it is crucial from the point of view of the child's development that she should be brought up in her own home. Thus, if the way in which parents are told about the diagnosis affects the likelihood of them bringing up the child themselves, this is yet another reason why a general policy should be adopted.

The parents may have to come to terms with particular aspects of their child's handicap: for example, that she will never see them; that she will never be able to hear them talk to her; that she will never walk; or that she may not attend a mainstream school. This adjustment may be very difficult for many parents and take a long time. It is essential that support services are set up and parents informed about them so that when they need help they know how to get it. It would be preferable if parents are able to gain the confidence of one or two particular people, so that when they need help they do not have to approach strangers. It is unfortunate in this respect that the recommendation of the Warnock Report for a 'named person' was not adopted in the 1981 Education Act (see p. 156).

Support in the form of help and information is necessary. The parents of the cerebral palsied children that Hewett studied illustrate this well. These parents made it clear that they could have been given more help. A number of the comments indicated that they would like professionals to show a greater awareness of the sort of things which would help their child and the family, and which would be appropriate for her. Some of the aids which were provided were inappropriate or impractical, like walking aids which were too heavy or chairs which were too big for the child to get on to. Parents also had suggestions of equipment which would be useful, like a tray which could fit on to a wheelchair with holes in which a cup, a bowl and toys could be fitted.

All this points to a need for a greater exchange of ideas between the people who care for the child and the people who make the equipment.

Parents need information. They need to be given as realistic a picture as possible of their child. In the case of Down's syndrome the old stereotype view must be avoided. These parents need to know that there is no simple relationship between the physical features of Down's syndrome and mental ability. They need to know that their Down's child will do many of the things that a normal child does. However, the view must be balanced. Parents should also be informed about problems which may arise in the future. For example, a number of Down's children have hearing difficulties and the child's hearing should be checked regularly. Poor hearing will exacerbate language difficulties and if something can be done it needs to be given priority. Parents of Down's children should also be made aware of the major sorts of health problem that these children have, especially those that can be fatal in the first year or two (notably respiratory diseases), so that immediate treatment can be obtained.

The parents of autistic children need to be given as clear information as is possible with such a complex and poorly understood handicap, and specialists should share their uncertainties about its actual nature. They should make it clear that the original view that parents caused the autistic behaviour by their treatment of the child is outdated and wrong. Parents need to be helped to try to accept that it may be impossible to change certain aspects of their child's behaviour. Autism is a handicap which disrupts social interaction in a way that many other handicaps do not. It must be all the more distressing for the parents and close family and friends. This will be further magnified by the fact that the incidence of autism is so small. The parents may not know of any other parents with autistic children and the general public may show less understanding than of more frequent handicaps.

Information should also be given to the parents about things which may happen as their child gets older. For example, parents of autistic children should be warned of the possibility that their child may start to have fits in adolescence. This sort of information could help parents to be more prepared for such an occurrence.

Particularly careful support may be needed for the parents of deaf children if it is to be recommended that they use a sign language. The majority of these parents will be able to hear, and the idea that their child may have difficulties communicating with them through spoken language must be particularly sad. They may be resistant to using signing and need a great deal of support, as well as information about the pros and cons of signing.

Parents need to be able to leave their handicapped child with someone else, for example, an experienced babysitter or a day centre, so that they can have some relief from their child. All parents need to have breaks from their children, and this may be very difficult to arrange in the case of a child who is handicapped. Parents may feel extremely hesitant at leaving their child in the care of anyone else unless they can be absolutely sure that they will be able to cope. A number of special schools and clubs for families with handicapped children organize babysitting by an approved group of people, and these should be encouraged.

Emotional support for parents of severely handicapped children who are keeping their children at home is an overlooked area. Yet it is quite clear from the literature that the attitudes of the parents of such children and the sorts of environment they provide for their child play a crucial role in their child's development, both intellectual and emotional. It is also quite clear from the literature that these families are often under a great deal of strain. For example, Pringle and Fiddes report that at least one-quarter of their 79 families with a thalidomide damaged or similarly handicapped child were living under overtly stressful circumstances: three sets of parents were divorced; two fathers were dead; four parents were receiving psychiatric help; two of the children were illegitimate and in care, and four legitimate children were also in care; three fathers were unemployed; and two fathers were in prison. Given that these parents are saving the authorities the cost of residential care, it seems right that more money should be available to help these parents care for their children at home. The parents of many physically handicapped children feel that more help could be provided in the early years. Once the child is receiving some form of education many more opportunities arise for the parents to talk to other people. It is in the period before this that more support needs to be made available.

All parents of handicapped children need to have the opportunity to discuss their children with other people, and here groups of parents with similarly handicapped children can be useful. The discovery that other people experience the same difficulties can be a great comfort, and other parents may have found ways of overcoming similar problems. It is encouraging that parent support groups are becoming much more common, often organized around useful facilities such as toy libraries, holiday play schemes and babysitting arrangements.

It is quite clear that a wide variety of support is needed for the parents of handicapped children. There is no single sort of support that all families need. Rather, different families will have different needs, and the same family's needs will change over time. Some families will seek out help, others will feel embarrassed to do so. Some will willingly accept support whilst others will reject any sort of offer. All people involved in supporting families with a handicapped child need to be extremely sensitive to the state of each family, whenever they seek support or it is offered to them.

## Changing attitudes

Handicapped people are part of society and able-bodied members of society should have a responsibility towards them. Many of the studies of handicapped children should serve to lessen the stereotyped and stigmatized view that many people in society have of the handicapped. The outcomes of these studies need to be made as widely available to the public as possible, so that people can understand more about handicap.

This may aid the acceptance of the handicapped by society. The parents of cerebral palsied children interviewed by Hewett wanted other people to take an interest, and not just to stare when they were out with their child. Hewett makes the point that society at one level pressures the handicapped to deny their disability, and on another level refuses to acknowledge that they are people. For example, society generally supports integration; it tells parents to treat their handicapped baby as though she were normal, and it encourages the handicapped to live as normal a life as possible. On the other hand, many members of society are outraged and somewhat disgusted when two physically handicapped people want to get married (e.g. *Like Other People*, 1972, Mental Health Film Council). In conversations, too, the handicapped person may not be treated as an individual, with questions being addressed to whoever she is with, as epitomized by the radio series entitled *Does he take sugar?*

Individual members of society ideally should make a positive effort to find out more about the handicapped. Another example of society's general denial of handicap is the emphasis which has existed for some time, and which is only gradually changing, on the deaf person learning spoken language. One of the objections in the past to sign language for the deaf has been that this will isolate the deaf person from the hearing community. This is a weak objection since the spoken language skills of the majority of deaf people are so poor as to isolate them anyway. Also, in their social lives, deaf adults mix more with one another than with hearing adults. It is the hearing members of society who are of the opinion that the deaf are missing a great deal and that everything should be done to encourage their participation within society as a whole by learning spoken language. An alternative is that people who can hear should learn to sign. Unfortunately, the deaf are a minority group, and it is unlikely that many people would be prepared to learn a language which they may never use. This is an extreme example, but it illustrates that, although society acknowledges the handicapped at one level, it is not prepared to make many adjustments towards them. Society needs to become much more aware of the position of the handicapped from the handicapped person's point of view, rather than looking at the situation from the point of view of the majority. Society needs to consider what the handicapped need.

# 8

# Some theoretical implications
## of the studies

## Introduction

This chapter considers what implications the development of handicapped children has for our understanding of development in general. The aim is not to present a new theory of development but rather to point to some factors which any complete account of development must be able to explain. The study of handicapped children's development provides an important way of examining our general understanding of development and of indicating inadequacies and limitations of existing theoretical accounts of developmental processes.

How may the development of handicapped children relate to the development of non-handicapped children? Five types of relationships have been outlined by Walker and Crawley (1983): delayed; abnormal; compensatory; absent; and normal. Delayed development is simply slower development than in the normal child, but the same stages are passed through and the same processes involved, although the handicapped child may ultimately reach a less advanced stage. By abnormal development, Walker and Crawley are referring to situations when the process of development is different from normal and the resulting behaviours or developments are not seen in normal children. In compensatory development, development takes a different route from that taken by normal children, although the end point is the same. When a development is absent, the handicapped child fails to develop in this particular area. Finally, aspects of the handicapped child's development may be normal, and develop within the range of variation reported for non-handicapped children. The compensatory type of development is of particular interest from the point of view of theory, since it may question existing theoretical assumptions about how a development comes about. Of course, within any handicap any or all of the five relationships to normal development may occur, since the handicap may affect different areas of development in different ways.

Let us look next at the theoretical implications which arise from each handicap considered in this book in turn. It is important to bear in mind that if a handicapped child develops differently from a non-handicapped child, it is very likely that the difference is due to the handicap. However, it may not be a direct consequence of the handicap. It may be caused by some other consequence of the handicap, for example, some restriction in the child's environment which is brought about by the handicap but which is not inevitable. All these possibilities need to be considered when examining the theoretical implications of the studies. The aim of any account of development should be to accommodate all the findings.

## The blind child

Studies of the development of blind children show quite clearly that vision makes a significant contribution to the way in which sighted children develop. Vision enables us to make sense of our environment quickly and efficiently. Sighted children integrate their different experiences at an earlier age than blind children and this gives them a head start. It is more difficult for blind children. Blind children can achieve levels of development in certain skills comparable to those of normal children. However, other aspects of their development may not reach the same levels as in sighted children. What is important from a theoretical point of view is that the child who is blind can achieve very similar developments to the child who is sighted. If vision were essential to making sense of the environment all blind children would fail to come to understand the world. For example, they would not develop an understanding of objects and people as permanent. It may be more of a struggle and take longer but, nevertheless, development can proceed successfully in the absence of vision. Study of the development of blind children makes it clear that there is not just one route to development but several.

I want to look at some particular instances of the blind child's development taking a different route from that taken by a sighted child. Consider first the development of reaching, and what it is that the child understands about objects at this stage. For a sighted child, Piagetian theory describes a series of stages which are prerequisite for reaching. In the first couple of months, the sighted baby will grasp objects which are put in her hand, and will look at objects and people and follow their movements, but she will not move her hands to grasp something that she sees, nor will she look at something she is grasping. At this stage, Piaget would argue that the actions of the eyes are quite separate from the actions of the hands. The actions are repeatable and can be thought of as having a structure, or schema. At around 2 months, the sighted baby begins watching her hands and this marks the beginnings of integration between the hand and the eye, the eye comes to see what the hand grasps, and the hand comes to grasp what the eye sees. This process of schemas coming together continues and can be seen in behaviours such as the baby watching her hands and glancing back and forwards between her hand and an object. At about 5 months, the sighted baby will see an object, lift up her hand and reach for it: the visual-motor schemas of eye-hand (looking at your hand) and eye-object (looking at an object) are integrated with the tactual-motor schema of the hand (grasping an object in your hand).

At the stage when she begins to reach for an object, she will stop reaching if the toy is completely covered up in front of her, although she will probably reach if a part of the toy remains in view. By around 8 or 9 months, the sighted baby will be able to retrieve a toy which has been completely hidden under a cloth. This development comes about because the child has begun to experiment with what she knows; she has begun to use familiar schemas in new situations, rather than merely repeating her existing schemas and discovering things by chance. This stage marks the point at which Piaget would argue that the sighted baby has some understanding of the permanence of objects in that she will search for an object which has been covered up. Towards the end of the first year a sighted baby, who is seated in a dark room, will reach out towards the sound made by an object. This demonstrates not only that she realizes that there is an object out there even though it is out of sight, but also that she realizes that the sound comes from an object. According to Piaget, for the sighted child to realize that a sound comes from an object, the visual-motor schema of eye-object must have become integrated with the auditory-motor schema of ear–object. This is likely to happen early on for the sighted child, and it has been argued that babies may be born with a capacity to locate a sound in space. The sighted child in the first few months will turn her head in the direction of a sound and locate where it comes from even though she may not initially associate particular objects with particular sounds.

Unlike the sighted child of about 6 or 7 months, the blind child does not reach out for an object which is removed from her grasp, nor will she orient towards sounds although she will listen attentively to them. A few months later the beginnings of a reach to an object which is removed can be observed in the blind child, at around the same time as she begins to turn her head towards a sound. Up until about 11 months, many blind children will reach for a toy they have been holding which is removed, but still they will not reach out when they hear a sound of something which they have not been holding. Reaching on sound cue alone usually happens first around the age of 1 year. This is much the same age as the sighted child reaches in the dark.

How does the blind child come to realize that objects exist beyond her immediate experience? From Fraiberg's (1977) observations, it seems that the experiences of holding an object and then retrieving it when it has been removed are vital. However, unlike the sighted child, the blind child has no reminder of the toy when it is removed unless of course it is making a noise, and even if it is, two pieces of evidence suggest that sounds do not come to be associated with objects for a blind child until towards the end of the first year. The first piece of evidence is that there seems to be no marked difference between the ages at which blind children reach for sound-making or soundless objects which are removed from their grasp. Second, the blind child reaches much later for objects which they have only heard, at around 12 months of age, compared with reaching for objects they have felt, at around 8 months. This evidence suggests that sound does not serve as an indicator of an object for a blind baby until she is about a year old.

Thus it seems that the blind child is initially only aware of the existence of an object through holding and feeling it. It is likely that through her experience of touching an object she comes to understand that objects are solid and tangible and this understanding leads her to search for an object when it is removed from her grasp. But this search is all within one modality. She is reaching for something she has already felt, and only knows that she has obtained it when she can feel it again. Only the tactual-motor schema of the hand is involved. This is characteristic of a much earlier stage in the sighted child, when she attempts to retrieve a dropped object not by looking for it, but by grasping after it. When the blind child begins to search for a recently removed object there is no requirement that separate schemas come together. For the blind child, it is not until the age of 8 or 9 months that the beginnings of the tactual-motor schema of the hand can be seen to be coming together with the auditory-motor schema of the ear as the child makes grasping movements when she hears the sound of an object. These schemas are fully integrated when the blind child reaches out purposefully on sound cue alone.

This integration of previously separate schemas marks a crucial step forward for the blind child. Her realization that sounds signify objects, many of which can be reached for, will guide her towards a much more active exploration of the world, and mobility.

This comparison of the development of reaching in blind and sighted children illustrates the difference between the possible routes taken by blind and sighted children. It is quite clear that the route is hazardous for the blind child, and yet the fact that most blind children succeed in the end argues strongly for the idea that this development can proceed along more than one route.

The difference in the development of reaching in blind and sighted children also highlights a role of vision in the sighted child's development. For example, vision affords an association between the tactual and auditory properties of an object, and although this association does eventually occur for the majority of blind children it takes much longer in the absence of sight.

The motor development of the young blind child illustrates this delay well. Although blind children achieve certain motor developments at the same age as sighted children, other motor developments are considerably delayed. These delayed developments are characterized as postures and movements which the child herself must initiate: for example, raising herself up on to her arms whilst lying on her stomach; getting up into a sitting position; crawling; and walking. For the sighted child, these developments seem to follow from a visual curiosity: sitting up to look around or walking towards something on the other side of the room. This same enticement is not available for the blind child. Sound does not indicate something out of reach in the same way as sight, and until the blind child discovers that sound can signify something which she can reach for and, through this, that she is surrounded by objects which can be explored, she will not be encouraged to venture out into the environment. For the sighted child, vision provides a path for mobility and other sorts of self-initiated movement, whereas for the blind child, mobility can be seen to be delayed because sound does not convey until much later the presence of things which can be contacted. Her path into self-initiated movement is different from the path taken by the sighted child.

The blind child's understanding of people and her understanding of herself in particular, as an individual amongst other individuals, further illustrates this idea of other routes for development. Blind children commonly use the third person or their own name to refer to themselves, rather than the first person. That is, they refer to themselves as other people would refer to them. Fraiberg (1977) has made extremely detailed observations of this particular phenomenon and draws parallels with other developments such as the blind child's delayed ability to recreate a situation in play, and to represent herself in play. These particular delays are not related to any cognitive impairment, occurring as they do in bright and otherwise extremely able blind children. Why is it so hard for the blind child to construct an image of herself and others?

From an early age, the sighted child has countless opportunities to experience the relationship between the different parts of her body, realizing, for example, the control she has over the action of her hands. She can see other people, the way they relate to one another and to her in space, and she will probably have the experience of seeing herself in a mirror. All these experiences are afforded by vision. The blind child cannot bring together, in the same way, all her separate experiences, tactual, auditory, kinaesthetic and so on. Fraiberg argues that for the blind child to develop an accurate self-image, amongst the images of other people, she must infer from her own experiences of herself what it is that she has in common with others and that these others themselves must also have self-images.

An alternative explanation of the difficulty that blind children have with referring correctly to themselves is that they have difficulty making sense of deictic words. These are words such as I/you and here/there whose meaning depends on the context in which they are used. Without vision, the blind child has to find another way to discover how these words are used.

Whatever the explanation for the difficulty that blind children have in referring to themselves correctly, the task is much more difficult for blind children than it is for children who can see. Blind children's route to a self-image is much harder and more perilous, with some never achieving a real understanding of themselves and others as separate individuals. But the fact that some succeed argues for an alternative route to this particular development.

A fourth area of development in which the blind child can be seen to be taking a different route from the sighted child is in language acquisition. Fraiberg compared the early stages of language amongst her blind babies with the norms for sighted children on the relevant items of the Bayley Mental Scale (Bayley, 1969). Although the blind children tended to be slightly behind the sighted children, most of them fell within the normal range. However, the blind children were especially delayed in two respects, namely reaching a vocabulary of two words and, later on, in being able to combine two words. Fraiberg argues that these items present particular difficulties for blind children. As evidence for this, she points out that the blind children were within the sighted range on an item of intermediate difficulty, that of making wants known, whereas several of the blind children were below the sighted range on the two items in question. Also, as these children get older, they do become competent language users on the whole. Fraiberg argues that these particular difficulties in reaching a vocabulary of two words, and later in combining two words, 'can be fairly examined as an impediment of blindness but one which need not have permanent effects'. Why are these two items so noticeably delayed?

The blind child is slow to reach a vocabulary of two words because she does not have the impetus afforded by vision. She has no experience of objects and people beyond her immediate space, and because her mobility is delayed she is less likely to bring herself into contact with objects further afield. The process by which the blind child comes to identify objects is much more laborious, relying on non-visual experiences. On the other hand, the blind child expresses her needs within the sighted age range, because these desires are generated from within herself: she wants to be tickled, she wants a drink and so on. Unlike the sighted child, she will not request things of which she has no experience, like a new object that a sighted child might see on the windowsill.

Why is the blind child delayed in combining two words? As with the first few words, the sighted child at this stage is describing objects she sees: she is linking people and objects with what she sees them doing, or with modifiers to describe some particular attribute of them that she sees, for example: 'allgone milk', 'byebye car' and 'big dog'. Without sight, the blind child has less access to these sorts of experience and this holds her back in producing combinations. Indeed, her first combinations are likely to be centred on herself: for example, describing what she is doing. This relates to Dunlea's (1984) observation that young blind children are delayed in realizing that words are symbols. Dunlea found that the early words of blind children tend to remain fixed to the original context in which they occur and are not initially generalized to other situations. But these difficulties are overcome. The blind child discovers what other people are doing and what they are like in other ways and she gets there in the end, producing sentences of increasing complexity. She is taking a different and more arduous route from the sighted child, but a route which is necessitated by the nature of her handicap.

## The deaf child

The opportunities for development which are afforded by sound are enormous. However, it is clear from studies of young deaf children that sound is not essential for most aspects of development. The deaf infant seems to understand about people and objects and to be able to manipulate symbols at a young age, as evidenced by her early use of signs and pretend play. Young deaf children appear to develop the necessary skills for symbolic reasoning in the absence of sound. However, it does seem as though the nature of this development may be different from that of a hearing child. The deaf child cannot use the same cues as the hearing child, and her development must necessarily take a different route.

Sound is not necessary for cognitive development in the early stages, but as the child gets older the environment becomes increasingly influential. If this environment is normally brought to the child through the medium of spoken language, the deaf child, who has no alternative means of communication, will be at a disadvantage. The provision of some alternative can overcome this. Thus there are other routes to development. Spoken language is not that crucial although some means of communication is necessary.

The study of the cognitive development of deaf children has confirmed that spoken language is not necessary for normal cognitive development to occur. However, aspects of their understanding, for example, of opposites, may be less good than that of hearing children. In the case of opposites, and also the deaf child's understanding of the words more and less, it seems that the nature of the language to which the child is exposed can influence her understanding. Thus, although spoken language is not necessary for normal cognitive development, the language of the child may influence the child's understanding. This is consistent with Vygotsky's account of the relationship between language and thought (see p. 63).

At a later stage of development, the deaf adolescent may experience difficulties in abstract reasoning. It appears that the environment, in particular the educational one, is especially crucial for the development of abstract reasoning. Although deaf adolescents attend school, their educational achievement is limited. Deafness seems to prevent them from benefiting from the school environment to the same extent as hearing children. The implication for theory is that the formal nature of school may facilitate, more than other experiences, the development of abstract reasoning.

It seems quite clear, from studies of deaf children, that some of the impetus for communication comes from within the child. The study by Feldman et al. (1978) is exciting, despite Gregory and Mogford's (1981) failure to replicate its findings. It demonstrates that at least the beginnings of communication may be child-generated. The children in this study devised their own idiosyncratic signs and used them in a relatively sophisticated way without any apparent guidance from their parents. They were not as sophisticated as their hearing contemporaries, but the fact that these children devised means of communicating highlights some of the child's contribution to the language process, which has implications for accounts of the language acquisition process. These have moved from very child orientated accounts of language acquisition towards accounts attributing a great deal to the interaction between parents and their children. These latter accounts have emphasized the importance of the parents' active interpretation of what the child is doing or saying. Perhaps theory should take greater account of the input which the child makes to the interaction. With the hearing child this is intimately bound up with the parents' contribution and is hard to disentangle.

It is clear, from the Feldman et al. study, that other speakers are important to the child's cracking of the language code since none of the deaf children developed into fluent speakers. So although theory should reflect the child's contribution, the emphasis on joint action and the parental role in interaction is also important.

Observations of deaf children of deaf signing parents can illuminate the process of language acquisition. The time that language takes to appear depends on the modality, not on the stage of development that the child has reached beyond some minimum level: if the visual modality is used, as in signing, children start to 'talk' much earlier. Unless there is something very exceptional about the abilities of deaf children born to deaf signing parents, it follows that the hearing child must have things to talk about long before she does. This clearly refutes Piaget's view that the child needs to have attained the last stage of the sensorimotor period and be able to represent objects symbolically before language is possible. Deaf signing children may have a large vocabulary by this stage, and be combining gestures. Symbolic representation, as defined by the end of the sensorimotor period, is not a prerequisite for language.

Signing children can also provide a way of identifying characteristics of the language process which are not just peculiar to spoken language. For example, early signs seem to have some equivalence to whole phrases, as do early words. Many of the first signs seem to be variants of the adult form, like baby talk. Deaf children overgeneralize the meaning of their signs just as hearing children do. Any explanations of these phenomena cannot be dependent on the modality.

## The child with a motor handicap

Theoretically, children physically handicapped from birth should provide evidence concerning the degree to which various aspects of development are dependent on motor activity. In practice the variability in the exact pattern of motor handicap which occurs in individual children makes this difficult. However, it should be possible to identify whether or not particular motor skills are necessary for particular developments by examining the development of individual children alongside their means of acting on the environment. Unfortunately, most of the studies do not give sufficient details about the individual children for this to be possible.

Several studies have found that the relationship between the physically handicapped child's motor disability and other aspects of her development, such as her cognitive development, is poor. Other factors, such as the quality of the environment, are much better indicators of the child's level of cognitive functioning than her physical handicap. This points to the relative unimportance of a physical handicap except in the sense of it having other influences on the child's circumstances and environment. But, without details about individuals, it cannot be concluded that action is not necessary for cognition, since the children in these studies can usually act on their environment in some way or other. However, it is clear that many of them are not able to act in a conventional way. We can therefore ask if any particular sort of action or experience is necessary for cognitive development.

The two most useful studies are those of Kopp and Shaperman (1973), and Gouin Décarie (1969). Gouin Décarie's study of children damaged by thalidomide at first sight suggests that for a child to be able to reach the end of Piaget's sensorimotor period, when objects can be represented in their absence, she needs to be able to bring her hands together, and be able to get her hand up to her mouth. In Piaget's account of the sensorimotor period these two behaviours represent an opportunity to coordinate previously separate schemas. If the child can bring her two hands together, she has the necessary action for the coordination of eye, hand and object. She will be able to watch objects and hold objects, and, if she can bring her hands together, she will be able to watch her hands as she holds and manipulates objects. Of course, it is possible for the coordination of eye, hand and object to occur if the child cannot bring her two hands together. However, there are several reasons why this development is more likely to happen if she can bring both hands together: any action involving both hands is more likely to occur at the front of the body and so be visible to the child; it is much harder to manipulate an object with only one hand; with two hands there are many more ways of manipulating an object and the child is more likely to attend to a spectacle if it is interesting and changing, and, even in the absence of an appropriate object, the development can occur when one of the hands holds and explores the other. In a similar way, if the child can bring her hand up to her mouth this provides the opportunity for her to coordinate the holding of an object with the mouthing of an object. Her hand can bring an object she is holding up to her mouth for her to suck on it. This study of thalidomide damaged children therefore suggests that the opportunity for the coordination of schemas such as these may be necessary for the child to develop to the end of the sensorimotor period. However, even this study is not clear. Although the two children who had not yet reached the end of the sensorimotor period could not achieve either of these behaviours, they were also younger than the age at which the end of the sensorimotor stage is reached by non-handicapped children.

The study by Kopp and Shaperman suggests that being able to bring the hands together and get a hand to the mouth may not in fact be crucial. The child in this study had no arms or legs and yet had obviously reached the end of the sensorimotor period. Unfortunately, he was not formally tested until three months after an artificial arm was fitted, and this may have provided him with the necessary opportunities. But, with one arm, he still could not have experienced the bringing together of two hands, so it seems unlikely that this is necessary. This case study again raises the question as to what is necessary for cognitive development. Kopp and Shaperman's child did have ways of experiencing his environment: he could roll over from 5 months, and by a year could push a ball along the ground. These two observations show that by a year separate schemas had become coordinated. Presumably at 5 months he was watching objects, demonstrating the schema of eye-object, and as he rolled around he must have come into contact with objects and furniture, a roll-object schema. By a year, he was showing that he had coordinated his looking schema with his rolling schema by pushing a ball around. Thus even this child, with relatively few opportunities to interact with his environment motorically, had sufficient to discover ways in which he could act on the environment.

Are we to conclude therefore that provided the child has some ability to interact with her environment she will develop cognitively, at least in the first few years? Can we say anything about the sort of interaction and the amount of interaction which is necessary? The cases examined suggest that the nature of interaction is not especially important provided that there is the opportunity for separate behaviours to become coordinated. The conclusion has to be that cognitive development can occur in the presence of very little motor activity. However, the question of whether development can occur in the complete absence of motor activity remains unanswered and is perhaps unanswerable.

What are the implications for theory? Piaget's theory of cognitive development stresses the role of action. The studies certainly do not negate the role of action, although it is quite clear that cognitive development can occur when the child has very few ways of acting on the environment. On the other hand, they do not disprove the converse, that cognitive development cannot occur in the absence of action. They also make clear that a variety of different types of action seem to give the child a way into cognition. There is no one particular route. Provided that the child has sufficient movement to bring her into contact with her environment, and provided that some of these behaviours can become linked together to provide higher order behaviours, then we see developments. But it is unclear what would be the limiting case, the minimum necessary for development to occur.

At this point we have to reconcile two things. One is the conclusion that very minimal action on the environment can foster cognitive development. The other is that many physically handicapped children, even those who do not have any known brain damage, appear to be impaired cognitively. The first thing to notice is that the evidence on the role of action has come from studies of very young children, mainly children of 2 years and under. It may be that the sorts of experience which are available to these children are sufficient for the sorts of development which occur in this period. Later developments may depend on other experiences, experiences of which the physically handicapped child is deprived. Some of the evidence supports this type of explanation. The physical handicaps of these children will lead them to experience many deprivations. Some of them will be institutionalized and others, even though at home, will live in relatively impoverished environments because of their inability to get about and their resulting isolation. Thus, although they may be quite capable of acting on their environment in various ways, the opportunities that they have for this may be severely diminished. Such a deprivation may account for the discrepancy between the relatively normal early developments of some of these children, and their subsequently impaired developments.

Such factors need to be taken into account in any valid theory of the process of development. The opportunities for interaction which are afforded the child, as well as the manner of her interactions, are of crucial importance to development.

Similar conclusions are reached when other aspects of development are considered, for example social development. Gouin Décarie (1969) demonstrated that substitute channels are available to the child damaged by thalidomide, and that through these channels she can demonstrate some of the same sorts of social behaviour as a child who can use the more conventional channels, provided that the environment offers appropriate experiences. If the environment is deprived by, for example, not providing the opportunity for the child to form stable relationships, then her social development may deviate from the norm. But, if the environment provides appropriate experiences, the child will find a way to express herself and form relationships. In other words, the conventional routes are not the only ones.

## The child with Down's syndrome

One of the main reasons for examining the development of children with Down's syndrome is to try to answer the question of whether these children's development is like that of normal children, but slowed down, or whether they actually develop differently by means of different processes. Support for either position would be of value theoretically. If development is delayed, then Down's children would provide a way of looking at developmental processes in slow motion. If their development follows a different course, then any adequate theory of development must be able to explain the differences. Unfortunately, the studies of Down's children which have been considered fail to provide a clear answer to the question. Some researchers argue that their data support the delay position, while others argue for the difference position. In some cases, it may be that the behaviour that is being looked at is achieved later by Down's children than by normal children and that the behaviour has achieved by a different route from that usually followed by normal children. Unless the development of particular abilities is followed in detail it will continue to be unclear whether the development of Down's children is different or just delayed. It is noteworthy that Morss's (1983, 1985) studies, which looked in detail at the emergence of a specific ability, support the difference model. Morss's studies question the Piagetian model of sensorimotor development. Down's children do not use their past experiences of errors and successes in the same way as normal children. They do not build on previous achievements. The processes involved must be different, although in a way which is as yet unclear.

Further theoretical implications come from those studies which have examined the relationships between a variety of different behaviours in the Down's child. For example, Moore et al. (1977) found that the Down's child's language ability, as assessed by the mean length of utterance, was related to the understanding that she had of objects, and it was not related to either chronological age or to mental age. This supports the view that language emerges out of the child's knowledge and understanding of objects. In normal children this relationship is harder to see because their chronological and mental ages are very similar. The Down's child provides a way of separating out various different developments which in the normal child usually develop side by side.

The study by Crawley and Spiker (1983) is interesting too, since it emphasizes the role of the parent. Children who played in harmony with their mothers were more competent than those who did not. Development does not happen in isolation. This, together with other studies, supports the view that the social context in which development occurs is of vital importance. Crawley and Spiker's study also points to the importance of individual differences, and for the need for the behaviours of the adult and the child to adjust to each other in order for development to be optimized. Similarly, all the studies concerning the consequences of institutionalization indicate that any theory of development must take account of the environment.

## The autistic child

The theoretical implications which follow from studies of autistic children are far less clear than those which arise from the previous handicaps. The reason is that the primary problems underlying autism are not known. A survey of recent literature shows that, among researchers in the UK alone, some consider the primary problem to be cognitive (e.g. Rutter, 1983; Baron-Cohen et al., 1985), some consider the primary problem to be social (e.g. Tinbergen and Tinbergen, 1983), and at least one suggests that the primary problem may be connative (Hobson, 1986). A consequence of this disagreement is that it is not possible to trace the course of autistic development forwards from a known starting point. This is very different from the situation with the other handicaps, especially the sensory handicaps. As a result the aim of much of the research with autistic children is to try to make sense of their behaviour at various stages of development, and from this to infer the underlying causes of autistic behaviour. It is therefore not possible to make comparisons between the course of normal children's development and the course of autistic children's development. The implications which the study of autism has for understanding development are therefore different in kind from the implications which have arisen from the other handicaps discussed in this book.

Perhaps the most striking implication which the study of autism has for our understanding of development is to demonstrate the extent of our ignorance about the prerequisites for and processes underlying normal development. In particular, it demonstrates how little is known, after many years of research, about the foundations of human behaviour, and about the complex interactions between different aspects of behaviour in the course of development.

Take, for example, the question of face recognition ability. It is clear that the ability to recognize familiar faces is essential for normal social development. It is also clear that the ability to recognize familiar faces and to form social relationships is critically important for cognitive, linguistic and other non-social developments. If a baby cannot recognize her parents, bonding will not occur, and the baby will lack the important early relationships in the context of which so much learning normally occurs. The autistic-like behaviour of some blind children who, for one reason or another, fail to compensate for their lack of vision, illustrates this point clearly. Theoretically, therefore, impaired face recognition could explain a great deal of autistic behaviour. In addition, the experimental findings of both Langdell (1978) and Hobson (1986) suggest that abnormalities of face processing do exist in autism. However, even if an inability to process faces normally is of critical importance in the genesis of autistic behaviour, we cannot say whether or not this is a primary problem. The reason for this is that the prerequisites and processes underlying normal face recognition are not agreed. Familiar face recognition is thought by some to be an innate species-specific ability. Others consider it to be a highly developed aspect of visual processing in general, its remarkable development in the normal person being accounted for in terms of an inbuilt motivation to attend to faces. Depending on which of these viewpoints one accepts, impaired face recognition ability in autism may reflect a deficit in the visual processing of social objects as Langdell suggests, or a high level cognitive deficit in visual processing such as Rutter might suggest, or a motivational abnormality which would relate to Hobson's views. The implication is for more research with both normal and handicapped children, specifically directed towards understanding the processes of development.

The study of the development of autistic children has a second implication for our understanding of development. The development of autistic children is very uneven. This has implications for our understanding of how different areas of development relate to one another. The development of autistic children in one area may be quite normal, or even superior to that found in non-handicapped children, whilst development in another area may be impaired. This range of development can even be seen within single areas of development. Consider language development in the autistic child. Spoken language development may be absent in cases of autism where there is overall mental retardation. However, language does develop in some more able autistic children after an initial delay. Once speech begins to appear in these children, articulation may quite rapidly become normal. Correct grammar develops more slowly, following a course of distinctively abnormal errors. However, this can eventually become entirely normal. On the other hand, vocabulary and semantics are never entirely normal. Some autistic people do acquire large vocabularies of mainly concrete substantive words, but idiomatic speech, allusion and metaphor are never fully achieved. Similarly, the way in which autistic people use language and non-verbal aspects of speech (prosody) to convey meaning remain abnormal in all cases. It seems very likely that more able autistic children learn language, after an initial delay, using compensatory mechanisms. Thus within a single area of development it is possible to identify all five of Walker and Crawley's (1983) types of relationship between the development of normal children and the development of handicapped children (see p. 179). To attempt to draw out possible theoretical implications of such uneven development is beyond the scope of this discussion. However, it is clear that the dissociations (or partial dissociations) between, for example, the ability to learn concrete, substantive words and the ability to learn idiomatic speech, and between the relative ease with which articulation is achieved, compared with the persistent abnormality of prosody, have potential value for understanding the processes underlying the acquisition of spoken language.

A final theoretical implication for our understanding of development arises from a consideration of the high abilities of some autistic children. These children may have intact senses and motor development, high non-verbal intelligence, a reasonable vocabulary and normal grammar, excellent rote and associate memory and even superior musical or drawing ability, yet aspects of their behaviour are still bizarre. It is clear that some necessary prerequisites are lacking. When, eventually, the fundamental behaviour deficits in autism are identified, the implications for the necessary and sufficient prerequisites for the normal development of behaviour will be immense.

## Conclusions

It is crucial that theories of development should pay attention to the development of handicapped children. Study of these children can clarify the processes underlying development. They can point to other routes to development, and they can identify features of development which may have been overlooked in the study of non-handicapped children. It is only by studying the development of handicapped children and of non-handicapped children that a realistic theory can be constructed. This is a task for the future, but by acknowledging the value of studies of handicapped children I hope to encourage more research and theorizing in this area. If theory does take account of the development of handicapped children then not only will the development of non-handicapped children be better understood, but practitioners working with handicapped children will have a much sounder base from which to begin.

# References

Abercrombie, M. L. J. 1964: *Perceptual and Visuo-Motor Disorders in Cerebral Palsy.* Little Club Clinics in Developmental Medicine No. 11. London: Spastics Society and Heinemann.

Adelson, E. and Fraiberg, S. 1974: Gross motor development in infants blind from birth. *Child Development,* 45, 114-26.

Ainscow, M. and Tweddle, D. A. 1979: *Preventing Classroom Failure: An Objectives Approach.* Chichester: Wiley.

Ainsworth, M. D. S. and Wittig, B. A. 1969: Attachment and exploratory behavior of one-year-olds in a strange situation. In B. M. Foss (ed.), *Determinants of Infant Behaviour,* 4. London: Methuen.

Anderson, E. M. and Spain, B. 1977: *The Child with Spina Bifida.* London: Methuen.

August, G. J., Stewart, M. A. and Tsai, L. 1981: The incidence of cognitive disabilities in the siblings of autistic children. *British Journal of Psychiatry,* 138, 416-22.

Babson, S. G. and Benson, R. C. 1971: *Management of High-risk Pregnancy and Intensive Care of the Neonate.* St Louis Missouri: Mosby.

Bach-y-Rita, P. 1972: *Brain Mechanisms in Sensory Substitution.* London: Academic Press.

Bancroft, D. M. R. 1985: 'The Development of Temporal Reference: A Study of Children's Language'. Unpublished Ph.D. thesis, University of Nottingham.

Baron, J. 1972: Temperament profile of children with Down's syndrome. *Developmental Medicine and Child Neurology,* 14, 640-3.

Baron-Cohen, S., Leslie, A. M. and Frith, U. 1985: Does the autistic child have a theory of mind? *Cognition,* 21, 37–46.

Baron-Cohen, S. In press: Autism and symbolic play. *British Journal of Developmental Psychology.*

Barraga, N. (ed.) 1970: *Visual Efficiency Scale.* Louisville, Kentucky: American Printing House for the Blind.

Bartak, L. and Rutter, M. 1976: Differences between mentally retarded and normally intelligent autistic children. *Journal of Autism and Childhood Schizophrenia,* 6, 109-20.

Bartak, L., Rutter, M. and Cox, A. 1975: A comparative study of infantile autism and specific developmental receptive language disorder. 1. The children. *British Journal of Psychiatry,* 126, 127-45.

Bax, M. C. O. 1964: Terminology and classification of cerebral palsy. *Developmental Medicine and Child Neurology*, 6, 295-7.

Bayley, N. 1969: *Bayley Scales of Infant Development*. New York: Psychological Corporation.

Bayley, N., Rhodes, L. and Gooch, B. 1966: A comparison of the growth and development of institutionalized and home-reared mongoloids. A follow-up study. *California Mental Health Research Digest*, 4, 104-5.

Behrmann, M. (ed.) 1984: *Handbook of Microcomputers in Special Education*. Windsor: NFER/Nelson.

Bell, S. M. 1970: The development of the concept of the object as related to infant-mother attachment. *Child Development*, 41, 291-311.

Bellugi, U. 1980: Clues from the similarities between signed and spoken language. In U. Bellugi and M. Studdert-Kennedy (eds), *Signed and Spoken Language: Biological Constraints on Linguistic Form*. Berlin: Verlag Chemie.

Bellugi, U. and Klima, E. S. 1972: The roots of language in the sign talk of the deaf. *Psychology Today*, 6, 61-76.

Bemporad, J. R. 1979: Adult recollections of a formerly autistic child. *Journal of Autism and Developmental Disorders*, 9, 179-98.

Benda, C. E. 1949: *Mongolism and Cretinism*. New York: Grune and Stratton.

Berg, J. M., Crome, L. and France, N. E. 1960: Congenital cardiac malformations in mongolism. *British Heart Journal*, 22, 331-46.

Berger, J. and Cunningham, C. C. 1981: Early development of social interactions in Down's syndrome and non-handicapped infants. In A. Teirikko, R. Vihavainen and T. Nenonen (eds), *Finland Speaks. Report of the European Association for Special Education Conference: Communication and Handicap*. Helsinki, Finland: The Finnish Association for Special Education.

Berger, J. and Cunningham, C. C. 1983: Development of early vocal behaviors and interactions in Down's syndrome and nonhandicapped infant-mother pairs. *Developmental Psychology*, 19, 322-31.

Berry, P., Gunn, P. and Andrews, R. 1980: Behavior of Down syndrome infants in a strange situation. *American Journal of Mental Deficiency*, 85, 213-18.

Berry, P., Gunn, P., Andrews, R. and Price, C. 1981: Characteristics of Down syndrome infants and their families. *Australian Paediatric Journal*, 17, 40-3.

Bertenthal, B. I. and Fischer, K. W. 1978: Development of self-recognition in the infant. *Developmental Psychology*, 14, 44-50.

Bishop, D. V. M. 1983: Comprehension of English syntax by profoundly deaf children. *Journal of Child Psychology and Psychiatry*, 24, 415-34.

Blank, M. 1974: Cognitive functions of language in the preschool years. *Developmental Psychology*, 10, 229-45.

Blank, M. and Bridger, W. H. 1966: Conceptual cross-modal transfer in deaf and hearing children. *Child Development*, 37, 29-38.

Bonvillian, J. D., Orlansky, M. D. and Novak, L. L. 1983: Early sign language acquisition and its relation to cognition and motor development. In J. G. Kyle and B. Woll (eds), *Language in Sign: An International Perspective on Sign Language*. London: Croom Helm.

Bower, T. G. R. 1974: *Development in Infancy*. San Francisco: Freeman.

Bower, T. G. R. 1977: Blind babies see with their ears. *New Scientist*, 73, 255-7.

Bradford, L. J. and Hardy, W. G. (eds) 1979: *Hearing and Hearing Impairment*. New York: Grune and Stratton.

Bradshaw, J. 1975: *The Financial Needs of Children*. London: Disability Alliance.

Brask, B. H. 1970: A prevalence investigation of childhood psychosis. 16th Scandinavian Congress of Psychiatry. Cited in L. Wing (ed.) 1976: *Early Childhood Autism*. Oxford: Pergamon.

Brinkworth, R. 1975: The unfinished child: Early treatment and training for the infant with Down's syndrome. *Royal Society of Health Journal*, 95, 73-8.

Bruner, J. S. 1975: The ontogenesis of speech acts. *Journal of Child Language*, 2, 1-19.

Buckhalt, J. A., Rutherford, R. B. and Goldberg, K. E. 1978: Verbal and nonverbal interaction of mothers with their Down's syndrome and nonretarded infants. *American Journal of Mental Deficiency*, 82, 337-43.

Buckley, S. 1985: Attaining basic educational skills: Reading, writing and number. In D. Lane and B. Stratford (eds), *Current Approaches to Down's Syndrome*. London: Holt, Rinehart and Winston.

Buium, N., Rynders, J. and Turnure, J. 1974: Early maternal linguistic environment of normal and Down's syndrome language-learning children. *American Journal of Mental Deficiency*, 79, 52-8.

Burlingham, D. 1965: Some problems of ego development in blind children. *Psychoanalytic Study of the Child*, 20, 194-208.

Burlingham, D. 1979: To be blind in a sighted world. *Psychoanalytic Study of the Child*, 34, 5-30.

Cantor, G. N. and Girardeau, F. L. 1959: Rhythmic discrimination ability in mongoloid and normal children. *American Journal of Mental Deficiency*, 63, 621-5.

Cantwell, D., Baker, L. and Rutter, M. 1978: A comparative study of infantile autism and specific developmental receptive language disorder. IV. Analysis of syntax and language function. *Journal of Child Psychology and Psychiatry*, 19, 351-62.

Carr, J. 1970: Mental and motor development in young mongol children. *Journal of Mental Deficiency Research*, 14, 205-20.

Carr, J. 1975: *Young Children with Down's Syndrome*. London: Butterworth.

Carter, C. O. 1974: Clues to the aetiology of neural tube malformations. *Developmental Medicine and Child Neurology*, Supplement 32, 3-15.

Carter, G. and Jancar, J. 1983: Mortality in the mentally handicapped: A 50 year survey at the Stoke Park Group of Hospitals (1930-1980). *Journal of Mental Deficiency Research*, 27, 143-56.

Centerwall, S. A. and Centerwall, W. R. 1960: A study of children with mongolism reared in the home compared to those reared away from home. *Paediatrics*, 25, 678-85.

Chomsky, N. 1975: *Reflections on Language*. New York: Pantheon Books.

Cicchetti, D. and Pogge-Hesse, P. 1982: Possible contributions of the study of organically retarded persons to developmental theory. In E. Zigler and D. Balla (eds), *Mental Retardation: The Developmental-Difference Controversy*, Hillsdale, New Jersey: Erlbaum.

Cicchetti, D. and Schneider-Rosen, K. 1983: Theoretical and empirical considerations in the investigation of the relationship between affect and cognition in atypical populations of infants. In C. Izard, J. Kagan and R. Zajonc (eds), *Emotions, Cognition and Behaviour*. New York: Cambridge University Press.

Cicchetti, D. and Serafica, F. C. 1981: Interplay among behavioral systems: Illustrations from the study of attachment, affiliation, and wariness in young children with Down's syndrome. *Developmental Psychology*, 17, 36-49.

Cicchetti, D. and Stroufe, L. A. 1976: The relationship between affective and cognitive development in Down's syndrome infants. *Child Development*, 47, 920-9.

Cicchetti, D. and Stroufe, L. A. 1978: An organization view of affect: Illustration from the study of Down's syndrome infants. In M. Lewis and L. A. Rosenblum (eds), *The Development of Affect*. New York: Plenum.

Clark, P. and Rutter, M. 1977: Compliance and resistance in autistic children. *Journal of Autism and Childhood Schizophrenia*, 7, 33-48.

Clark, P. and Rutter, M. 1979: Task difficulty and task performance in autistic children. *Journal of Child Psychology and Psychiatry*, 20, 271-85.

Clark, P. and Rutter, M. 1981: Autistic children's responses to structure and to interpersonal demands. *Journal of Autism and Developmental Disorders*, 11, 201-17.

Clements, P. R., Bates, M. V. and Hafer, M. 1976: Variability within Down's syndrome (trisomy 21): Empirically observed sex differences in IQ. *Mental Retardation*, 14, 30-1.

Cole, M. and Scribner, S. 1974: *Culture and Thought*. New York: Wiley.

Connolly, J. A. 1977: Down's syndrome incidence: Practical and theoretical considerations. *Journal of the Irish Medical Association*, 70, 126-8.

Connolly, J. A. 1978: Intelligence levels of Down's syndrome children. *American Journal of Mental Deficiency*, 83, 193-6.

Conrad, R. 1979: *The Deaf School Child: Language and Cognitive Function*. London: Harper and Row.

Conrad, R. 1981: Sign language in education: Some consequent problems. In B. Woll, J. G. Kyle and M. Deuchar (eds), *Perspectives on BSL and Deafness*. London: Croom Helm.

Conrad, R. and Weiskrantz, B. C. 1981: On the cognitive ability of deaf children of deaf parents. *American Annals of the Deaf*, 126, 995-1003.

Cornwell, A. C. and Birch, H. G. 1969: Psychological and social development in home-reared children with Down's syndrome (mongolism). *American Journal of Mental Deficiency*, 75, 341-50.

Cowie, V. A. 1970: *A Study of the Early Development of Mongols*. Oxford: Pergamon.

Crawley, S. B. and Spiker, D. 1983: Mother-child interactions involving two-year-olds with Down's syndrome: A look at individual differences. *Child Development*, 54, 1312-23.

Cromer, R. F. 1973: Conservation by the congenitally blind. *British Journal of Psychology*, 64, 241-50.

Cromer, R. F. 1974: The development of language and cognition: The cognition hypothesis. In B. M. Foss (ed.), *New Perspectives in Child Development*. Harmondsworth: Penguin Books.

Cruickshank, W. M. 1964: The multiple-handicapped child and courageous action. *International Journal for the Education of the Blind*, 14, 65-75.

Cruickshank, W. M. (ed.) 1976: *Cerebral Palsy, a Developmental Disability*. New York: Syracuse University Press.

Cunningham, C. C. and McArthur, K. 1981: Hearing loss and treatment in young Down's syndrome children. *Child: Care, Health and Development*, 7, 357-74.

Cunningham, C. C. and Sloper, P. 1976: *Down's Syndrome Infants: A Positive Approach to Parent and Professional Collaboration*. Manchester: Hester Adrian Research Centre, University of Manchester.

Cunningham, C. C., Morgan, P. and McGucken, R. B. 1984: Down's syndrome: Is dissatisfaction with disclosure of diagnosis inevitable? *Developmental Medicine and Child Neurology*, 26, 33-9.

Cutsforth, T. D. 1951: *The Blind in School and Society*. New York: American Foundation for the Blind.

Daly, B., Addington, J., Kerfoot, S. and Sigston, A. 1985: *Portage: The Importance of Parents*. Windsor: NFER/Nelson.

Dameron, L. E. 1963: Development of intelligence of infants with mongolism. *Child Development*, 34, 733-8.

Deacon, J. J. 1974: *Tongue Tied: Fifty Years of Friendship in a Subnormality Hospital*. London: National Society for Mentally Handicapped Children.

DeMyer, M. K., Barton, S., Alpern, G. D., Kimberlin, C., Allen, J., Yang, E. and Steele, R. 1974: The measured intelligence of autistic children. *Journal of Autism and Childhood Schizophrenia*, 4, 42-60.

Denhoff, E. and Holden, R. H. 1951: Pediatric aspects of cerebral palsy. *Journal of Pediatrics*, 39, 363-73.

Denmark, J. C., Rodda, M., Abel, R. A., Skelton, U., Eldridge, R. W., Warren, F. and Gordon, A. 1979: *A Word in Deaf Ears. A Study of Communication and Behaviour in a Sample of 75 Deaf Adolescents*. London: Royal National Institute for the Deaf.

Department of Education and Science 1968: *The Education of Deaf Children*. London: HMSO.

Dicks-Mireaux, M. J. 1966: Development of intelligence of children with Down's syndrome - Preliminary report. *Journal of Mental Deficiency Research*, 10, 89-93.

Dicks-Mireaux, M. J. 1972: Mental development of infants with Down's syndrome. *American Journal of Mental Deficiency*, 77, 26-32.

Dobree, J. H. and Boulter, E. 1982: *Blindness and Visual Handicap: The Facts*. Oxford: Oxford University Press.

Donaldson, M. 1978: *Children's Minds*. London: Fontana.

Down, J. Langdon H. 1866: Observations on an ethnic classification of idiots. *Clinical Lectures and Reports by the Medical and Surgical Staff of the London Hospital*, 3, 259-62.

Drotar, D., Baskiewicz, A., Irvin, N., Kennell, J. and Klaus, M. 1975: The adaptation of parents to the birth of an infant with a congenital malformation: a hypothetical model. *Pediatrics*, 56, 710-17.

Dunlea, A. 1984: The relation between concept formation and semantic roles: Some evidence from the blind. In L. Feagans, C. Garvey and R. Golinkoff (eds), *The Origins and Growth of Communication*. Norwood, New Jersey: Ablex Publishing Corporation.

Dunst, C. J. and Rheingrover, R. M. 1983: Structural characteristics of sensorimotor development among Down's syndrome infants. *Journal of Mental Deficiency Research*, 27, 11-22.

Eisenberg, L. and Kanner, L. 1956: Early infantile autism, 1943-1955. *American Journal of Orthopsychiatry*, 26, 556-66.

Erbs, R. C. and Smith, G. F. 1962: Unpublished observations. In L. S. Penrose and G. F. Smith (1966), *Down's Anomaly*. London: J. and A. Churchill.

Fantz, R. L. and Miranda, S. B. 1975: Longitudinal development of visual selectivity and perception in Down's syndrome and normal infants. Cited by R. L. Fantz, J. F. Fagan and S. B. Miranda, Early visual selectivity: As a function of pattern variables, previous exposure, age from birth and conception, and expected cognitive deficit. In L. B. Cohen and P. Salapatek (eds), *Infant Perception: From Sensation to Cognition*. Vol. 1. Basic Visual Processes. New York: Academic Press.

Fantz, R. L., Fagan, J. F. and Miranda, S. B. 1975: Early visual selectivity: As a function of pattern variables, previous exposure, age from birth and conception, and expected cognitive deficit. In L. B. Cohen and P. Salapatek (eds), *Infant Perception: From Sensation to Cognition*. Vol. 1. Basic Visual Processes. New York: Academic Press.

Farrell, P. T. 1982: An evaluation of an EDY course in behaviour modification techniques for teachers and care staff in an ESN(S) school. *Special Education: Forward Trends*, 9 (2), 21-5.

Feldman, H., Goldin-Meadow, S. and Gleitman, L. 1978: Beyond Herodotus: The creation of language by linguistically deprived children. In A. Lock (ed.), *Action, Gesture and Symbol: The Emergence of Language*. London: Academic Press.

Ferrari, M. and Matthews, W. S. 1983: Self-recognition deficits in autism: Syndrome-specific or general developmental delay? *Journal of Autism and Developmental Disorders*, 13, 317-24.

Ferrier, L. J. 1978: Some observations of error in context. In N. Waterson and C. Snow (eds), *The Development of Communication*. Chichester: Wiley.

Fishler, K., Share, J. and Koch, R. 1964: Adaptation of Gesell developmental scales for evaluation of development in children with Down's syndrome. *American Journal of Mental Deficiency*, 68, 642-6.

Fisichelli, V. R. and Karelitz, S. 1966: Frequency spectra of the cries of normal infants and those with Down's syndrome. *Psychonomic Science*, 6, 195-6.

Fisichelli, V. R., Haber, A., Davis, J. and Karelitz, S. 1966: Audible characteristics of the cries of normal infants and those with Down's syndrome. *Perceptual and Motor Skills*, 23, 744-6.

Folstein, S. and Rutter, M. 1977: Infantile autism: A genetic study of 21 twin pairs. *Journal of Child Psychology and Psychiatry*, 18, 297-321.

Fraiberg, S. 1968: Parallel and divergent patterns in blind and sighted infants. *Psychoanalytic Study of the Child*, 23, 264-300.

Fraiberg, S. 1977: *Insights from the Blind*. London: Souvenir Press.

Fraiberg, S. and Adelson, E. 1975: Self-representation in language and play: Observations of blind children. In R. Lenneberg and E. Lenneberg (eds), *The Foundations of Language Development: Multi-disciplinary Approach*. Vol. 2. New York: Academic Press.

Fraiberg, S., Siegel, B. L. and Gibson, R. 1966: The role of sound in the search behavior of a blind infant. *Psychoanalytic Study of the Child*, 21, 327-57.

Frank, S. M., Allen, D. A., Stein, L. and Meyers, B. 1976: Linguistic performance in vulnerable and autistic children and their mothers. *American Journal of Psychiatry*, 133, 909-15.

Fraser, J. and Mitchell, A. 1876: Kalmuck idiocy: Report of a case with autopsy, by J. Fraser, MB, with notes on sixty-two cases, by Dr A. Mitchell, Commissioner in Lunacy. *Journal of Mental Science*, 22, 161-79.

Freudenberg, R. P., Driscoll, J. W. and Stern, G. S. 1978: Reactions of adult humans to cries of normal and abnormal infants. *Infant Behavior and Development*, 1, 224-7.

Furth, H. G. 1966: *Thinking without Language*. London: Collier MacMillan.

Furth, H. G. 1973: *Deafness and Learning: A Psychological Approach*. Belmont, California: Wadsworth.

Fyffe, C. and Prior, M. 1978: Evidence for language recoding in autistic, retarded and normal children: A re-examination. *British Journal of Psychology*, 69, 393-402.

Garreau, B., Barthelemy, C., Sauvage, D., Leddet, I. and LeLord, G. 1984: A comparison of autistic syndromes with and without associated neurological problems. *Journal of Autism and Developmental Disorders*, 14, 105-11.

Garwood, S. Gray 1983: *Educating Young Handicapped Children. A Developmental Approach*. 2nd edition. Rockville, Maryland: Aspen Systems Corporation.

Gath, A. 1972: The mental health of siblings of a congenitally abnormal child. *Journal of Child Psychology and Psychiatry*, 13, 211-8.

Gath, A. 1973: The school-age siblings of mongol children. *British Journal of Psychiatry*, 123, 161-7.

Gath, A. 1974: Sibling reactions to mental handicap: A comparison of the brothers and sisters of mongol children. *Journal of Child Psychology and Psychiatry*, 15, 187-98.

Gath, A. 1978: *Down's Syndrome and the Family*. London: Academic Press.

Gibbs, M. V. and Thorpe, J. G. 1983: Personality stereotype of noninstitutionalized Down syndrome children. *American Journal of Mental Deficiency*, 87, 601-5.

Gibbs, N. 1981: Reflections on visually handicapped children I have known. *The British Psychological Society Division of Educational and Child Psychology Occasional Papers*, 5, 48-50.

Gillberg, C. 1984: Infantile autism and other childhood psychoses in a Swedish urban region. Epidemiological aspects. *Journal of Child Psychology and Psychiatry*, 25, 35-43.

Gillberg, C. and Gillberg, I. C. 1983: Infantile autism: A total population study of reduced optimality in the pre-, peri-, and neonatal period. *Journal of Autism and Developmental Disorders*, 13, 153-66.

Glenn, S. M. and Cunningham, C. C. 1982: Recognition of the familiar words of nursery rhymes by handicapped and nonhandicapped infants. *Journal of Child Psychology and Psychiatry*, 23, 319-27.

Glenn, S. M. and Cunningham, C. C. 1983: What do babies listen to most? A developmental study of auditory preferences in nonhandicapped infants and infants with Down's syndrome. *Developmental Psychology*, 19, 332-7.

Glenn, S. M., Cunningham, C. C. and Joyce, P. F. 1981: A study of auditory preferences in non-handicapped infants and infants with Down's syndrome. *Child Development*, 52, 1303-7.

Glenting, P. 1976: Variations in the population of congenital (pre- and perinatal) cases of cerebral palsy in Danish counties east of the Little Belt during the years 1950-1969. Cerebral Palsy Registry of Denmark Report No. 3 (*Danish*). *Ugeskrift for Laeger*, 138, 2984-91.

Golinkoff, R. M. (ed.) 1983: *The Transition from Prelinguistic to Linguistic Communication*. Hillsdale, New Jersey: Erlbaum.

Gomulicki, B. R. 1961: The development of perception and learning in blind children. Cambridge University: The Psychological Laboratory. Cited by J. Juurmaa, 1973: Transposition in mental spatial manipulation: A theoretical analysis. *Research Bulletin, American Foundation for the Blind*, 26, 87-134.

Gordon, A. M. 1944: Some aspects of sensory discrimination in mongolism. *American Journal of Mental Deficiency*, 49, 55-63.

Goss, R. N. 1970: Language used by mothers of deaf children and mothers of hearing children. *American Annals of the Deaf*, 115, 93-6.

Gottesman, M. 1973: Conservation development in blind children. *Child Development*, 44, 824-7.

Goueffic, S., Vallencien, B. and Leroy-Boisivon, A. 1967: La voix des mongoliens. *Journal Français d'Oto-Rhino-Laryngologie, Audio-Phonologie et Chirurgie Maxillo-Faciale*, 16, 139-41.

Gouin Décarie, T. 1969: A study of the mental and emotional development of the thalidomide child. In B. M. Foss (ed.), *Determinants of Infant Behaviour, 4*. London: Methuen.

Gouin Décarie, T. and O'Neill, M. 1973/4: Quelques aspects du développement cognitif d'enfants souffrant de malformations dues à la thalidomide. *Bulletin de Psychologie*, 27, 286-303.

Gould, J. 1986: The Lowe and Costello Symbolic Play Test in socially impaired children. *Journal of Autism and Developmental Disorders*, 16, 199-213.

Graham, E. E. and Shapiro, E. 1953: Use of the performance scale of the WISC with the deaf child. *Journal of Consulting Psychology*, 17, 396-8.

Green, W. W. 1981: Hearing disorders. In A. E. Blackhurst and W. H. Berdine (eds), *An Introduction to Special Education*. Boston, Massachusetts: Little, Brown.

Greenwald, C. and Leonard, L. 1979: Communicative and sensorimotor development of Down's syndrome children. *American Journal of Mental Deficiency*, 84, 296-303.

Gregory, S. 1976: *The Deaf Child and his Family*. London: George Allen and Unwin.

Gregory, S. and Mogford, K. 1981: Early language development in deaf children. In B. Woll, J. G. Kyle and M. Deuchar (eds), *Perspectives on BSL and Deafness*. London: Croom Helm.

Griffiths, R. 1954: *The Abilities of Babies*. London: University of London Press.

Gulliford, R. 1971: *Special Educational Needs*. London: Routledge and Kegan Paul.

Gunn, P., Berry, P. and Andrews, R. J. 1981: The temperament of Down's syndrome infants: A research note. *Journal of Child Psychology and Psychiatry*, 22, 189-94.

Gunn, P., Berry, P, and Andrews, R. J. 1982: Looking behavior of Down syndrome infants. *American Journal of Mental Deficiency*, 87, 344-7.

Gunn, P., Berry, P. and Andrews, R. J. 1983: The temperament of Down's syndrome toddlers: A research note. *Journal of Child Psychology and Psychiatry*, 24, 601-5.

Hagberg, B. 1975: Pre-, peri- and postnatal prevention of major neuropediatric handicaps. *Neuropädiatrie*, 6, 331-8.

Hagberg, B., Hagberg, G. and Olow, L. 1975a: The changing panorama of cerebral palsy in Sweden 1954-1970. I: Analysis of the general changes. *Acta Paediatrica Scandinavica*, 64, 187-92.

Hagberg, B., Hagberg, G., and Olow, L. 1975b: The changing panorama of cerebral palsy in Sweden 1954-1970. II: Analysis of various syndromes. *Acta Paediatrica Scandinavica*, 64, 193-200.

Harris, D. B. 1963: *Goodenough-Harris Drawing Test*. New York: Harcourt Brace Jovanovich.

Hatwell, Y. 1966: *Privation Sensorielle et Intelligence*. Paris: Presses Universitaires de France.

Hermelin, B. 1976: Coding and the sense modalities. In L. Wing (ed.), *Early Childhood Autism*. 2nd edition. Oxford: Pergamon Press.

Hermelin, B. and Frith, U. 1971: Psychological studies of childhood autism. Can autistic children make sense of what they see and hear? *Journal of Special Education*, 5, 1107-17.

Herren, H. and Dietrich, M.-J. 1977: Functions of language in perceptual identification from intermodal transfer in deaf and hearing children (translation). *Journal de Psychologie Normale et Pathologique*, 74, 203-26.

Hewett, S. 1970: *The Family and the Handicapped Child: A Study of Cerebral Palsied Children in their Homes*. London: Allen and Unwin.

Hill, P. and McCune-Nicolich, L. 1981: Pretend play and patterns of cognition in Down's syndrome children. *Child Development*, 52, 611-17.

Hobson, R. P. 1982: The autistic child's concept of persons. In D. Park (ed.), *Proceedings of the 1981 International Conference on Autism, Boston, USA*. Washington, DC: National Society for Children and Adults with Autism.

Hobson, R. P. 1984: Early childhood autism and the question of egocentrism. *Journal of Autism and Developmental Disorders*, 14, 85-104.

Hobson, R. P. 1986: The autistic child's appraisal of expressions of emotion. *Journal of Child Psychology and Psychiatry*, 27, 321-42.

Hodgson, A. 1984: Integrating physically handicapped pupils. *Special Education: Forward Trends*, 11(1), 27-9.

Holmes-Siedle, M., Lindenbaum, R. H. and Galliard, A. 1982: Vitamin supplements and neural tube defects. *Lancet*, 1, 276.

Hook, E. B. and Cross, P. K. 1982: Paternal age and Down's syndrome genotypes diagnosed prenatally: No association in New York State data. *Human Genetics*, 62, 167-74.

Hunt, H. 1981: Organization of, and experience in, a multi-disciplinary visual assessment team in a local authority. *The British Psychological Society Division of Educational and Child Psychology Occasional Papers*, 5, 19-29.

Illingworth, R. S. 1958: *Recent Advances in Cerebral Palsy*. London: J. and A. Churchill.

Itard, J. M. G. 1801/1807: Mémoire et rapport sur Victor de l'Aveyron. In L. Malson, 1964: *Les Enfants Sauvages*. Paris: Union Générale d'Editions.

Jacobs, P. A., Baikie, A. G., Court Brown, W. M. and Strong, J. A. 1959: The somatic chromosomes in mongolism. *Lancet*, 1, 710.

Johnson, R. C. and Abelson, R. B. 1969: Intellectual, behavioral and physical characteristics associated with trisomy, translocation and mosaic types of Down's syndrome. *American Journal of Mental Deficiency*, 73, 852-5.

Jones, O. 1977: Mother-child interaction with pre-linguistic Down's syndrome and normal infants. In H. R. Schaffer (ed.), *Studies in Mother-Infant Interaction*. London: Academic Press.

Jongbloet, P. H. 1975: Aging Gametes. *Proceedings International Symposium, Seattle* Basle: S. Karger AG.

Kanner, L. 1943: Autistic disturbances of affective contact. *Nervous Child*, 2, 217-50.

Kanner, L. 1949: Problems of nosology and psychodynamics in early infantile autism. *American Journal of Orthopsychiatry*, 19, 416-26.

Kanner, L. 1973: *Childhood Psychosis: Initial Studies and New Insights*. Washington, DC: Winston.

Kay, L. and Strelow, E. 1977: Blind babies need specially designed aids. *New Scientist*, 74, 709-12.

Keeler, W. R. 1958: Autistic patterns and defective communication in blind children with retrolental fibroplasia. In P. H. Hoch and J. Zubin (eds), *Psychopathology of Communication*. New York: Grune and Stratton.

Kehoe, L. 1978: Poor hearing exacerbates Down's syndrome. *New Scientist*, 80, 341.

Kiernan, C. 1983: The use of nonvocal communication techniques with autistic individuals. *Journal of Child Psychology and Psychiatry*, 24, 339-75.

Koegel, R. L. and Wilhelm, H. 1973: Selective responding to the components of multiple visual cues by autistic children. *Journal of Experimental Child Psychology*, 15, 442-53.

Kolk, C. J. V. 1977: Intelligence testing for visually impaired persons. *Journal of Visual Impairment and Blindness*, 71, 158-63.

Kopp, C. B. and Shaperman, J. 1973: Cognitive development in the absence of object manipulation during infancy. Extended report. Brief report published in *Developmental Psychology*, 9, 430.

Krakow, J. and Kopp, C. 1982: Sustained attention in young Down syndrome children. *Topics in Early Childhood Special Education*, 2, 32-42.

Kučera, J. 1969: Age at walking, at eruption of deciduous teeth and response to ephedrine in children with Down's syndrome. *Journal of Mental Deficiency Research*, 13, 143-8.

Kyle, J. G. 1981: Reading development in deaf children. *Journal of Research in Reading*, 3, 86-97.

Kyle, J. G. and Allsop, L. 1982a: Communicating with young deaf people. *Teacher of the Deaf*, 6, 89-95.

Kyle, J. G. and Allsop, L. 1982b: Deaf People and the Community. Final report to the Nuffield Foundation. Bristol: School of Education, Bristol University. Cited in J. G. Kyle and B. Woll, 1985: *Sign Language: The Study of Deaf People and their Language*. London: Cambridge University Press.

Kyle, J. G. and Woll, B. 1985: *Sign Language. The Study of Deaf People and their Language.* London: Cambridge University Press.

Landau, B. and Gleitman, L. R. 1985: *Language and Experience. Evidence from the Blind Child.* Cambridge, Massachusetts: Harvard University Press.

Langdell, T. 1978: Recognition of faces: An approach to the study of autism. *Journal of Child Psychology and Psychiatry,* 19, 255–68.

Langdon-Down, R. L. 1906: Some observations on the mongolian type of imbecility. *Journal of Mental Science,* 52, 187–190.

Lenneberg, E. H., Nichols, I. A. and Rosenberger, E. F. 1962: Primitive stages of language development in mongolism. In *Disorders of Communication,* 47, 119–37. Research Publications, Association for Research in Nervous and Mental Disease. Baltimore, Maryland: Williams and Wilkins.

Levinson, A., Friedman, A. and Stamps, F. 1955: Variability of mongolism. *Pediatrics,* 16, 43–53.

Lewis, V. A. and Bryant, P. E. 1982: Touch and vision in normal and Down's syndrome babies. *Perception,* 11, 691–701.

Lieven, E. V. M. 1982: Context, process and progress in young children's speech. In M. Beveridge (ed.), *Children Thinking through Language.* London: Edward Arnold.

Lind, J., Vuorenkoski, V., Rosberg, G., Partanen, T. J. and Wasz-Höckert, O. 1970: Spectographic analysis of vocal responses to pain stimuli in infants with Down's syndrome. *Developmental Medicine and Child Neurology,* 12, 478–86.

Lindsten, J., Marsk, L., Berglund, K., Iselius, L., Ryman, N., Annerén, G., Kjessler, B., Mitelman, F., Nordenson, I., Wahlström, J. and Vejlens, L. 1981: Incidence of Down's syndrome in Sweden during the years 1968–1977. In G. R. Burgio, M. Fraccaro, L. Tiepolo and U. Wolf (eds), *Trisomy 21. An International Symposium, Italy, 1979.* Berlin: Springer-Verlag.

Lockyer, L. and Rutter, M. 1969: A five to fifteen year follow up study of infantile psychosis: III Psychological aspects. *British Journal of Psychiatry,* 115, 865–82.

Loeffler, F. and Smith, G. F. 1964: Unpublished observations. Reported in L. S. Penrose and G. F. Smith, 1966: *Down's Anomaly.* London: J. and A. Churchill.

Lorber, J. 1971: Results of treatment of myelomeningocele. *Developmental Medicine and Child Neurology,* 13, 279–303.

Lorimer, J. 1981: The limitations of Braille as a medium for communication and the possibility of improving reading standards. *The British Psychological Society Division of Educational and Child Psychology Occasional Papers,* 5, 63–72.

Lorimer, J. and Tobin, M. J. 1980: Modified Braille codes, reading rates and space saving. *New Beacon,* 64, 281–4.

Lotter, V. 1966: Epidemiology of autistic conditions in young children: I Prevalence. *Social Psychiatry,* 1, 124–37.

Lotter, V. 1967a: 'The Prevalence of the Autistic Syndrome in Children'. Unpublished Ph.D. thesis, University of London.

Lotter, V. 1967b: Epidemiology of autistic conditions in young children: II Some characteristics of the parents and children. *Social Psychiatry,* 1, 163–73.

Lotter, V. 1974: Factors related to outcome in autistic children. *Journal of Autism and Childhood Schizophrenia,* 4, 263–77.

Lowenfeld, B. 1948: Effects of blindness on the cognitive functions of children. *Nervous Child*, 7, 45–54.

Lyle, J. G. 1960: The effect of an institution environment upon the verbal development of imbecile children. III The Brooklands Residential Family Unit. *Journal of Mental Deficiency Research*, 4, 14–23.

McBride, V. G. 1974: Explorations in rapid reading in Braille. *New Outlook for the Blind*, 68, 8–12.

McBrien, J. 1981: Introducing the EDY project. *Special Education: Forward Trends*, 8 (2), 29–30.

MacDougall, J. C. and Rabinovitch, M. S. 1971: Early auditory deprivation and sensory compensation. *Developmental Psychology*, 5, 368.

McHale, S. M., Simeonsson, R. J., Marcus, L. M. and Olley, J. G. 1980: The social and symbolic quality of autistic children's communication. *Journal of Autism and Developmental Disorders*, 10, 299–310.

McIntire, M. L. 1977: The acquisition of American Sign Language hand configurations. *Sign Language Studies*, 16, 247–66.

Mans, L., Cicchetti, D. and Stroufe, L. A. 1978: Mirror reactions of Down's syndrome infants and toddlers: Cognitive underpinnings of self recognition. *Child Development*, 49, 1247–50.

Meadow, K. P. 1967: 'The effect of early manual communication and family climate on the deaf child's development'. Unpublished doctoral dissertation, University of California, Berkeley.

Meadow, K. P. 1968: Parental responses to the medical ambiguities of deafness. *Journal of Health and Social Behavior*, 9, 299–309.

Meadow, K. P. 1980: *Deafness and Child Development*. London: Edward Arnold.

Melyn, M. A. and White, D. T. 1973: Mental and developmental milestones of non-institutionalized Down's syndrome children. *Pediatrics*, 52, 542–5.

Millar, S. 1981: Tactual shapes. *The British Psychological Society Division of Educational and Child Psychology Occasional Papers*, 5, 58–62.

Miller, C. K. 1969: Conservation in blind children. *Education of the Visually Handicapped*, 1, 101–5.

Mills, A. E. (ed.), 1983: *Language Acquisition in the Blind Child. Normal and Deficient*. London: Croom Helm.

Ministry of Education 1962: *Children with Impaired Hearing*. Circular 10/62. London: HMSO.

Miranda, S. B. 1976: Visual attention in defective and high-risk infants. *Merrill-Palmer Quarterly*, 22, 201–28.

Miranda, S. B. and Fantz, R. L. 1973: Visual preferences of Down's syndrome and normal infants. *Child Development*, 44, 555–61.

Miranda, S. B. and Fantz, R. L. 1974: Recognition memory in Down's syndrome and normal infants. *Child Development*, 45, 651–60.

Mirenda, P. L., Donnellan, A. M. and Yoder, D. E. 1983: Gaze behavior: A new look at an old problem. *Journal of Autism and Developmental Disorders*, 13, 397–409.

Mittler, P. 1970: *The Psychological Assessment of Mental and Physical Handicaps*. London: Methuen.

Mittwoch, U. 1952: The chromosome complement in a mongolian imbecile. *Annals of Eugenics*, 17, 37.

Mohay, H. 1982: A preliminary description of the communication systems evolved by two deaf children in the absence of a sign language model. *Sign Language Studies*, 34, 73-90.

Montague, J. C., Brown, W. S. and Hollien, H. 1974: Vocal fundamental frequency characteristics of institutionalized Down's syndrome children. *American Journal of Mental Deficiency*, 78, 414-18.

Moore, M. K., Clark, D., Mael, M., Rajotte, P. and Stoel-Gammon, C. 1977: 'The relationship between language and object permanence development: A study of Down's infants and children'. Paper presented at the meeting of the *Society for Research in Child Development*, March, New Orleans, Louisiana.

Morss, J. R. 1983: Cognitive development in the Down's syndrome infant: Slow or different? *British Journal of Educational Psychology*, 53, 40-7.

Morss, J. R. 1985: Early cognitive development: Difference or delay. In D. Lane and B. Stratford (eds), *Current Approaches to Down's Syndrome*. London: Holt, Rinehart and Winston.

Motti, F., Cicchetti, D. and Stroufe, L. A. 1983: From infant affect expression to symbolic play: The coherence of development in Down syndrome children. *Child Development*, 54, 1168-75.

Myklebust, H. R. 1964: *The Psychology of Deafness: Sensory Deprivation, Learning and Adjustment*. 2nd edition. New York: Grune and Stratton.

Nagera, H. and Colonna, A. B. 1965: Aspects of the contribution of sight to ego and drive development. *Psychoanalytic Study of the Child*, 20, 267-87.

Nelson, K. 1973: Structure and strategy in learning to talk. *Monographs of the Society for Research in Child Development*, 38. Chicago: University of Chicago Press.

Niswander, K. R. and Gordon, M. (eds) 1972: *The Collaborative Perinatal Study of the National Institute of Neurological Diseases and Strokes: The Women and their Pregnancies*. Philadelphia: W. B. Saunders.

Norris, M., Spaulding, P. J. and Brodie, F. H. 1957: *Blindness in Children*. Chicago: University of Chicago Press.

O'Connor, N. and Berkson, G. 1963: Eye movements in normals and defectives. *American Journal of Mental Deficiency*, 68, 85-90.

O'Connor, N. and Hermelin, B. 1961: Visual and stereognostic shape recognition in normal children and mongol and non-mongol imbeciles. *Journal of Mental Deficiency Research*, 5, 63-6.

Oléron, P. and Herren, H. 1961: L'acquisition des conservations et langage: étude comparative sur des enfants sourds et entendants. *Enfance*, 14, 203-19.

Øster, J. 1953: *Mongolism*. Copenhagen: Danish Science Press.

Øster, J., Mikkelsen, M. and Nielsen, A. 1975: Mortality and lifetable in Down's syndrome. *Acta Paediatrica Scandinavica*, 64, 322-6.

Petitto, L. 1983: From gesture to symbol: The acquisition of personal pronouns in ASL. Unpublished paper, McGill University, Montreal, Canada. Cited in J. G. Kyle and B. Woll (eds), 1985: *Sign Language. The Study of Deaf People and Their Language*. Cambridge: Cambridge University Press.

Piaget, J. 1953: *The Origin of Intelligence in the Child*. London: Routledge and Kegan Paul. First published 1936.

Piaget, J. 1967: *Biologie et Connaissance*. Paris: Gallimard.

Piaget, J. 1983: Piaget's theory. In P. H. Mussen (ed.), *Handbook of Child Psychology*. 4th Edition. New York: Wiley.

Piaget, J. and Inhelder, B. 1969: *The Psychology of the Child*. London: Routledge and Kegan Paul.

Pringle, M. L. Kellmer and Fiddes, D. O. 1970: *The Challenge of Thalidomide*. London: The National Bureau for Co-operation in Child Care.

Prior, M. R. 1979: Cognitive abilities and disabilities in infantile autism: A review. *Journal of Abnormal Child Psychology*, 7, 357-80.

Report of the Ad Hoc Committee to Define Deaf and Hard of Hearing 1975: *American Annals of the Deaf*, 120, 509-12.

Richards, B. W. and Siddiqui, A. Q. 1980: Age and mortality trends in residents of an institution for the mentally handicapped. *Journal of Mental Deficiency Research*, 24, 99-105.

Ricks, D. M. 1975: Vocal communication in pre-verbal normal and autistic children. In N. O'Connor (ed.), *Language, Cognitive Deficits, and Retardation*. London: Butterworths.

Ricks, D. M. and Wing, L. 1975: Language, communication, and the use of symbols in normal and autistic children. *Journal of Autism and Childhood Schizophrenia*, 5, 191-221.

Ridler, M. A. C. 1971: Banding patterns of metaphase chromosomes in Down's syndrome. *Lancet*, 2, 603.

Rodewald, A., Zang, K. D., Zankl, H. and Zankl, M. 1981: Dermatoglyphic peculiarities in Down's syndrome. Detection of mosaicism and balanced translocation carriers. In G. R. Burgio, M. Fraccaro, L. Tiepolo and U. Wolf (eds), *Trisomy 21. An International Symposium, Italy, 1979*. Berlin: Springer-Verlag.

Rogers, S. C. and Weatherall, J. A. C. 1976: Anencephalus, spina bifida and congenital hydrocephalus. England and Wales, 1964-1972. *Studies on Medical and Population Subjects*, 32. London: HMSO.

Rollin, H. R. 1946: Personality in mongolism with special reference to the incidence of catatonic psychosis. *American Journal of Mental Deficiency*, 51, 219-37.

Rondal, J.-A. 1981: Language acquisition in Down's syndrome children: Recent studies and problems. In A. Teirikko, R. Vihavainen and T. Nenonen (eds), *Finland Speaks. Report of the European Association for Special Education Conference: Communication and Handicap*. Helsinki, Finland: The Finnish Association for Special Education.

Rosenthal, J., Massie, H. and Wulff, K. 1980: A comparison of cognitive development in normal and psychotic children in the first two years of life from home movies. *Journal of Autism and Developmental Disorders*, 10, 433-44.

Rutter, D. R. 1984: *Looking and Seeing: The Role of Visual Communication in Social Interaction*. Chichester: Wiley.

Rutter, M. 1978: Diagnosis and definition. In M. Rutter and E. Schopler (eds), *Autism: A Reappraisal of Concepts and Treatment*. New York: Plenum.

Rutter, M. 1983: Cognitive deficits in the pathogenesis of autism. *Journal of Child Psychology and Psychiatry*, 24, 513-31.

Rutter, M. and Lockyer, L. 1967: A five to fifteen year follow-up study of infantile psychosis: I Description of sample. *British Journal of Psychiatry*, 113, 1169-82.

Rutter, M., Bartak, L. and Newman, S. 1971: Autism - a central disorder of cognition and language? In M. Rutter (ed.), *Infantile Autism: Concepts, Characteristics and Treatment*. Edinburgh: Churchill Livingstone.

Rutter, M., Greenfeld, D. and Lockyer, L. 1967: A five to fifteen year follow-up study of infantile psychosis: II Social and behavioural outcome. *British Journal of Psychiatry*, 113, 1183-99.

Ryan, J. F. Unpublished a: A longitudinal study of language development in young severely subnormal children: I Comparison of different verbal abilities.

Ryan, J. F. Unpublished b: A longitudinal study of language development in young severely subnormal children: II Developmental comparisons.

Ryan, J. F. 1975: Mental subnormality and language development. In E. H. Lenneberg and E. Lenneberg (eds), *Foundations of Language Development*. New York: Academic Press.

Rynders, J. E., Spiker, D. and Horrobin, J. M. 1978: Underestimating the educability of Down's syndrome children: Examination of methodological problems in recent literature. *American Journal of Mental Deficiency*, 82, 440-8.

Sapir, E. 1912: Language and environment. *American Anthropologist*, n.s., 226-42. Reprinted in D. G. Mandelbaum (ed.) 1958: *Selected Writings of Edward Sapir in Language, Culture and Personality*. Berkeley and Los Angeles: University of California Press.

Schiff, W. and Dytell, R. S. 1971: Tactile identification of letters: A comparison of deaf and hearing childrens' performances. *Journal of Experimental Child Psychology*, 11, 150-64.

Schlesinger, H. S. 1978: The acquisition of signed and spoken language. In L. S. Liben (ed.), *Deaf Children: Developmental Perspectives*. New York: Academic Press.

Schlesinger, H. and Meadow, K. 1972: *Sound and Sign: Childhood Deafness and Mental Health*. Berkeley: University of California Press.

Schwam, E. 1980: 'MORE' is 'LESS': Sign language comprehension in deaf and hearing children. *Journal of Experimental Child Psychology*, 29, 249-63.

Scott, E. P., Jan, J. E. and Freeman, R. D. 1977: *Can't Your Child See?* Baltimore, Maryland: University Park Press.

Scott, R. A. 1969: The socialization of blind children. In D. A. Goslin (ed.), *Handbook of Socialization Theory and Research*. Chicago: Rand McNally.

Scully, C. 1973: Down's syndrome. *British Journal of Hospital Medicine*, 10, 89-98.

Searle, J. R. 1969: *Speech Acts*. Cambridge: Cambridge University Press.

Séquin, E. 1846: *Le traitement moral, l'hygiène et l'éducation des idiots*. Paris: J. B. Baillière.

Seidel, U. P., Chadwick, O. F. and Rutter, M. 1975: Psychological disorders in crippled children: A comparative study of children with and without brain damage. *Developmental Medicine and Child Neurology*, 17, 563-73.

Selfe, L. 1977: *Nadia: A Case of Extraordinary Drawing Ability in an Autistic Child*. London: Academic Press.

Selfe, L. 1983: *Normal and Anomalous Representational Drawing Ability in Children*. London: Academic Press.

Serafica, F. C. and Cicchetti, D. 1976: Down's syndrome children in a strange situation: Attachment and exploratory behaviors. *Merrill-Palmer Quarterly*, 22, 137-50.

Shah, A. and Frith, U. 1983: An islet of ability in autistic children: A research note. *Journal of Child Psychology and Psychiatry*, 24, 613-20.

Shipe, D. and Shotwell, A. M. 1965: Effect of out-of-home care on mongoloid children: A continuation study. *American Journal of Mental Deficiency*, 69, 649-52.

Shuttleworth, G. E. 1883: Physical features of idiocy in relation to classification and prognosis. *Liverpool Medico-Chirurgical Journal*, 3, 282-301.

Shuttleworth, G. E. 1900: *Mentally-deficient Children: Their Treatment and Training*. London: P. Blakiston's.

Simmons, F. B. 1977: Automated screening test for newborns. The Crib-o-gram. In B. F. Joffe (ed.), *Hearing Loss in Children*. London: University Park Press.

Sisco, F. H. and Anderson, R. J. 1980: Deaf children's performance on the WISC-R relative to hearing status of parents and child-rearing experiences. *American Annals of the Deaf*, 125, 923-30.

Smithells, R. W., Sheppard, S., Schorah, C. J., Sellar, M. J., Nevin, N. C., Harris, R., Read, A. P., Fielding, D. W. and Walker, S. 1981: Vitamin supplementation and neural tube defects. *Lancet*, 2, 1424-5.

Spiker, D. and Ricks, M. 1984: Visual self-recognition in autistic children: Developmental relationships. *Child Development*, 55, 214-25.

Stedman, D. J. and Eichorn, D. H. 1964: A comparison of the growth and development of institutionalized and home-reared mongoloids during infancy and early childhood. *American Journal of Mental Deficiency*, 69, 391-401.

Stene, J., Stene, E., Stengel-Rutkowski, S. and Murken, J. D. 1981: Paternal age and Down's syndrome. Data from prenatal diagnosis (D.F.G.). *Human Genetics*, 59, 119-24.

Stern, D. 1977: *The First Relationship: Infant and Mother*. London: Open Books.

Sterritt, G. M., Camp, B. W. and Lipman, B. S. 1966: Effects of early auditory deprivation upon auditory and visual information processing. *Perceptual and Motor Skills*, 23, 123-30.

Stoneman, Z., Brody, G. H. and Abbott, D. 1983: In-home observations of young Down's syndrome children with their mothers and fathers. *American Journal of Mental Deficiency*, 87, 591-600.

Stratford, B. and Ching, E. Y. -Y. 1983: Rhythm and time in the perception of Down's syndrome children. *Journal of Mental Deficiency Research*, 27, 23-38.

Sutherland, G. A. 1899: Mongolian imbecility in infants. *Practitioner*, 63, 632-42.

Swisher, L. 1976: The language performance of the oral deaf. In H. A. Whitaker and H. Whitaker (eds), *Studies in Neurolinguistics*, 2. New York: Academic Press.

Templin, M. 1967: Methodological variations in language research with deaf subjects. *Proceedings of International Conference on Oral Education of the Deaf*, 11, 1428-40. Washington, DC: Alexander Graham Bell Association.

Tew, B. J. and Laurence, K. M. 1972: The ability and attainments of spina bifida patients born in South Wales between 1956-1962. *Developmental Medicine and Child Neurology*, Supplement 27, 124-31.

Tiegerman, E. and Primavera, L. H. 1984: Imitating the autistic child: Facilitating communicative gaze behaviour. *Journal of Autism and Developmental Disorders*, 14, 27-38.

Tillman, M. H. 1967a: The performance of blind and sighted children on the Wechsler Intelligence Scale for Children: Study I. *International Journal for the Education of the Blind*, 16, 65-74.

Tillman, M. H. 1967b: The performance of blind and sighted children on the Wechsler Intelligence Scale for Children: Study II. *International Journal for the Education of the Blind*, 16, 106-12.

Tillman, M. H. 1973: Intelligence scales for the blind: A review with implications for research. *Journal of School Psychology*, 11, 80-7.

Tinbergen, N. and Tinbergen, E. A. 1983: *'Autistic' Children: New Hope for a Cure*. London: Allen and Unwin.

Tizard, J. 1960: The residential care of mentally handicapped children. *Proceedings of London Conference on the Scientific Aspects of Mental Deficiency*, 2, 659-66.

Tjio, J. H. and Levan, A. 1956: The chromosome number in man. *Hereditas* 42, 1-6.

Tobin, M. J. 1972: Conservation of substance in the blind and partially sighted. *British Journal of Educational Psychology*, 42, 192-7.

Tobin, M. J., Tooze, F. H. G., Chapman, E. K. and Moss, S. C. 1978: *Look and Think: A Handbook on Visual Perception Training for Severely Visually Handicapped Children*. London: Schools Council.

Tredgold, A. F. 1908: *Mental Deficiency (Amentia)*. London: Baillière, Tindall and Cox.

Treffert, D. A. 1970: Epidemiology of infantile autism. *Archives of General Psychiatry*, 22, 431-8.

Urwin, C. 1978: 'The development of communication between blind infants and their parents: Some ways into language'. Unpublished Ph.D. thesis, University of Cambridge.

Urwin, C. 1981: Early language development in blind children. *The British Psychological Society Division of Educational and Child Psychology Occasional Papers*, 5, 78-93.

Urwin, C. 1983: Dialogue and cognitive functioning in the early language development of three blind children. In A. E. Mills (ed.), *Language Acquisition in the Blind Child*. London: Croom Helm.

Vernon, McC. 1967: Relationship of language to the thinking process. *Archives of General Psychiatry*, 16, 325-33.

Vernon, M. D. 1972: *The Report of the Vernon Committee on the Education of the Visually Handicapped 1968-1972*. London: HMSO.

Volterra, V. 1983: Gestures, signs and words at two years. In J. G. Kyle and B. Woll (eds), *Language in Sign: An International Perspective on Sign Language*. London: Croom Helm.

Vygotsky, L. S. 1962: *Thought and Language*. Cambridge, Massachusetts: MIT Press/New York: John Wiley.

Waardenburg, P. J. 1932: *Das menschliche Auge und seine Erbanlagen*. The Hague: Martinus Nijhoff.

Walker, J. A. and Crawley, S. B. 1983: Conceptual and methodological issues in studying the handicapped infant. In S. Gray Garwood and R. R. Fewell (eds),

*Educating Handicapped Infants: Issues in Development and Intervention.* Rockville, Maryland: Aspen Systems Corporation.

Warnock, H. M. 1978: *Special Educational Need. Report of the Committee of Enquiry into the Education of Handicapped Children and Young People. 1974–1978.* London: HMSO.

Warren, D. H. 1977: *Blindness and Early Childhood Development.* New York: American Foundation for the Blind.

Watson, J. B. 1913: Psychology as the behaviorist views it. *Psychological Review,* 20, 158–77.

Watson, J. B. 1919: *Psychology from the Standpoint of a Behaviorist.* Philadelphia: Lippincott.

Wechsler, D. 1974: *Manual for the Intelligence Scale for Children.* Revised edition. New York: The Psychological Corporation.

Weinberg, B. and Zlatin, M. 1970: Speaking fundamental frequency characteristics of five- and six-year-old children with mongolism. *Journal of Speech and Hearing Research,* 13, 418–25.

Whorf, B. L. 1940: Science and linguistics. *Technology Review,* 42, 227–31, 247–8. Reprinted in J. B. Carroll (ed.) 1956: *Language, Thought and Reality: Selected Writings of Benjamin Lee Whorf.* Cambridge, Massachusetts: MIT Press/New York: John Wiley.

Wiegersma, P. H. and Van der Velde, A. 1983: Motor development of deaf children. *Journal of Child Psychology and Psychiatry,* 24, 103–11.

Williams, M. 1956: *Intelligence Test for Children with Defective Vision.* Birmingham: University of Birmingham.

Williams, M. 1968: Superior intelligence of children blinded from retinoblastoma. *Archives of Diseases of Childhood,* 43, 204–10.

Williams, M. 1971: Braille reading. *The Teacher of the Blind,* 59, 103–16.

Wills, D. M. 1968: Problems of play and mastery in the blind child. *British Journal of Medical Psychology,* 41, 213–22.

Wills, D. M. 1970: Vulnerable periods in the early development of blind children. *Psychoanalytic Study of the Child,* 25, 461–80.

Wills, D. M. 1978: Early speech development in blind children. *Psychoanalytic Study of the Child,* 34, 85–117.

Wills, D. M. 1981a: Work with mothers of young blind children. *The British Psychological Society Division of Educational and Child Psychology Occasional Papers,* 5, 34–41.

Wills, D. M. 1981b: Entry into boarding school and after. *The British Psychological Society Division of Educational and Child Psychology Occasional Papers,* 5, 42–7.

Wilson, M. M. 1970: Children with cerebral palsy. *Education Survey,* No. 7. London: HMSO.

Wing, L. 1969: The handicaps of autistic children – a comparative study. *Journal of Child Psychology and Psychiatry,* 10, 1–40.

Wing, L. 1971: Perceptual and language development in autistic children: A comparative study. In M. Rutter (ed.), *Infantile Autism: Concepts, Characteristics and Treatment.* Edinburgh: Churchill Livingstone.

Wing, L. (ed.) 1976: *Early Childhood Autism.* 2nd edition. Oxford: Pergamon Press.

Wing, L. and Gould, J. 1979: Severe impairments of social interaction and associated abnormalities in children: Epidemiology and classification. *Journal of Autism and Developmental Disorders*, 9, 11–29.

Wing, L., Yeates, S. R., Brierley, L. M. and Gould, J. 1978: The prevalence of early childhood autism: Comparison of administrative and epidemiological studies. *Psychological Medicine*, 6, 89–100.

Witkin, H. A., Oltman, P. K., Chase, J. B. and Friedman, F. 1971: Cognitive patterning in the blind. In J. Hellmuth (ed.), *Cognitive Studies*, 2. New York: Bruner/Mazel.

Wode, H. 1983: Precursors and the study of the impaired language learner. In A. E. Mills (ed.), *Language Acquisition in the Blind Child: Normal and Deficient*. London: Croom Helm.

Wolchik, S. A. 1983: Language patterns of parents of young autistic and normal children. *Journal of Autism and Developmental Disorders*, 13, 167–80.

Wood, D. 1981: Some developmental aspects of prelingual deafness. In B. Woll, J. G. Kyle and M. Deuchar (eds), *Perspectives on BSL and Deafness*. London: Croom Helm.

Wood, D., Wood, H., Griffiths, A. and Howarth, I. 1986: *Teaching and Talking with Deaf Children*. Chichester: Wiley.

Woodburn, M. 1973: *Social Implications of Spina Bifida - A Study in S. E. Scotland*. Edinburgh: Eastern Branch Scottish Spina Bifida Association.

Wynn, M. and Wynn, A. 1979: *Prevention of Handicap and the Health of Women*. London: Routledge and Kegan Paul.

Zekulin, X. Y., Gibson, D., Mosley, J. L. and Brown, R. I. 1974: Auditory-motor channeling in Down's syndrome subjects. *American Journal of Mental Deficiency*, 78, 571–7.

Zigler, E. 1967: Familial mental retardation: A continuing dilemma. *Science*, 155, 292–8.

# Index